RELIGION
AND MODERN LIFE

RELIGION AND MODERN LIFE

LECTURES GIVEN FOR THE
(PHILLIPS BROOKS HOUSE ASSOCIATION,
HARVARD UNIVERSITY)

Essay Index Reprint Series

BOOKS FOR LIBRARIES PRESS
FREEPORT, NEW YORK

First Published 1927
Reprinted 1972

BL
50
.P5
1972

Library of Congress Cataloging in Publication Data

Phillips Brooks House Association, Harvard University.
    Religion and modern life.

    (Essay index reprint series)
    Reprint of the 1927 ed.
    1. Religion--Addresses, essays, lectures.
I. Title.
BL50.P5 1972   200   75-39104
ISBN 0-8369-2713-3

PRINTED IN THE UNITED STATES OF AMERICA
BY
NEW WORLD BOOK MANUFACTURING CO., INC.
HALLANDALE, FLORIDA 33009

TO

ARTHUR BEANE

CLASS OF

1911

INTRODUCTORY NOTE

THESE lectures on religious beliefs new and old the world over, and on religious questions of to-day, were given at Phillips Brooks House, Harvard University, in the academic years 1924–6. The speakers were chosen by the Graduate Schools Society and the Christian Association of the Phillips Brooks House Association, who assigned to each a subject which they thought him peculiarly fitted to discuss. These speakers prepared for informal meetings which ended with questions and answers. Their lectures were not designed for publication; and when their personal distinction and the success of the meetings created a demand for it, some of them were obliged to amplify and reconstruct notes which, months earlier, they had done with and set aside. For this additional labor of love the Association would express a lasting gratitude.

The book is dedicated to the memory of Arthur Beane, from 1911 to 1918 Secretary of Phillips Brooks House Association and its moving spirit: a man trained to hard work and rejoicing therein; filled with faith, hope, and greatest of all with love; strong in the constancy of his earnestness and the humanity of his religious belief.

[vii]

After his service at Phillips Brooks House he went into business, in which he soon began to prosper and was rising rapidly; but neither the exactions of business nor the increase of prosperity could dull his understanding of those who needed human counsel and more than human aid. He worked always for the welfare of those about him, and leavened any community in which he lived. He died on March 15, 1925, at the age of forty-five.

L. B. R. BRIGGS.

CONTENTS

CONTENTS

RELIGION AND MODERN LIFE

RELIGION FOR MODERN YOUTH

CHARLES WILLIAM ELIOT

THE first question which I want to say something about is whether modern young people think about religion at all. If at all, how much? Again, do young men think of religion as much as young women? My own experience leads me to think that most young men—what we call modern young men—do think about religion a good deal after they are well grown up, not much when they are children. I cannot say confidently whether girls think of religion more than boys; because I have never had much opportunity to study girls passing from the stage of childhood to womanhood, never having had any daughters myself. Later, I have had some opportunities of studying young girlhood's attitude toward religion; because I have had several granddaughters and granddaughters-in-law. But in general I speak with little confidence about the attitude of girls and young women toward religion; because my opportunities for observation have been scanty.

Another very interesting question about modern youth is how much they talk about religion and the fundamental problems of life, the conduct of life, the philosophy of life; how much they talk about it among themselves. It is my observation that boys and adolescents are extremely reticent on those subjects with their own kindred, with their fathers and mothers and brothers and sisters; but when they get older, when they go to college, for example, I think they talk a good deal with their intimates and close friends about religious subjects and in general about the philosophy and conduct of life. I hope that is the case with all of you, that you talk about these grave and profoundly interesting subjects with your comrades and friends. It is a very improving thing to do.

Almost all educated youth acquire and cherish motives which may fairly be called religious. At least, that is my observation of educated youth. As a matter of fact, they do acquire before they are grown up many motives which it is fair to call religious; although some kinds of devout people do not use that name for these youthful motives. That is, I believe, a solid fact with modern youth. They do, as a matter of fact, acquire during their education and growth these motives of a religious kind. I believe that they usually acquire one motive in particular, namely, the motive, the wish, the purpose to be serviceable in their world—serviceable to comrades and friends, serviceable to their families, serviceable in their town or city, serviceable to their nation. I can testify that that is a common and strong motive with graduates of Harvard College, and I believe it to be inherent in the graduates of almost all American colleges and universities—this desire to be serviceable.

Next I must inquire into the development of this desire to be serviceable. How does it begin? What is the order of its development?

It seems to me that it begins in childhood, with very small children; but of course they have no conception of the modes of being serviceable with which they are afterward to become familiar. I think it starts from the suggestions or advice or silent example of the mother. This mode of treating little children is much more ancient than people suppose. There has been comparatively little change in the last three centuries in the mode in which mothers begin to teach their children to pray, for example, to uplift the forming mind to something higher and larger than itself.

But these modes which mothers use, and long have used, are in many instances little understood by the children, and never have been. I came lately on an interesting instance of that lack of understanding in children of the religious suggestions of the mothers. The mother of a large family, who was well known to me, adopted the following method with her children: she had them sing before breakfast the following verse. They sang it, did not simply repeat it— they sang it:

> "Father, we thank Thee for the night,
> And for the pleasant morning light;
> For rest and food and loving care
> And all that makes the day most fair."

That mother was somewhat taken aback when the youngest of her children, grown to be a man, informed her one day that he always supposed that the Father they addressed in that song was his own father.

This sort of experience of mothers with their children is, I believe, very common—that the mother herself does not know what the child thinks about the little prayer he recites or the verse he sings. Of course, the children I have just spoken of did not in the least know what "rest" meant in the third line of the verse they sang. They probably had a vivid conception of what "food" meant. The fundamental misunderstanding of that child is something you may prudently look for in all sorts of exhortations of parents to children when they are hoping to inculcate religious ideas.

As a matter of fact, most Christian children get their early religious impressions from some Bible story or parable about God or about some saintly man or woman, or from stories about pagan deities that inhabited groves and temples, or represented terrible forces of nature like tempests, floods, volcanoes, and earthquakes, and were able either to protect trembling man or to destroy him. Such ideas are still perpetuated in the minds of children by what they are taught or by what they choose to read. From poetry and fiction, and from music, a child takes in many influences and impressions without saying anything about them.

Another question in regard to the development of religion in the rising generation is very interesting. Are they being better taught than they were formerly? Are the prayers they put up more intelligible to them and more intelligently repeated than they used to be?

I remember very distinctly and vividly the first religious idea that I got when a little boy. It came to me from a doggerel verse which I was instructed to repeat when I lay down between the sheets on my little bed:

> "Now I lay me down to sleep,
> I pray the Lord my soul to keep.
> If I should die before I wake
> I pray the Lord my soul to take."

That was the first thing I was taught in the way of prayer. I repeated that verse for years and years without in the least understanding what was meant by "my soul." And in the third line it said, "If I should die before I wake." I had not the slightest notion of what "death" meant, no glimmer of an idea about death. "I pray the Lord"—what or who was the Lord? I had no idea. And yet I repeated that prayer for years when I first got into bed in the evening.

There are many things of that sort still going on in the Christian world; mothers and fathers still trying to impart to children religious ideas by poetry or fables or myths which do not enter into the child's comprehension in the least. So the subject we have before us to-day, "Religion for Modern Youth," is one of keenest interest.

The next question which I want to bring to your attention is what the actual state of the modern youth's mind is with regard to past beliefs of the human race. In regard to past beliefs I suppose— I believe—that the modern youth rejects almost all the tenets, dogmas, and creeds of the past; that he comes to the question of religion with a mind free from the terrible obstacles which the common Christian dogmas and creeds have imposed upon past generations. The modern youth does not believe in the least the Genesis story of creation, or of God, Adam, and Eve in the garden of Eden. He does not believe in the total depravity of mankind as taught in the ordinary evangelical creeds and manuals. He has rejected those things, his mind is free from them, and therefore the problem what to believe is all the more interesting and stirring.

But what to believe? There lies the interest of the modern youth's discussion with his comrades—what to believe? Here, too, I know that the scope of my own observations is limited. I was born and brought up a Unitarian, and have always remained so—have always retained connection with a Unitarian church, and my religious guides and exemplars have been Unitarian ministers and authors. That is not the history of most modern youths. The modern youth may come out of any religious denomination or out of the great mass of the unchurched. He comes more and more out of a large variety of Christian denominations with all kinds of questions and all kinds of purposes and all kinds of teachers and preachers. But that is one of the most delightful and admirable features of the present flux about philosophy and religion. That is one of the most cheerful signs with regard to the progress of mankind—this new tendency in youth to take a liberal, open-minded view of religion and of their hopes, their own hopes—to realize that this is the happiest age the world has ever known, that the field before the youth as they grow up and go out into life is the fairest field into which any generation has ever entered; that their prospects for the future—the prospects of mankind, the prospects of the family, the prospects of religion —are wider and freer than they have ever been before.

How delightful is this prospect for modern youth, how free a field, how hopeful a field! We all of us reverence the lessons of the past, but how much more hopeful are the lessons of the future! How much more joy there is in them than ever before in the world! The modern youth has before him a prospect of happiness and power and influence which no other generation has possessed.

I feel the need of reading you some things which are in print, most of them my own earlier writings; because I have learned by experience that I used to be able to write better than I can now, and as I wish to give you the best I have to give, I must read some things to you. But the first thing I want to read to you is a portion of an address given about a fortnight ago by Professor Evans at the opening of the Harvard Theological School:

"No man can truly understand the profound significance nor adequately appreciate the supreme value of religion who does not bring all the powers of his mind to its study." Notice that phrase—"*all* the powers of his mind to its study." But Professor Evans goes on: "As Carlyle said of his father, 'He was religious with the consent of all his faculties,'" so may we say that it requires all our faculties to know our subject. It makes requisition on our critical intellect, creative imagination, keen-edged conscience, and the winged power of soul.

"The men who teach and study here ["here" is the Harvard Theological School] find, in the noble words of Augustine, the true ideal of the teacher and pupil:

"'Neither will I shrink from inquiry, if I am anywhere in doubt; nor be ashamed to learn, if I am anywhere in error. Further let me ask of the reader, wherever, like myself, he is certain, there to go with me; wherever, like myself, he hesitates, there to join with me in inquiring; wherever he recognizes himself to be in error, there to return to me; wherever he recognizes me to be so, there to call me back; so that we may enter together upon the path of charity and advance toward Him of whom it is said: "Seek His face evermore." ' "

I wanted to read you that because it states admirably the new atmosphere in which religious teachings are given in the schools of theology and by men who are thoroughly religious in temper and yet open-minded and fair-minded. That is a great change and a most delightful change in the attitude of teachers of theology, not in one sect only, but in many sects, in many denominations—Christian denominations. You see that this religious teacher has advanced into the position of the scientist.

Next I want to call your attention to Pasteur's statement of the difference between knowledge and belief. You know that Pasteur was the greatest scientist by far of the nineteenth century. He conferred upon mankind the greatest benefits a scientist has conferred in any generation. His discoveries were made through exact experimentation guided by imaginative insight. He was the son of a private soldier in the armies of Napoleon I who was himself a devout Roman Catholic, and an ardent follower of the first Napoleon as soldier and ruler. Pasteur's mother was also a devout Catholic; and Pasteur himself was a Catholic in practice all his life. When he uttered his incomparable statement about the difference between knowledge and belief he was sitting at the bedside of his dying daughter, holding her hand and hoping for some responsive pressure:

I *know* only scientifically determined truth, but I am going to *believe* what I wish to believe, what I cannot but believe. I expect to meet this dear child again in another world.

Now, that attitude of Pasteur, that state of his mind, pervaded his whole career. He was constantly distinguishing between what he knew and what he imagined or believed and chose to believe. That discrimination is what we all need when we contemplate the difference between science and religion, or between knowledge and faith.

I have just read you a passage from Doctor Evans's latest address in which he shows conclusively how the theologian is approaching the attitude of the scientist. Now, I have told you of Pasteur, who illustrates perfectly the approach of the scientist to religion. The distinction he drew between knowledge and belief goes nowadays through all scientific reasonings and processes, and particularly the play of the human imagination in physical science runs through all the processes of invention and discovery. In the region of preventive medicine, you probably know something of the part that imagination has played in the discovery of new preventives against old and new diseases. Quite lately the subjects of chemistry and physics have illustrated vividly the play of the human imagination in scientific discovery.

We are indeed coming to a state of the world when the old conflict between science and religion will disappear, partly because scientific methods approach those of theology and those of theology approach those of science, but also because we realize in all sections or areas of human thinking that progress depends on the free play of the human imagination.

But now, because my time is short, I must turn to another field of religious growth and progress. I want to read you a few passages from previous writings of mine. This is from a tract called *The Religion of the Future:*

The new religion will magnify and laud God's love and compassion, and will not venture to state what the justice of God may, or may not, require of himself, or of any of his creatures. This will be one of the great differences between the future religion and the past religions. Institutional Christianity as a rule condemned the mass of mankind to eternal torment; partly because the leaders of the churches thought they understood completely the justice of God, and partly because the exclusive possession of means of deliverance gave the churches some restraining influence over even the boldest sinners, and much over the timid. The new religion will make no such pretensions, and will teach no such horrible and perverse doctrines. . . .

All these objects of worship (the deified powers of nature, the various gods and goddesses that inhabited sky, ocean, mountains, groves, and streams, or the numerous deities revered in the various Christian communions— God the Father, the Son of God, the Mother of God, the Holy Ghost, and the host of tutelary saints) have greatly moved the human soul, and have inspired men to thoughts and deeds of beauty, love, and duty. Will the new religion do as much? It is reasonable to expect that it will. The sentiments of awe and reverence, and the love of beauty and goodness, will remain, and will increase in strength and influence. All the natural human affections will remain in full force. The new religion will foster powerfully a virtue which is comparatively new in the world—the love of truth and the passion for seeking it, and the truth will progressively make men free; so that the coming generations will be freer, and therefore more productive and stronger than the preceding. The new religionists will not worship their ancestors; but they will have a stronger sense of the descent of the present from the past than men have ever had before, and each generation will feel more strongly than ever before its indebtedness to the preceding.

The two sentiments which most inspire men to good deeds are love and hope. Religion should give freer and more rational play to these two sentiments than the world has heretofore witnessed; and the love and hope will be thoroughly grounded in and on efficient, serviceable, visible, actual, and concrete deeds and conduct. . . .

Now the new religion affords an indefinite scope, or range, for progress and development. It rejects all the limitations of family, tribal, or national religion. It is not bound to any dogma, creed, book, or institution. *It has the whole world for the field of the loving labors of its disciples;* and its fundamental precept of serviceableness admits an infinite variety and range in both time and space. It is very simple, and therefore possesses an important element of durability. It is the complicated things that get out of order. Its symbols will not relate to sacrifice or dogma; but it will doubtless have symbols, which will represent its love of liberty, truth, and beauty. It will also have social rites and reverent observances; for it will wish to commemorate the good thoughts and deeds which have come down from former generations. It will have its saints; but its canonizations will be based on grounds somewhat new. It will have its heroes; but they must have shown a loving, disinterested, or protective courage. It will have its communions, with the Great Spirit, with the spirits of the departed, and with living fellow men of like minds. Working together will be one of its fundamental ideas,—of men with God, of men with prophets, leaders, and teachers, of men with one another, of men's intelligence with the forces of nature. It will teach only such uses of authority as are necessary to secure the co-operation of several or many people to one end; and the discipline it will advocate will be training in the development of co-operative good-will. . . .

I find in my studies of industrial strife that the most fruitful subject is the one I just mentioned, the development of co-operative good-will. That is one of the cheerful prophecies of the ceasing of industrial strife.

Finally, this twentieth-century religion is not only to be in harmony with the great secular movements of modern society—democracy, individualism, social idealism, the zeal for education, the spirit of research, the modern tendency to welcome the new, the fresh powers of preventive medicine, and the recent advances in business and industrial ethics—but also in essential agreement with the direct, personal teachings of Jesus, as they are reported in the Gospels. The revelation he gave to mankind thus becomes more wonderful than ever.

I had intended to read you some other passages, but I desire to abandon that purpose in favor of an opportunity to answer questions from the floor.

Question: Doctor Eliot, do you believe that the new religion will attempt to answer definitely questions regarding ultimate things, such as God and a future existence, or will it realize that there can be no definite answer?

Doctor Eliot: I think it is quite clear that the new religion will not maintain that there is anything *ultimate* within its knowledge. It will conceive of all religious questions as subject to continuous development and will never think of them for a moment as final truth deposited in a casket or a vase or a church —in any branch or institution of Christianity. It will see an open field, a field constantly shifting, conditions of human life constantly shifting, and therefore will not pretend to make any final or ultimate recommendations of any sort.

Question: President Eliot, those who adhere to the older forms of belief, even among young men and women, do so, I believe, largely because of the element of personal loyalty to a supreme being. Shall we find that in a newer religion—any form of personalism?

Doctor Eliot: The finite man, a little speck of a being, who lives a few seconds on a little speck of an earth, cannot expect, I think, to arrive by any effort of his own at an adequate conception of God's personality. Why should he expect to? Why should an inhabitant of this very insignificant earth expect to be able to comprehend, or to enjoy, what may fairly be called the companionship of God? The word "companion" does not apply to God's relation to man. The finite mortal cannot expect by any effort of his own to understand God. What may he expect? We have learned in history of the existence of a small number of men and women who thought themselves to have had a vision of God. All the prophets and seers of the world have believed that they had a vision of God. It is perfectly clear that Jesus Christ believed that he had a vision of God when the dove descended on him as he stepped out of the river Jordan where John the Baptist had baptized him. All the seers have had that conception, that they personally had a vision of God. Now the priests of the new religion—there will be priests of the new religion just as there have been of every other religion—may not necessarily share that conception. Is there any substitute for that belief—the belief that a given individual has had a vision of God? For myself, I see no equally moving substitute for that belief available to-day. The views of thinking people about the means of human progress, the means of improving the condition of mankind are changing rapidly. They have undergone a very profound change during the past few years. This is a clear outcome of the increasing attention to individualism in family, school, industry, and government. Therefore I think the question just asked is one that cannot be answered categorically, and to which every individual is free to construct his own answer.

Question: What might be our vision of punishment or reward in the future world?

Doctor Eliot: All religions have taught that the greater part of the human race is going to extinction, transmigration, purgatory, or hell-fire, and a small, selected portion is going to something called heaven or paradise. For my own part I have never seen any description of heaven which was not intolerable. The common notion of the suffering human being who has had a hard life and is dying, perhaps in torment, is that heaven is going to give rest from pain and agony, or rest from hard labor and monotonous drudgery—that heaven is a place of rest. Now that is a most formidable idea. That heaven would be a place of rest is for me, and for any other man or woman who knows what joy in work is, simply intolerable, not to be thought of at all. The ancient conceptions of reward and punishment in the future world will be abandoned. The new religion will change them absolutely. Neither reward nor punishment as heretofore conceived of is to be thought of any more. For the future the new religion will, we may all hope, look forward to another life, not with confidence of knowledge, but as Pasteur looked forward to rejoining his daughter in another world. We may believe what we choose to believe, what we cannot help believing. We must not think or imagine for a moment that we *know* anything about either rewards or punishments in a future life.

Question: Would not a religion of service be as good for a nation if it omitted all speculations on metaphysics and Deity?

Doctor Eliot: The purpose to be serviceable is in my belief the best guide for a modern youth about his own future, his own life work. But I find it difficult to believe that this life of service, actually carrying out the purpose to be serviceable, can be conducted without something beside the love of men and the love of women. The love of the neighbor seems to me to lead perfectly straight to the love of God. It seems to me, in fact, that it is sure to bring any human being who works hard because of love to his neighbor face to face with the Eternal Goodness.

Question: President Eliot, is it absurd to hope for a common religion on the earth in future?

Doctor Eliot: One of the readings from a former paper of mine, which I was obliged to omit, dealt with that matter—the hope, as I understand you, for a universal religion?

The Questioner: Yes.

Doctor Eliot: That is, of course, something which must remain in the condition of a hope. It will take generations to answer out of human experience that question; so that generations to come may fairly assert that the love of men does lead straight and inevitably to the love of God. But surely that is a hope which young men and women everywhere may naturally and rightfully cherish.

RELIGION AND THE MIND

JAMES BISSETT PRATT

IT will be difficult to deal intelligently with the subject suggested in the title of this lecture unless we first come to some understanding as to what we shall mean by the term religion. The word has been given so many varying and even contradictory definitions that it would be altogether unsafe to take for granted that we all agree as to its meaning. Moreover, the answers we should give to the questions we shall have to face in pursuing our subject will vary greatly according to the way in which we interpret the word religion. Some people will define it as belief in a personal God; others will tell you it means merely social morality—visiting the fatherless and the widows in their affliction, keeping oneself unspotted from the world, organizing movements for better housing conditions, going slumming, preaching mild forms of socialism, and generally participating in "uplift." My own use of the word religion shall be somewhere midway between these extremes. I do not think we should identify religion with belief in a personal God nor with any other specific doctrine of theology. For if we look at the actual religions of the world, not from the theological but from the historical and psychological point of view, we shall find such a variety of doctrines that no doctrinal definition of religion would be really significant. Yet, on the other hand, there can be no doubt that the word religion, as it has almost universally been used, certainly connotes something more than morality. The attempt to identify religion with some particular philosophical or theological doctrine is wrong in being too narrow and too specific: but it is right in feeling that religion is essentially cosmic in its nature. Religion is not simply a way of acting toward one's fellow men. It is a way of acting and a way of feeling and a way of thinking toward or about the Universe. So at least it seems to me. For the purposes of this lecture, therefore, I shall use the word religion to mean man's attitude toward the ultimate cosmic Power. But I do not mean by this a merely theoretical or academic attitude toward a purely theoretical Being. Religion is no mere philosophical position. It is a felt attitude of a practical nature. It has always to do with the practical question of destiny. Throughout its whole history it has been knit up with the question, which combines both theory and practice, What is going to become of me? What is going to become of us? All of these considerations I should wish to combine into a tentative definition which should interpret religion as one's attitude toward the Determiner of Destiny.

Before taking up the more specific questions which we must face in this lecture, we should consider very briefly one additional matter of a general sort—namely, the nature of the psychology of religion, its tasks and limitations. For whether we take psychology in the introspective sense, as a description of consciousness and its processes, or in the behavioristic sense, as a description of stimuli and response, its field is sharply limited, and the psychology of religion is, after all, psychology. The mistake is often made of expecting too much of the psychology of religion. We must not demand that it go beyond its sphere, nor confuse its task with that of metaphysics. Unless we are careful about this matter we shall be open to a very considerable danger. The psychology of religion will tell us about the idea of God and its effects upon the reactions of men. From the fact that psychology cannot, in the nature of things, find God but only the idea of Him, many absent-minded students of the subject conclude that only the idea of God is of any human consequence and that God himself, as a Reality outside of the mind, can be banished from our thought as an outgrown dogma. To draw such a conclusion, whether explicitly or implicitly, is, of course, to confuse psychology with theology. The further consequence of such inadvertence is to psychologize the whole of theology and to make religion merely a subjective matter. Such a procedure is really fatal not only to theology, but to the psychology of religion as well. For the religious mind means the objects of its thought and emotion objectively; and if they were taken by it in merely subjective fashion, they would soon cease to be of any consequence; they would cease to be at all. In one sense, to be sure, religion is a subjective matter—it has a subjective aspect and this psychology studies. But religion means to be objective as well; it is an attitude toward the Determiner of Destiny. And however the Determiner of Destiny be interpreted, it has at least this in common with the God of Christian Scholasticism, that in the mind of the religious man it is the *Ens realissimum*. Forget this; make it over into a mere subjective idea; and you have missed the central characteristic of the object of your study.

With so much prefaced as to the nature of religion and the nature of psychology we are in a position where we may deal intelligently with the first of the questions proposed by your committee for this lecture: "Is the mind naturally religious?" The mind is certainly not naturally religious in the sense of having an innate belief in one personal God, nor of enjoying an inborn tendency to go slumming. But if the question be put in terms of our definition so as to read, does the mind naturally take some attitude toward the Determiner of Destiny? the question becomes a very different and a very much more instructive one. And here we are faced with the problem of a religious instinct. The phrase religious instinct is, as you all know, very common. It is met with in all sorts of popular books on religion, it is heard repeatedly in sermons, it is prominent in the magazines. What is the justification of this use of words? What is the truth about the so-called instinct of religion?

I think the right answer to this question can be put in one phrase: there is no religious instinct, but man is instinctively religious. Let me explain what I mean. If the word instinct is to retain enough meaning to be worth using at all it must be used to refer to something specific as well as innate. It must mean some specific way of acting, or of feeling or attending. It is for this reason that you will not find an "instinct of religion" set down in any of the current lists of instincts suggested by various psychologists. If the word instinct is to be used in so large and loose a way as to allow us to speak of a religious instinct, then almost anything that man comes to feel or to do might properly be explained by postulating an instinct for it. Thus we should have an instinct for reading the newspapers, for working the typewriter, for running a motor-car, or breaking the Volstead Act. If the word instinct be used in so wide a sense, it becomes useless. The psychologists, therefore, are amply justified in denying the existence of a religious instinct.

None the less it is true that man is instinctively

religious. By this I mean that a creature endowed with man's equipment of instincts and reason is bound to develop an attitude toward the Determiner of Destiny. Let us take, for example, Professor McDougall's analysis of reverence—"the religious emotion *par excellence*." This, he tells us, is composed of the primary (or instinctive) emotions of wonder, negative self-feeling, fear, and tender emotion. In other words, given a being endowed with these specific instinctive emotions, in certain natural and common situations he will inevitably feel the emotion of reverence. And given a being endowed with these emotions plus curiosity and reason, he will surely develop an attitude of combined feeling and action and thought toward the cosmic realities behind the immediate presentation of the senses; he will come to think about and have a feeling for the Determiner of Destiny.

It follows from this that until human nature becomes so changed in its fundamental outlines as to make man something else than man, he will necessarily remain religious. The forms of activity by which religion expresses itself will change, the symbols through which the intellect pictures or conceives the Determiner of Destiny will change—as indeed they always have changed—but the cosmic sense, the religious attitude, will endure as long as man is man.

All men, therefore, are religious at least potentially. Doubtless all men are actually religious at occasional moments. But the degree to which religion actually dominates and colors the mind will vary greatly with different individuals. We are therefore justified in using the common phrase "religious people," meaning by these words those individuals within whose conscious life thought and feeling for the Determiner of Destiny play an important and masterful rôle. If, now, we wish to discover the effect of religion on the mind, we can do so best by studying these people in whose lives it is most dominant—noting what it does for them and in what ways, if any, they differ from others.

One effect of religion on the mind must be already obvious from what has been said of the nature of religion and of religious people. Religion almost inevitably gives one a larger horizon than one would otherwise have. In one sense, indeed, this statement is almost tautological—almost an "analytic proposition" in Kant's sense of the term. For a wide horizon is in effect synonymous with a cosmic attitude. To cultivate some sort of cosmic attitude—some sort of religious sense—widens one's habitual horizon, widens the world in which one consciously lives. Religious people are not more learned than others, they are not more clever, but they do tend to put things in a larger setting—to make a larger picture with a larger frame. It may be that some of you will feel that this conclusion is not borne out by the character of many religious people whom you know. And there is no doubt that many religious people have rather little minds. Some of them have a dogmatic point of view with a nice little universe, all neatly planned out, with no room for the mysterious or the awful—at the top of it a "magnified non-natural man" of perfect deportment, who laid out a definite "plan of salvation" and created man on a certain Friday morning. Religious people with narrow horizons like this there are. But let me point out two relevant considerations. In the first place, religion should not be identified with the narrow sort of theology of the people we have here in mind. Religion is a much larger thing than that—much larger even in the lives of these people than that. Their religion is the totality of their attitude—emotional and volitional as well as creedal—toward the Determiner of Destiny. Not only are they not typical religious people: their religion is much larger than their theology. And furthermore, if the horizon of these people be small, that fact is due not so much to the nature of religion as to the nature of their minds. Little minds can hardly have large horizons. For the really significant question is not as to the actual size of the horizon of these little-minded people, but rather as to the effect religion has had upon it. If they had had no religion how wide would their horizon have been? Questions of this sort are, of course, incapable of certain answer; but we can tell with a fair degree of probability what the answer should be by turning our gaze upon other people who seem in most respects similar except for the lack of religion. These little-minded non-religious people— how large are their thoughts, with what are their emotions and activities concerned? They are not occupied with the anthropomorphic Deity of the Book of Genesis—No! For they are thinking about the price of Steel Common, and the latest movies, and the baseball scores. When Sunday gives them leisure from the daily round they do not turn to their Bibles; they dive into the interminable middle sections of the Sunday papers, the latest scandals, and the sporting news. Doubtless the Book of Genesis has its limitations; but it is a far cry from the description how in the beginning God created the heavens and the earth to the colored illustrations of the delectable doings of Mutt and Jeff.

The effect of religion upon the mind is in some ways similar to the effect of philosophy. Both philosophy and religion tend to give the mind which occupies itself with them a larger outlook, a broader and more impersonal setting, a certain freedom from the dominance of the immediate and the particular. In some ways they differ. Philosophy is more stimulating to intellectual activity; religion more productive of spiritual peace. Philosophy continually stirs one up to ask new questions; religion satisfies one with a large and general answer. Philosophy urges one on to the sceptical attitude; religion brings the emotion of certitude and confidence.

And this brings us to the question of the effect of religion upon happiness. If we trust what religious people themselves say on this matter we must conclude that the effect is very great. Whoever has talked with religious people on this subject must have been impressed with this fact. Some years ago I circulated a questionnaire which included, among other things, the following question: "If you should become thoroughly convinced that there was no God, would it make any great difference in your life—either in happiness, morality, or in other respects?" Out of the fifty people who answered this question forty asserted that the loss of belief would diminish their happiness. Typical among the answers were the following:

"He is as much a necessity to my spiritual existence as the elements of pure air are to my physical system in the preservation of life and health." "If I were convinced there was no God, I fear a sense of loneliness would become intolerable." "It would be like blotting out the sun." "It would plunge me in darkness and despair, but no one could make me believe it, for I have the witness in myself." "If I became convinced that there was no God, . . . it would make the greatest difference in my life both in happiness, which is largely dependent upon hope, and in morality. I should 'live, drink and be merry' with a vengeance and indulge myself in many excesses. I am sure of this." "I should go mad, I think. . . . There would be no I, no anything. He is the life of life to me, in everything making the vital meaning of even small things—flowers—

all beauty. He is the hidden strength of my strength and the stay of my weakness—some one to understand me and to be there always, requiring, reproving, but loving." "If I should become convinced that there is no God, then life for me would not be worth living. All my ideas and ideals must needs undergo complete modification. I should have no zest for pleasure, no courage to bear pain, no aims in life. I should fear death, yet long for death to end the farce of living." "As for any repose or ability to face life and death with composure, any incentive to be perfect in things hidden from outsiders, any exhilaration in living and trying to do my best—I cannot conceive it without the idea of God. . . . To live, on the contrary, with this constant feeling of common nature and common work with God is educative and constructive in itself, and gives, to me at least, in spite of innumerable shortcomings, the exhilaration of untold attainments and possibilities in the future, and puts a dignity as well as a joy into everything."

I think these responses represent pretty fairly the feelings and opinions of many or most religious people. There is no doubt that they believe a large part of their happiness comes from their religion, and that almost all of it would be destroyed should their religion be lost. We are not bound, however, to accept their opinion about themselves as necessarily correct. Religious people may not overestimate the contribution which religion makes to their happiness, but most of them probably do overestimate the loss in happiness they would suffer if they lost their religion. For they do not take into consideration the fact that there are partial substitutes for religion and that non-religious people, who have no belief in

God or immortality, are happy. Many a devoted wife or mother is perfectly certain that she could never have another happy moment should her husband or her child be taken away. Yet, such is the recuperative power of human nature that, after at most a few years, happiness of a sort returns. The normal course of a healthy physical and healthy moral life, with plenty of work and something worth while to accomplish, almost inevitably brings happiness. Most of us who have reached mature years have outlived several social situations or creedal situations which once seemed to us the necessary condition for our personal happiness. If the whole world should lose all faith in God and all hope of anything beyond the grave, it would soon adjust itself, after a fashion, to the new situation, and the song of the bird, the beauty of the sea, the exhilaration of youth and of physical health, the delights of artistic and intellectual pursuits, the stimulus of successful and difficult work, the joys of friendship and love and of family life would still breed happiness as they always have.

It might be a happy world still; but it would have lost something out of it which through ignorance might not be missed but which would be a real loss none the less. It would be a happy world, but one kind of happiness which those who know it often prize more highly than all others, it would not have. Religious people may be mistaken—they doubtless are mistaken—when they assert that without religion they would be forever wretched; but when they tell us that a large part of the happiness which they now possess comes from their religion, we have no reason to doubt their word. Here they are dealing not with conjectures as to the future, or as to some condition contrary to fact; they are making an immediate self-analysis and this analysis is worth as much as any other product of introspection on their part. I do not say it is decisive—mistakes in introspective analysis are common enough. But when one finds such uniform and emphatic agreement on a subject such as this, the evidential value is considerable. Especially is this the case where, as here, the testimony of those involved coincides so closely with what we should from *a priori* reasons be led to expect. For there can be no doubt that the cosmic attitude of all the actual great historical religions is of a consoling and hope-giving and inspiring nature. Surely this point need not be labored.

Furthermore, many religious people are in a position peculiarly fortunate for determining what religion actually does in the creation of happiness: I refer to those who for years were practically without religion and who through some conversion experience, to use their own phrase, "got religion." The change that comes about in such a situation is always marked, and often extraordinary. Nor can the expression of the joy of conversion with which we are all familiar be set down as due, in any large extent, to conventional Christian language. The same transformation in the hedonic life from depression to peace and steady elation, is testified to by converts in other religions who had never heard of Christianity or of our Western conventions. One has only to turn the pages of Mrs. Rhys David's translations of the *Psalms of the Early Buddhists* to find this familiar refrain, this repeated chorus, echoing from every one of those ancient brethren and sisters. Life for them was transformed. They had found a new joy, a peace which the world could neither give nor take away.

That religion does increase happiness—or add a new kind of happiness—will, I believe, be further attested by a comparison of religious and non-religious people as they impress a careful observer. That, at any rate, is my personal conclusion. Religious people seem to me notably happier than others. The difference seems to be observable both in every-day life and at times of emergency and trial. The religious man shares with the philosopher a point of view which enables him to see beyond the immediate events which loom so large in the eyes of one to whom cosmic realities are nothing and who lacks the confidence of religious faith. The typically religious people that I have known give one the impression of not having put all their eggs in one basket; or, if they have, that basket is in some realm where thieves do not break through nor steal. They refuse to take the chances and changes of their immediate fate too seriously. They possess a certain quiet calm and a certain inner joy through all the drudgery of the common day. And in the hour of trial their faces are often radiant. They had prepared themselves for just such moments. In short, I find in religious people a certain *depth*, a certain stability which in non-religious people of corresponding native equipment I fail to discern.

The whole matter of happiness and religion will be plainer if we ask ourselves what we mean by happiness. Happiness plainly is not pleasure. Those who lead lives of pleasure are frequently the most unhappy. Happiness in fact is consistent not only with the absence of pleasure but with the presence of a good deal of actual pain. To be brief—for we have no time for an elaborate analysis—happiness consists in the unified and successful working of our instincts and purposes. The unified and successful life is the happy life. Now unity is not a thing easily achieved. The natural man finds himself the prey of various strong and divergent impulses and aims. He is torn in opposite directions by his passions and his ideals. He is frequently in a state of civil war— than which nothing can be more miserable, no matter what pleasures may incidentally accompany it. As Professor Royce pointed out long ago, the way to unity, and the only way, is through loyalty. And the larger the loyalty, provided it be intense and dominating, the larger will be the portion of man's total life that it will unify. Now religion has the unique advantage of bringing at the same time the largest of loyalties and the most lasting of devotions. Hence it is that a deeply religious man is almost invariably a man of unified loyalty and of deep-lying happiness.

And this brings us to the question of the effect of religion on the will and on the moral conduct of life, for the same unity which is the condition of happiness is also the condition of real and efficient virtue. Most religious people assert not only that religion is a great help to morality, but also that without it their own virtue would suffer. Half of my respondents asserted that if they should lose their faith in God their morals would be seriously undermined or destroyed. This, I think, is a mistake. The influence of religion on morality is probably considerably overestimated by enthusiastically religious people. A good man whose habits and purposes have been already formed will pretty surely remain a good man even should he lose all his religious faith. While this is true, however, we must remember that the formation of the good man's habits and purposes is usually largely influenced by religion—by his own religion and by that of his parents and teachers. And even within the life of the adult the glowing inspiration that often comes from the religious attitude is a welcome reinforcement to the influence of that colder Daughter of the Voice of God.

Religion influences the morality of the individual, both during his formative years and in his mature life, in two ways—as a deterrent and as an inspiration. The deterrent influence of religion has been utilized, relied upon, and extolled out of all proportion to its relative value. In past generations and in less advanced communities, doubtless the fear of hell has worked a good deal of decency; but in the America and Europe of our common acquaintance it has lost or is fast losing most of its power. Much more important—because both more worthy and more enduring—is the positive assistance which religion brings to the moral life. The cosmic attitude, just because of its larger view, enables one to see straight, to ignore the petty, to adjudge values correctly, to think justly, and to put first things first. The religious attitude, therefore, must always give a certain preliminary advantage: it must tend to make the moral view—i. e., the rational view—dominant in the guidance of conduct. But further than that, as an empirical fact, the actual religions of to-day—Christianity, Buddhism, Hinduism, Mohammedanism, and Confucianism, so far as this can be called a religion—are inextricably bound up with moral teachings, which almost invariably are of an uplifting, and often of an ennobling nature. In the minds of their more intelligent followers these great religions *mean* morality. And the cosmic or more strictly religious parts of these systems are so nicely adapted to the ethical parts that the moral teachings get a natural enforcement of immense emotional power. It is in this positive way that religion makes its greatest contribution to morality: not as criminal judge or executioner or warning Fury, but as a giver of new strength and inspiration. The man who feels that in obeying the moral law he is putting himself on the side of the great cosmic forces, that he is not alone in the moral struggle but that God is on his side, has an immense advantage in the achievement of noble deeds over the good man who feels himself almost alone. The central principle of the moral life is, in one sense, loyalty to the larger good, to the greatest cause one knows. Now loyalty to the race in its future course demands a large imagination and a large mind. For most ordinary men these things are cold. But identify this aim with loyalty to a spiritual Being who is, or symbolically stands for, the cosmic Whole; if necessary personalize this Being in the form of the Christ or the Buddha—and you have a power which can act on the imagination of the simple mind, and which as a fact in millions of cases has made moral heroes out of very ordinary material.

The influence of religion upon the mind is made more clear if we turn to the more specific question of the influence of prayer upon the mind. For as

Professor James has said, "prayer is religion in act." Prayer at its best is not petition, but is the immediate and intense realization of oneself and of the Determiner of Destiny and of the actuality of some sort of relation between the two. The moments given to this meditative recognition bring strength, consolation, confidence, insight, new direction of the will, new self-concentration and fulfilment. So, at least, all sorts of religious people testify. For illustration of the sort of thing that prayer does let us turn again to some of the answers of my respondents. "The help is very practical," writes one woman. "Many times as a teacher I have gone to the classroom utterly unequal to the work, or to meet a crisis, and depending entirely on the promise of wisdom and strength to be given. At such times I have done my best and most successful work." Another woman writes: "In this matter more than in the other things about which you have asked, I rest on personal evidence. In time of perplexity about important matters I have found my judgment clarified and my decision shaping itself as a result of prayer, in much the same way that I have found myself affected by consultation with a wise friend. . . . I have still the feeling that I am left to make up my own mind but that my mind is working at its best. . . . I know that prayer makes possible the carrying of heavy burdens with serenity, and doing one's ordinary work with an undivided mind in spite of anxiety and sorrow. I know that prayer creates an atmosphere of the spirit, an elevation above pettiness and irritation, a warmth of affection for others, and a triumph over selfishness that no amount of philosophizing or reasoning with oneself can produce." "Essentially," writes one man, "I pray to enjoy a higher communion than is possible for me with any human soul." "Prayer is to spiritual life what breathing is to natural life." "I pray because I want to and like to, and feel that God understands, and I like the sympathy of it." "Prayer is natural, *not* one-sided. I feel that there is an *interchange* of something, I know not what, between me and that unseen, but felt-to-be present, being." "I pray—not in set terms very much—but I turn to God in all places and at all times, more or less, and I have felt real communion, hindered or dulled often by tired nerves or a whirlwind of emotion more earthly, or by sin more often, but I sometimes have it; and more constantly, if not quite communion, yet a strong dimmed sense of response—something I cannot quite hold, but feel."

Such are the subjective effects of prayer. Has prayer, in addition to this, any objective effects? Does one in prayer really come into contact with some Power or Being other than oneself? Or is prayer, as your committee has expressed it, "purely psychological?" This question, I think, is hardly one for me to answer. The subject assigned to me was, as you know, "Religion, Its Psychology." The question whether prayer is more than psychological belongs rather to the philosophy of religion. For plainly the psychology of religion can say nothing final on this question. It can, however, say something of a preliminary sort. The task of the psychology of religion, as I understand it, is roughly two-fold: first, to describe the facts of the religious consciousness as accurately as possible, and then to explain them in the scientific sense of explanation—*i. e.*, to generalize them and put them in order under laws of regular sequence. Both of these tasks it is seeking to accomplish. It has to some extent described the prayer state, and the effects that religion in general and prayer in particular have upon the mind. Some of these effects are of the sort that seem to indicate an outside source of inflowing power. Such is usually the conclusion, at any rate, of the prayerful mind itself. But psychology is bound to go on and see if the facts of prayer and its conditions and effects may not be so correlated with each other and with general psychological and physiological conditions as to be capable of generalization without appeal to any hypothetical entity outside of the human circle. To a considerable extent psychology is succeeding in building up such a generalization. The facts of prayer probably follow, *i. e.*, are capable of being described by means of, certain regular sequences.

We must be careful, however, not to draw from this the unjustified conclusion that therefore the prayerful consciousness is mistaken when it supposes itself in contact with something not itself. The fact, if it be a fact, that events follow each other regularly and are capable of being generalized by descriptive laws or formulæ may mean merely that the soul is in the presence of a constant and steady influence, and that the changes which it experiences are due to the combination of this influence with varying physiological and psychological conditions. Since these latter are the only ones that change and since they are also the only ones that psychology can get at and study, it is justified in expressing its so-called explanation (which, be it remembered, is only a description) in terms of these human conditions.

There is therefore nothing in the facts which psychology has discovered, nor in the explanation which it offers and the theory which it is enabled to build up, in any way incompatible with the conviction of the religious consciousness that under certain conditions the soul comes into touch with a Power not itself and receives from this Power the increased strength and insight which, as an indubitable fact, it experiences. It may well be that, given certain favorable conditions of body and mind, the act of prayer is, as it were, the throwing open of a window toward the East, and that through this the constant and eternal Light flows in.

Whether this is true, or only a possible hypothesis, it is not for psychology but for philosophy to decide. Each of you must take your own stand upon this question. I have wished merely to point out that there is nothing in the psychology of religion to make such an hypothesis at all improbable. The religious man is convinced that prayer is not merely psychological. He feels that in prayer at its best something objective takes place, that in it the soul realizes its inner nature, that it stands face to face with the Determiner of Destiny, and that some kind of interchange and communion is actualized between part and Whole, between the finite spirit and a Power not merely itself yet to which it is akin. Unless we take a view of the Universe so thoroughly and narrowly naturalistic as to leave no room for the spiritual, we should have no more justification from philosophy than from psychology in labelling as improbable this testimony of the religious consciousness. We cannot indeed prove that this testimony is justified. Whether it is or not each must decide for himself. Personally I believe that it is.

CHRISTIANITY AND OTHER RELIGIONS

DANIEL EVANS

THE contact of individuals, racial groups, and nations makes possible various attitudes and reactions. Some may remain indifferent, others hostile, while still others may be interested and curious, sympathetic and co-operative. We observe these attitudes and reactions in our own experiences and in the conduct of others, also in our own social group and not infrequently in our own nation and in other nations.

Now, in like manner, we find the same attitudes and reactions upon the part of various religions of the world. For centuries these contacts have been growing, until in our day, practically all the religions of the world are confronted with the problem of the right attitude toward one another. And this is particularly true of the Christian religion. Through travellers, traders, and missionaries it has been taken into all the world and the problem of the proper attitude toward other religions has become more and more acute. It must be said that there are some representatives of the Christian religion (whether they truly represent it may be questioned) who maintain an attitude of indifference: they will have nothing to do with the representatives of other religions: they pursue the policy of isolation. They fear they will dishonor the Christian religion by any recognition of other religions, and degrade it by comparing it with them. The then Archbishop of Canterbury refused on these grounds to attend "The World's Parliament of Religions" in Chicago in 1893.

There are others who take a hostile attitude toward other religions. They controvert them and do all they can to destroy them. Such persons appear to measure their love for and loyalty to the Christian religion by the intensity and fierceness of their hate of other religions.

There are persons, however, who are deeply interested in other religions than their own. Some are, of course, just curious: they want to know how other human beings relate themselves to the deity, and the experiences they have in this ultimate relation of life, and find some pleasure in studying these religions. Others have a far profounder interest; they desire to understand the religious life of other people and to appreciate the craving of the human spirit for fellowship with the Divine, and to feel the vital unity of the religious consciousness beneath the surface differences.

In all the great religions, as well as in the Christian religion, we find these several attitudes and these different reactions. No one religious group has a monopoly of indifference, or hostility, or interest, or friendliness. The explanation for these different attitudes and reactions must be sought in the conceptions entertained of the nature of the religions other than one's own. Back of the temper of mind is the idea of the character of these other religions. We confine ourselves now almost wholly to some traditional notions entertained by Christians of other religions in comparison with their own. Thus, some have regarded the Christian religion as true and all other religions as false. Others have divided all religions into revealed and natural: the Christian religion is a revealed religion; in and through it, God has disclosed His reality and purpose, through nature, history, great prophetic minds, and last and greatest of all in his Son. The natural religions are the products of the unaided reason of men, the results of their complex experiences without religious truth and certainty, and with much error. Still others have regarded the Christian religion as the sole pure religion and all others as really nothing but superstitious corruptions. The Christian religion is the pure life-stream that flows through the history of the race and the other religions are stagnant ponds, or dead seas. There linger still in some books on Christianity and other religions, even in our day, these traditional conceptions.

We observe, however, that there has always been

a far different conception of Christianity and other religions, cherished by the better and nobler representatives of the Christian religion on the one side and of the other religions on the other. In our own day, most educated Christians no longer think and speak of other religions as false, or "natural," or corrupt and superstitious, but regard them as true, revealed, and expressions of the great vital needs of the soul. And they respect other religions, and desire to learn about them from their own representatives, or from their sacred Scriptures. One striking manifestation of this, was "The World's Parliament of Religions," held in Chicago, in 1893, in connection with the World's Fair. The leaders in all the Christian Churches in this country invited the leaders of all the other great living religions to come and expound their religions before this parliament, and they came from all parts of the world, and a strange and splendid spectacle they presented, in all their differences of garments, colors, speech, and races, nationalities, and religions. Both the Christians and the others were in the true spiritual succession of liberal and fair-minded men of their respective religions. It was not the first time in the history of the world when men of different religions got together. The Emperor Akbar, a contemporary of Queen Elizabeth, invited to his court, Jews, Christians, Mohammedans, Brahmans, and Zoroastrians, and listened to their discussions, weighed their arguments, and came to the conclusion that there were good and sensible men in all religions. And one wise and liberal Mussulman once wrote:

One is born a pagan, another a Jew, and a third a Mussulman. The true philosopher sees in each a fellow-seeker after God.

And Mohammed himself said:

Every nation has a quarter of the heaven (to which they turn in prayer): it is God who turneth them toward it. Hasten then emulously after the good wheresoever ye are: God will one day bring you all together.

The same liberal spirit is found in the other religions, and these fine sentiments can be matched from them.

The Christian Fathers of the fourth century credited Demetrius Phalereus, the large-minded librarian of Ptolemy Philadelphus, about 250 B. C. with the attempt to secure the sacred books not only of the Jews, but also of the Ethiopians, Indians, Persians, Babylonians, Assyrians, Chaldeans, Romans, Phœnicians, Syrians, and Greeks.

And within the Christian religion there have always been liberal-minded men, who have recognized in other religions the disclosure of God, and their place in the divine providence. Justin Martyr believed and taught that the seed of the Divine Logos was implanted in men of every race: and that whatever truth was uttered anywhere was the property of Christians. And Clement of Alexandria, one of the noblest thinkers of the early Church, said that "the way of truth was like a mighty river ever flowing, and as it passed it was ever receiving fresh streams on this side and that." And the work of Greek philosophy was like the law and Gospel, an actual covenant, as that at Sinai: and as the law was a tutor for the Jews to bring them to Christ, so was philosophy for the Greeks.

And Eusebius, with a broad sweep of learning, passed in review the religions of Egypt, Phœnicia, Greece, and Rome, and maintained that all the higher culture was due to participation in the Logos, which had been continuously present in the hearts of man and providing the rudiments of the Divine Laws. The whole cultured life, in ethics, art, science, and philosophy, was thus brought within the scope of Revelation, and served as a *Preparation for the Gospel*. A book with this title, J. E. Carpenter says, "Is the first great work on comparative religion which issued out of Christian theology." Augustine, Abelard, Zwingli, and other great representatives of the Christian religion took the same attitude toward other faiths.

From this finer temper of mind, and true conception of religion in general and of the Christian religion in particular, there has grown a new historical interest in, and study of, religion and its significance and value in human life.

The historian of any country now recognizes that

it is impossible to explain its history without taking
into account the part religion has played in its career.
No man gets at the genius of a people or learns its
secret, without understanding its religion. Religion
is always the Hamlet of its drama. Neither its politics, nor its economics, nor its art, nor its education,
nor its events, nor the soul of the people can be
understood apart from its religion. The historian is
fully aware of this, and writes now from this point
of view.

The historian of religion itself, while he narrows
the range of his study, deepens it in giving his attention to this central reality in the life of a people, or
humanity. His specialized interest in religion has
made us see that religion is one of the great, if not
the supreme interest of human beings. And he is
making us recognize and appreciate the individuality
of religions. Each religion has its own distinctive
nature. It has its own character. There is something
unique in it. It is the expression and satisfaction of
the vital needs of the people. It has its own peculiar
glory: it is its own justification for being. This does
not mean, however, that all religions are on the same
level and are of equal worth and have the same
significance. On the contrary, what the history of
religions makes plain is the development of the religious consciousness and the stages through which
it has passed, and the emergent types of religion
characteristic of the stage. So, at the present time,

on the basis of the work done by the historians of primitive and historical religions, the philosophers of religion give us a new classification of religions. They are not satisfied with the traditional, dogmatic classifications into true and false, revealed and natural, pure and corrupt, nor are they satisfied with the classifications based on more and better historical data, such as polytheistic and monotheistic, or national and universal, or personal and mass-religions; they classify them rather in accordance with their primary interests and functions, and thus we have the newer classifications of nature-religions, morality-religions, and redemption-religions. It is, however, recognized that there is no rigorous line of demarcation here, any more than in other vital growths: here as elsewhere there are transitional features. This classification seeks to grade religions by the function they serve and the values they seek to secure and conserve. Thus, the nature-religions are primarily concerned with economic or survival values. The problem of subsistence and self-preservation is primary in the earlier stages of existence. Their life is precarious. Dangers threaten them on every hand. Hostile forces surround them. Food, shelter, preservation, and posterity, are their urgent interests. Their religion has chiefly to do with these values. They seek the gods in their behalf and maintain favorable relations with them for these purposes.

The morality-religions are on a higher level. They

are characteristic of the greater civilizations. With the consolidation of tribes, and the growth of nations, and the increasing complexity of social life, new needs are developed and moral values have a higher place, and are more needed for the purity and safety of civilization. In the interests of righteousness, justice, truth, and all such moral values, men seek their God, convinced of his interest in these values, and that they exist in his character, and express his purpose and demands, and that they may appeal for his help in their behalf, and that they themselves must be the servants of these moral values.

The next stage is that reached by the redemption-religions. These mark the stage when the profounder needs of the human spirit are keenly felt, when the ruling passion is for life in the spiritual order, or with the Divine Reality. The time came when men could not remain satisfied with the values of time and the earth: when they felt the inadequacy of the natural order and human society to meet the cravings of their souls. They had needs which these could not minister to. They felt they must pass through the material to the spiritual, through the temporal to the eternal, through the finite to the infinite, and through the human to the Divine. They were in search for the ultimate Reality behind or above or beyond this world of appearance. They felt a spiritual nostalgia for the ultimate Reality.

They were prevented from returning and arriving there by many things. Some were hindered by this material world which for them was so opaque that the spiritual could not shine through, or so massive that there was grave danger of thinking it the most real of all realities: or so alluring and deceitful that it holds the mind captive to its illusion. Others found in their bodies the great hindrance, in the demands of the senses, in the clamor of the passions, in the urge of their instincts and impulses; or in their minds with their blindness, obtuseness, deception, or obstinacy. Release was sought from these hindrances, that the human spirit might live its true life in the world of the Eternal Spirit and there be at home and at rest. Redemption from these hindrances, and freedom for the life of the spirit, became the greater interest of life, and the human spirit passionately craved for God Himself as its salvation. Religion then as a fact of history and an experience in human life has passed from the natural through the moral to those ultimate spiritual values and realities of the Universe.

Now it is within this general framework that we can best fit in the various religions of the world, and see their place in history and the values in which they have been interested and the function they have served. There are still many living religions which belong to the stage of the nature-religions. There are also some living religions which belong to the stage of morality-religions: and there are also living redemption-religions. It is then within this framework of reference that we shall consider the religions which we are asked to compare with the Christian religion and shall endeavor to view them as near to their original sources as possible: to get back to their personal founders, for the religions of personal founders have their own peculiar character since they bear the impress of the geniuses from whom they are derived. This method will not give us full knowledge, for this would require us to know these religions in their history, and all the changes they have undergone, and their present condition, but this method will give us a clear insight into their distinctive nature and enable us to appreciate their significance and worth.

We turn attention first to Confucianism which has played such an important part in China. From its early veneration of Confucius China passed in 1906 to his worship, and temples have been raised in his honor all through the country. He was born 551 B. C. He had the privilege of a good education, and was fortunate in securing a position as counsellor with the political ruler of his time and later was promoted to a magistracy, and went still higher in the state and was made superintendent of public works, and was so successful that crime ceased and great moral improvement was made. After leaving this position he went from court to court offering his good counsels to the rulers.

It is evident from the positions he held and the

service he rendered that he considered his task in life to be a moral counsellor and practical statesman. His primary interest was in moral matters. He was a practical thinker. He was a moral servant of the state. His primary interest was ethical nationalism. He sought to establish good order and to secure the welfare of the nation by moral education through wise counsel. For him the cardinal virtue was filial piety. The good son will make a good brother, friend, neighbor, and subject. *Reciprocity* was his *golden* rule, stated, however, in the negative: "What you do not want done to yourself, do not do to another." Reciprocity, however, requires that one requite injury with justice, and kindness with kindness. Men should be dealt with according to their deserts. He held that men are fundamentally good by nature and they can not blame Heaven for being what they are, for if and when they are not good, this is not due to their nature, but to their bad education, ignorance, and parental neglect. His ideal is that of the "Superior Man," who knows the right and proper thing to do in every situation. He is "a man not only of faultless virtue, but also of faultless propriety." (G. F. Moore.)

By his ideal, and counsels and also by his practical activity, Confucius moved almost wholly in the ethical sphere. In matters of the state ritual of religion, he was punctilious; but in matters of conviction and thought about the ultimate spiritual reality, about the divine or spiritual beings, he had little to say. It is true, however, that in times of strain and stress he felt himself sustained by the thought that "Heaven knew him" and had interest in him. His conception of Heaven, however, was that of a *moral order* of the world which had some influence in nature and the human world, but there was no vivid sense of this Divine Order, and since it was not conceived in personal terms, prayer played little part in his life and less and less so until at last when ill, and urged to pray by a disciple, he replied: "It's a long time since I prayed." And concerning the after life, he maintained an agnostic position: he was silent. He had no wisdom to utter, no hope to cherish.

Confucius appears before us, then, as a moral counsellor, a practical thinker, a worker for a better national order. He moves largely, indeed almost wholly, in the moral sphere, in the practical world, in the region of the lesser interests and the secondary problem of life. He was not a progressive moral thinker: he did not consider himself as a reformer, but as a transmitter: he was not a profound philosopher concerned with the ultimate problems of life and the world: nor was he a religious genius to whom God is the greatest and most vivid of all realities in relation with whom the glory and wonder of life consist. His religion is at best a morality-religion with the emphasis on the morality rather than on the religion. It is in this sphere that he did his work, had his influence, and is of significance. He stands to Confucianism in a different relation from either Mohammed to Mohammedism, or Buddha to Buddhism, or Jesus to Christianity. He is a reviver of ancient customs, not an initiator of new movements.

The next religion we consider is Mohammedism, which derives its origin and character and genius from Mohammed, its founder. We have quite a different man in Mohammed from Confucius. He was born in 570 A. D. He was early left an orphan, and was brought up by his uncle, with whom he travelled much on business. He was later employed by a rich widow, whose capital was invested in caravans. He proved to be a good trader and successful financier and she a wise and daring woman, for she proposed a matrimonial partnership and, though much older than he, was accepted, and the marriage was blessed with six children and was very happy. While she lived, he took no other wives. When he was forty years of age he spent much time in solitude, in the mountains, near Mecca, engaged in the religious exercises of meditation, fasting, and prayer. He had come into contact with both Jews and Christians as well as his own more or less pagan folk. He was sorely troubled by the pagan customs and idolatrous practices of his own people. The burden of his soul was the gripping conviction of the impending judgment of God upon his people and the world. He brooded over this idea. It darkened the whole sky for him. Then there came the great conviction of God's revelation to him, and of his prophetic mission. The revelation and the mission were given in the message: "There is no god but God, and Mohammed is his prophet."

Here then it is made evident that Mohammed's problem was distinctively religious: his task was to get men to recognize and acknowledge God; to worship him in proper ways; to abandon all pagan practices and idolatrous customs and to live as Allah, the Great God, demanded of them. His mission was to proclaim this God, and to demand true worship, and a righteous life, and to warn against the terrific impending judgment. Allah, the great and true God, was a jealous God who would not tolerate other Gods, pagan or Christian; He was Lord of all Worlds, omnipotent savior and all merciful, whose will determined the destiny of all men.

Such a God demanded the moral reformation of his people. The social vices of gambling, drunkenness, infanticide of daughters, extra-marital sexual relations and lax divorces were condemned; and such social virtues as filial piety toward aged parents, duties of kinship, helpfulness to strangers, kindness to slaves, were enjoined.

To secure this reform of worship and of morals, he had recourse to the motives of the fear of hell and the hope of Paradise. The hereafter, therefore, played a large and vivid and powerful part in his thought and preaching. His imagination ran riot in picturing the torments and horrors of hell and the glories and bliss of heaven, and there was no hesitation in having recourse to very sensuous descriptions of both.

All persons who repented and accepted him as prophet composed a new religious brotherhood. They were fellow believers; they had great interests in common; they were bound to protect one another; their religious bond superseded their clan or tribal relations and duties and gave them safety and security.

Mohammed believed his mission was not for his own people alone, but for all mankind. He was the prophet of the one God for all men, for Jews and Christians as well as for the Arabs. His religion was the superior religion and required submission from all and he felt that his task required that he should impress his religion upon others and compel them, even by the sword, to accept it.

It is quite clear that we move here in a different world from that of Confucianism. That was primarily ethical; this is primarily religious; there Heaven or the Divine is the secondary consideration; here it is primary; there the other world plays no part; here it plays the chief part; there the moralist is gentle; here the religionist is stern. Mohammedanism belongs to the morality-type of religion and gains its significance and has its value as falling in this category. It has spread far and wide in the earth and has wielded great influence in the world, and has been a great blessing to the more backward races at the stage of the nature-religions, and it competes to-day with the Christian religion in the life of many peoples.

When we pass from China and Arabia into India we travel far in space, but farther in the world of thought and desire. Confucius refrained from thinking about ultimate matters, and confined his efforts to the practical moral problems of men in social and state relations, and Mohammed concerned himself with problems of religious worship, and moral reforms, with, however, an outlook into the transcendent future life. In India, men are concerned with very different problems; they move in different thought-worlds and are motivated by other needs. They are nothing if not metaphysical. They are profoundly philosophical. They deal with ultimate problems of life and thought. Their passion is for salvation. Their religions and philosophies are redemptive. They move in deeper regions, in more interior recesses of the soul, and in the transcendent order of Reality. We meet, in India, with two great types of redemption philosophies: the one is Brahmanism, the other Buddhism. Brahmanism is without a personal founder; Buddhism like the other religions has its great founder. The one bears the stamp of a general movement of thought to which many profound thinkers contribute: the other bears the stamp of the genius of one of the great souls of the human race. They are quite different from each other, but the second cannot be understood apart from the first.

We turn our attention first to Brahmanism. The religious thinkers who gave rise to this redemptive movement of life and thought were profoundly impressed with human sufferings and miseries. The religion of the day was too ritualistic, and too sensuous and too mixed with popular superstitions to satisfy them. Relief could not be found in and through it. They must seek further, and their search issued in this new philosophical religion of redemption. What deeply impressed them was the deceptive nature of this world of sense. It is the realm of the impermanent. It is the sphere of confusion. Life is a vortex forever whirling or a wheel forever turning. The world appears to be massively real, but is in fact phenomenal, illusional, and wrapped about with the veil of Maya, and so it is evil and the cause of sufferings, from which men must seek release. The inner world of the self is far more real than this outer world, and thither must men retreat. There they will find unity, not chaos; permanency, not transciency. Their own inner life which is so different from the outer world is not only similar, but in fact is identical with Brahma, the ultimate Reality.

Thus retreat from the outer world into the inner

life brings men into the region of the absolute. Here the Atman finds the Brahma and in finding the Brahma discovers that the Atman is identical with it, the self with the absolute. Nothing else is real; all else is illusion. Whatever is or thinks it is apart from the absolute is illusion.

The problem of life then for Brahmanism is salvation from this world of illusion. The evil from which men need redemption is the desire and the idea that one can live apart. This desire and thought involve men in the vortex, and make them subject to the causal-nexus which brings a succession of rebirths. Redemption from this evil comes when men see that they are fundamentally one with the absolute; when they realize this unity with Brahma; when they cease to think or desire to cherish their own individuality; when they literally surrender and lose themselves in the absolute. Salvation means to be without the desire of individual life, and to be one with the absolute. Thus "Brahma is he and in Brahma is he absorbed."

This salvation is obtained or attained, not by ritual practices, nor by the doing of meritorious good works, but by insight. Knowledge alone is the bridge to absorption in the absolute. This knowledge, however, is not discursive, nor rational, nor even intuitional. It is rather a psychical ecstatic state in which there comes about a loss of individual consciousness and blending and merging or swooning into the Divine Reality. This psychical state may be induced in many ways, and marvellous psychological devices and practices have been developed for this purpose. The goal of salvation is reached when there is complete absorption in the absolute without the slightest trace left of any desire or consciousness or individuality. This gospel of salvation from suffering and misery, from submersion in the world of illusion and whirling in the vortex of successive lives brought relief to men. It was a religion for the sorely afflicted. It did for men what neither the religion of ritual nor the religion of virtues could do. It gave men the consciousness of the absolute, and the arrival at the source and goal of all. "For a man in grief came seeking Knowledge, remarking, 'I have heard it said that he who knows the spirit passes beyond grief.'"

Yet the strange thing is that to pass beyond grief requires that one pass beyond life; to have the consciousness of the Absolute is to lose consciousness of all else and even of oneself; to arrive at the goal is to cease to be individual.

It was into this world of the popular religion and Brahmanism that Gotama was born, about 560 B. C. He was the son of a rich and noble landed proprietor of the Cakya clan. His early life and education and experiences were like those of others of his own station. He enjoyed all its advantages and privileges, in the way of sports and pleasures, and also of marriage.

Then came the great dissatisfaction, through the vivid discovery of the sufferings of life. These privileges and pleasures could no longer give him contentment. His mind was distraught. He became a seeker of salvation. He put himself under the guidance of religious experts, he practised rigorous self-mortification and went to ascetic extremes, but he could not find peace of mind.

Then there came the new and profound experience of enlightenment while he was meditating under the Bo-tree. He discovered that neither the life of indulgence, nor high-wrought psychical states, nor extreme asceticism availed; but illumination which came through insight and brought the peace desired. This enlightenment made him Buddha. It was a real, profound conversion which he experienced. It changed his whole life and made him one of the world's great saviors.

The fundamental problem of life and thought in India remained the same for him as for Brahmanism: how secure release from the sufferings of life. This was his problem, and his mission in life was its solution.

He broke with the popular religion and got rid of every remnant of faith in a Divine being; he broke, too, with the Brahminical philosophical speculation on the ultimate reality or the Absolute. The distinctively religious and the profoundly philosophical interests of life and thought did not appeal to him.

He was essentially atheistic and averse to metaphysics and confined himself to the practical moral problem of redeeming men from this world of suffering. His new wisdom was insight into the nature and cause of misery and the means and method for saving men therefrom. This wisdom made him a physician of souls. This was his interpretation of his task in life. His gospel was one of spiritual healing.

The cause of suffering he saw in the desire of man for life, accompanied by sensuous pleasures. This insight into desire as the cause of suffering is his central idea, the keystone of his whole system, and while the idea of desire had some place in Brahmanism, it did not have this central place and so Buddha gains his significance from this new conception. The removal of this cause of suffering is brought about only by the extinction of desire. As one puts out a fire, so must one extinguish desire. As one blows out or snuffs out a candle, so must one snuff out all desire. The problem of life then is to extinguish desire. Now in the attempt to solve this problem by extinguishing the flame of life, Buddha strikes out a new path and thus finds a new way of salvation. Other ways had failed him; his own new way was thoroughly ethical, in a twofold sense. First, the eightfold path in which one must walk is wholly ethical. The qualities of thought, speech, and conduct are all moral and they are essential in Buddhism, and only incidental in Brahmanism. Second, the way is thoroughly ethical also, because it is a moral achievement by one's own efforts. A man is thrown wholly upon his own moral resources. Every one is to work out his own salvation and there is no divine power to aid him.

The goal of salvation is complete cessation of being. It is not absorption in the absolute, but annihilation of the self, as far as there is any self in Buddhism. To attain to Nirvana in original Buddhism means not only the extinguishment of the flame of desire, but also of life itself. There is, therefore, an ethical and a metaphysical extinguishment. The continuance of the redeemed life had no place in his system of thought.

This was his gospel for suffering souls; to preach it was his mission, and to save all sorts and conditions of men was his passion; and to gather them into one fellowship was his aim. He went into the world with all its sufferings and sorrows and miseries with this message of salvation. In taking pity on men in their woeful condition, he came near to their hearts. In making the way of salvation ethical rather than ascetic or ritualistic or philosophical, he made an appeal to the deeper and nobler side of human life. And in his own noble character and greatness of soul was found an ideal that took their hearts captive. And from that day to this, in many lands, millions of human beings have found in Buddhism a faith by which to live well and die serenely.

The other religion which I am asked to discuss and with which these religions are to be compared is the Christian. Like Confucianism, Mohammedanism, and Buddhism, the Christian religion derives from a historical person whose genius is stamped upon it, and whose life and teaching and personality give it its distinctive character and content and power. The least thing that can be said of Jesus is that he was one of the world's great religious geniuses, whose soul was sensitive and hospitable to the Divine Reality. He had the great racial advantage of being a Jew, to whom had come a marvellously rich heritage in matters of faith and morals and into which he entered and assimilated its best parts into the very substance of his soul. He was, however, more than a product of his race; he was an emergent personality. He lived his own deep inner life; he reacted on all he inherited and on all he was taught; and there emerged in his soul a profounder and richer experience with God. This experience is the greatest thing in his life, out from which, as a centre, all other interests radiate, and out from which he moves to serve them. God is to him the first and final reality, the chief interest in life, the great companion in fellowship, the perfect standard for conduct, the absolute measure of all things in heaven and on earth, and whose sovereignty is to be recognized by all men on earth as it is in heaven, and in communion with whom in life and thought and will men in time and in eternity find the satisfaction of their desires and the enrichment of their lives and enhancement of their personalities.

These were his consuming interests: and the values to which he gave supreme place: this was the spiritual world in which he was thoroughly at home.

Now he conceived his problem in a thoroughly religious fashion, and so regarded his mission in life as the recovery of men from sin to God. The one great evil which hinders men from living their true life, and from which they need to be delivered, is not suffering but sin. The obstacles in the way of men's living with God and for his interests is not the physical world, nor the social environment, nor the natural instincts and desires, but the mind or heart or will. It is man himself that is his own worst foe, and the greatest hindrance to spiritual fellowship with God. It is the way he satisfies his natural cravings, the direction of his thought, the objects of his interests, and the self-centredness of his life. The real problem of redemption is to change a man's mind, to recover him to his true self, to have him find and love God, and devote his life to those interests in which all men can share for their moral and spiritual welfare. It was, therefore, upon the fact of sin and the problem of redemption that Christ concentrated his mind and consecrated his life. The mission of his life was to help men find their souls, love and live with God, and love and serve one another. He conceived the goal of salvation to be the fellowship of God and man; the Divine and human wills to be in concord; the soul of man to find its realization and satisfaction in the purposes of God. Here and now and forever, man is to live in and with and for God. And out from this divine and eternal centre man is to work in and take an appreciative and confident attitude toward the world of nature and the world of human beings, and also face with courage and hope the eternal world, as the sphere of his final destination wherein he is to be not absorbed nor extinguished, but conserved.

With these data before us, a comparison between the Christian religion and these other religions, in their original forms and at their sources, can be made. As compared with Confucianism, we observe that the problem of Confucius is secondary; that he was concerned simply with the right ordering of men in social relations, in the home, society, and the state; whereas Christ was concerned with the condition of the heart out from which come the issues of life and upon which all social life is dependent. And while with Confucius the distinctively religious life, with its vivid sense of God and spiritual realities, played a secondary and decreasing rôle, with Christ it played the chief rôle. The prayerless life of Confucius and the prayerful life of Christ indicate a radical difference in their lives and in their religions.

As compared with Mohammed, whose problem was

primarily religious and in this respect both move in the same thought-world, Mohammed was more concerned with the ritual of worship, submission to the will of God, eternal rewards, and the imposition of his will upon others by force and even by violence; whereas Christ was far more concerned with the inner attitude of the soul in prayer and love to God and in glad obedience to his will and in the springs of human conduct and the law of love and service with respect to others, and his appeal to men was to their experiences, their minds and consciences, and not to force or violence, and his conception of the future world was more ethical and spiritual.

In comparison with Brahmanism, the agreement is fundamental in one respect, but radically different in many others. The agreement lies in their profound interest in the ultimate Reality. Here man finds his true home, his abiding interest, his true blessedness. But the difference in the conception of this Reality is profound. In Brahmanism, this Reality is the undifferentiated Unity which grants no reality to the world, nor standing-room for man, and to which nothing can be real or good, and which will at last absorb into itself all souls, and neither it nor they will be the wiser or the better for it. Whereas in Christ's thought, this ultimate Reality is conceived in the terms of God, the Father, Lord of Heaven and Earth, a personality complete, a character perfect, a will omnipotent, a mind all-comprehending, a heart all-loving and all-cherishing, and communion with whom, not absorption, is the final goal of life and the realization of salvation.

The comparison with Buddhism also makes clear certain agreements and differences. Both Buddha and Christ were profoundly interested in suffering human beings; both were supremely interested in ethical matters, in the moral conduct and disposition, compassion, and service, and both were greater still in themselves, in their characters, and in the influence of their personalities. But Buddha was concerned primarily with the sufferings of man, Christ with their sins; Buddha with their release from the chain of rebirth, Christ with the new birth; Buddha with the extinguishment of the desire of life, Christ with its purification, that man might have life and have it more abundantly; Buddha with a man's redemption in his own naked strength, Christ with man's salvation by Divine Help; Buddha with a moral process of life that issued in nothingness, Christ with a moral process that issued in life eternal.

Our final consideration has to do with the question of superiority in religion. We remarked at the beginning that the old classifications of religions into true and false, revealed and natural, pure and corrupt are no longer maintained by modern thinkers, consequently the test of superiority based on these is no longer available. Moreover, it was declared that every religion is recognized as having its own individuality, and its own justification for existence. It might appear, then, that there is no place for the question of superiority in religion; that the very notion is a remainder of the old way of regarding religions; and that it smacks too much of the aristocratic temper, which has no room in a democracy of religions. As in a democracy every man is born equal and there is no place for inequality, so in religion are not each and all equal? Can there be any superiority?

While the question of superiority is primarily philosophical rather than historical, yet even the historian proceeds on the assumption that there are differences of values in religions and his judgments have to do with these values as well as with facts. Indeed, the very classification of religions into nature, morality, and redemptive types presupposes this judgment of value. How then shall we judge superiority in religion? There are three or four ways of judging, or tests to which we may have recourse.

The first is the test of the satisfaction of those vital needs out of which religion takes its rise, and which it is its function to fulfil. These needs as we have seen are numerous and various and graded. They range from those that have to do with subsistence and self-preservation and those that have to do with our higher cultural and moral interests up to those which are concerned primarily with the spiritual values of life in the soul's intimate relation to the ultimate reality. Some religions satisfy these lesser subsistence needs; others the higher ethical needs: but only a few the greatest needs of the human spirit. The religion then that ministers to these deepest needs is the best religion. The religion that makes for the completeness of life is the superior religion. In this respect, our religion declares the purpose or mission of its founder to be: "I am come that men may have life, and have it more abundantly."

Another test is the power of religion in the life of the race through the centuries. History is the crucible of all values. It is the acid test of claim to worth. The course of history is strewn with the bleached skeletons of many dead religions, and there is some dead stuff in most surviving religions. The religion then that can survive the deepening experience of men and their changing thought; that can successfully solve the critical problems of the race in its new situation and can confidently accept the challenge of new duties, is the one that has survival value, and the one that can do these things best is the superior religion. Now in the course of the centuries in the western world, the Christian religion has been able to meet this test. At the present time, the religions of the Far East are confronted with the gravest problems and the question is seriously raised by some thinkers of those religions whether they can solve them. We may take Doctor Anesaki as an instance. He writes in his book on *The Religious and Social Problems of the Orient:*

The problem for the Orient is how to adjust itself to this situation without losing its own best heritages. The future of Oriental culture by itself is a great uncertainty because it has so long been enwrapped in the immobility of a stagnant social life. But the crisis in its fate is brought to light and made acute by the contact of the Orient with the Occident, not only in its ideas, but industry and politics. . . . Science [as a quest for truth] is finding its way into the Orient, particularly into Japan, but this scientific attitude of mind is not congenial to the Oriental mind, either wedded to tradition or used for æsthetic employment. Moreover, in this sense it is not a good friend of the religious spirit [and he quotes a Japanese writer to the effect]: We have been experimenting much but have not experienced.

On another page Doctor Anesaki says:

We are compelled to confess that the same kind of doubts and questions face the Oriental religions. The Hindoo is proud of his profound spiritual inheritance, but can he declare that his precious heritage alone is sufficient to organize his life? China tried to establish Confucianism as her state religion, but its failure is too obvious. Japan has her Shinto and Buddhism, but is not the mind of the rising generation being steadily alienated from these religions? . . . The old religions [of Asia] have lost their positions of dominance and are being controlled or disturbed by the social changes that are taking place. Hinduism, hopelessly interwoven with the caste system, is pre-eminently a conservative, institutional force, and not an inspiring or regenerative power. Confucianism is a humanitarian ethic, but being an elaboration of a patriarchal system of politics and morals, its teachings are peculiarly static and formal— Shinto being a remnant of ancient nature worship and of the cult of the spirits, cannot hope to withstand the pressure of science, while its communal ethics is struggling for life in the face of the industrial régime. One religion that remains in the field with some hope is Buddhism. But it is hopelessly divided, its organizations are parochial, and its tenets often too metaphysical.

This is a situation which should make no true Christian or friend of religion rejoice, but give him grave concern, for while it may assure him of the superiority of his own religion, it must give him pause when he thinks of the spiritual interests of those great peoples. The very difficulty his own religion has had to meet in changing situations should make him sympathize with those other religions in their crisis.

There is one other test for judging the superiority in religion. It concerns the significance of the ideas or truths of religion. Every religion has its own *Weltanschauung*. It has its own distinctive truths, which it takes to be valid and which it believes to be in accord with reality. These truths have to do with the nature and destiny of man, the nature and purpose of the world, and the nature and character and purpose of the ultimate spiritual reality. Now in the light of all our knowledge from our own experience, and from science and philosophy, the question arises, which religion appears to give us the most adequate interpretation of man? Does the religion that makes man impersonal and robs or rather fails to grant him individuality, or the one that makes him a link in the chain of ancestry and posterity, or the one that makes him a tool of the Almighty, or the one that regards him as the child of God, an individual with the dignity of moral sovereignty and infinite spiritual worth? Again, which religion gives the most adequate interpretation of the world? The religion that peoples the world with spirits, or the one that makes it an illusion, or the one that regards it as a great causal-nexus with its endless recurrences, or the one that regards it as transparent and translucent, through which we see its Divine Creator and find in it reality, goodness, wonder, and a vast teleological drift, which carries humanity to a far-off divine event in which the divine purpose will be realized?

Once more we ask, which religion gives us the profoundest insight into the nature and purpose of the ultimate Reality? Does the religion that regards it as the impersonal heaven to which one does not direct his prayers; or the one that regards it as the bare abstract Almighty Will before which all must submit; or the one that considers it as the Absolute which grants no reality to anything and in which all souls are lost at last when disillusionment comes; or the one that sees only the causal-nexus as the law of Karma; or the religion that conceives the ultimate Reality in the terms of personality, whose mind is the truth of all things, whose will is the energy in, back of, and over all things, to whose love all human beings are precious, and whose character is best described as Christlike, and whose supreme interest is the moral and spiritual welfare of human beings in all worlds?

There are some of us who hold, on the basis of available knowledge and from the application of these various tests, that the Christian religion is the superior religion.

SIN, CONVERSION, FORGIVENESS, AND ATONEMENT

ANGUS DUN

THE four subjects which have been assigned to me for discussion—sin, conversion, forgiveness, and atonement—have this in common, that they all have to do with what religion does for people. Sin is the name which religion uses for what is wrong with people. Atonement, conversion, and forgiveness are all names which religion uses to describe the righting of this wrongness.

Sin is a distinctively religious term. It has reference to God. As the term "crime" has reference to the law of the community, or the term "social error" has reference to the demands of the book of etiquette, so the word "sin" has reference to the demands of God. Consequently for views of life which leave God out there can be no such thing as sin. For an exclusively biological view, for example, or the view-point of naturalistic psychology, there can be only maladaptation between the individual and his environment, or maladjustment within the self, conflict, repression, or what not. But sin, I repeat, is a religious idea and finds a place only within a religious view of life. It is that deed or that condition which separates a man from his rightful relation to God. This is what is common to the idea of sin wherever it appears within the bewildering variety of historical religions. In ancient Greece, you find it as the deed which has alienated the favor of the gods and brought disaster on the city. You find it in parts of the Old Testament as that from which a man must be cleansed before he can offer his sacrifices or enter into the holy place. In the teaching of Jesus, it is presented in terms of the Prodigal who turns his back on his Father's house and goes into a far country.

Since sin is that which separates men from God, it follows that the idea of sin in any particular religion corresponds to the idea of God. Where God is thought of primarily as a sovereign and lawgiver, uttering Ten Commandments from Sinai, there sin is breaking the laws of God. If God is the Presence sought in worship, then sin is whatever stands in the way of an entrance into that Presence or a consciousness of that Presence. For those to whom God is the Father of the household of men, sin is all that is unfilial and unbrotherly. The worst offense against a jealous God is flirtation with a rival God. The worst offense against a just God is injustice. The worst offense against a loving God is an offense against love.

It follows, in the second place, from the fact that sin is that which separates men from God, that the consciousness of sin, or what is frequently called the

conviction of sin, arises in connection with the consciousness of God. As the sight of a traffic policeman
makes us conscious that we are going thirty miles
an hour, as the presence of greatness makes us feel
small, or the presence of cleanness makes us feel
dirty, so the consciousness of God or of Holiness has
affected men. An Isaiah goes into the temple and
experiences an overwhelming impression of the
glory of God. And the immediate response is to cry
out, "Woe is me! for I am undone; because I am a
man of unclean lips, and I dwell in the midst of a
people of unclean lips: for mine eyes have seen the
king, the Lord of hosts." A Peter, in the act of be-
trayal, sees Christ looking at him, and he goes out
and weeps bitterly. The most insistent ideas of sin
arise out of an immediately felt conflict between
certain deeds or attitudes or conditions and the
awareness of God. The two things, God and sin, do
not go together. They are felt to be incompatible in
the same way that whistling "Yankee Doodle" is
incompatible with listening to a symphony, or
spitting is incompatible with an operating-room.
When the writer of one of the Psalms, a person, it is
worth remembering, of the same general constitution
as ourselves, says, "Who shall ascend into the hill of
the Lord? or who shall stand in his holy place? He
that hath clean hands and a pure heart; who hath
not lifted up his soul unto vanity, nor sworn deceit-
fully," he is reporting on religious experience. And

when Christ says, "The pure in heart shall see God," again we have a report of religious experience, of the kind of experience that has produced the idea of sin, and the conviction of sin.

With this preliminary glance at the idea of sin, let us turn to the three other religious ideas which we are considering, atonement, forgiveness, and conversion. As I have already said, they all have to do with the righting of the wrongness for which sin is a name. *Atonement* in its broader use means simply at-one-ment or reconciliation, the overcoming of the separation which sin creates between men and God. In a narrower but more common use it is that which makes amends for the sin, as we might say that the criminal atones for his crime by undergoing punishment or a nation atones for the damage done another nation in war by paying an indemnity. *Forgiveness* is that attitude on God's part which makes reconciliation possible, the declaration that hostilities are off, the receiving of the late enemy back into normal relations. *Conversion* is the change which must take place in the sinner if the separation is to be overcome. It may be a change of allegiance or of deed or of heart and character.

Just as the idea of sin varies with the idea of God, so the idea of atonement varies with the idea of sin. If sin is in the nature of a stain, then what is needed to be rid of it is something in the nature of a washing. Hence the great place which washings and baptisms have as preparation for worship or as initiation into the religious life. If sin is viewed as the drag which the body or matter exerts upon the spirit, then relief will be sought in disciplines that put the body under, in experiences which simulate escape from the body; and religious aspiration will centre on the time when the spirit can escape from its prison house. If sin is looked upon as the breaking of a sacred code of law, then the path of restoration involves the paying of the penalties which the broken law demands, the acceptance again into good legal standing, and in the future obedience to the law. But if sin is seen to issue from the character or will, then nothing will suffice as a means of reconciliation but a radical change in character. And then we have required something as drastic as what we usually mean by conversion. Then the forgiveness of God must be more than a pronouncement of good legal status. It must be acceptance back into friendly relations, into companionship and love.

A simple illustration may serve to clear our minds as to the general nature and relationship of the four ideas we are considering. Take as an analogy to the religious relationship, the connection of a student with Harvard University. The character of that institution determines what will be required of the student and what will threaten his connection with it. Since it is an institution for the furtherance of "sound learning and moral dispositions," persistent failure to progress in sound learning, and notorious evil living, will constitute the equivalent of sin and lead to a severance of friendly relations. How, then, is the relation to be restored, an at-one-ment made between Harvard University and the suspended student? Something in the nature of expiation or atonement may well be required, a more or less penal period of absence from college, of work in a bank, perhaps the making up of past work. Probably some general evidence will be demanded of a right-about face on the man's part, something remotely akin to conversion. And finally it will be necessary that the university authorities forgive the man, that is, restore him to good standing.

Having outlined the general meaning and relation of these four ideas, let us consider some of the variations that they have gone through in the history of religion. As has been suggested, the ruling idea in religion is the idea of God, and all other ideas and practices must ultimately adjust themselves to that. And the ruling motive in religion is the desire to be at-one with God, to possess His favor or come into His presence. This is the common thread of motive that one can follow through the bewilderingly complex maze of religious motives. The major variations in religion correspond to man's changing insight into the fundamental character of life, as to the Power or Reality or Law or Person with which or with whom he must ultimately reckon and as to the supreme good he may gain or lose.

At some of the earliest levels of religion into which we can enter with any imaginative sympathy and understanding, life appears to present itself to men as a realm of *things*, of good things and bad things, things he wants and things of which he is afraid. Among them are things holy or taboo. They are things like blood or the dead or the totem emblem that kindle in him a sense of unplumbed mystery and value and power beyond. This holiness he thinks of as another "something," rarer, more refined. At any rate, in it resides the secret, the power, the supreme value. The efforts of religion are directed toward gaining this thing, or keeping on good terms with it. At this level, sin is that other "something" which does not "go" with the holy, the thing that must be washed off or purged out or driven away, if one is to come near the holy. That which corresponds to what is later called atonement is the process of getting rid of the separating stain or pollution. For forgiveness and conversion there are no equivalents, for these can only arise when life and religion are interpreted in more personal terms.

A second great variation in religious outlook is to be seen where men interpret life in a more personal way. It is almost inevitable that men should attempt such an interpretation, for if we are to find meaning in life at all, meaning for us, we must find it in something akin to what we experience in ourselves as will or purpose. Accordingly, we find men forming ideas of mysterious persons or spirits as holding the key to the secret of life, as the powers with which they must ultimately reckon, and as the purveyors of good and evil. Religion is then the effort of men to keep on friendly terms with these gods. Sin is that which alienates the gods, which brings their disfavor on men and accounts for those tokens of divine disfavor, disaster, and evil. Men try to gain reconciliation with the alienated gods by making amends for their sins, by cleansing themselves or offering gifts or making sacrifices. They do it probably in much the same mood that we express when we say that we would "give anything" to undo some harm that we have done or wipe out some deed we have done. In some such spirit men "give anything," the most precious things they know, sheep, oxen, gold, fruit, their children, their own lives, to atone for their sins, and achieve the favor of the gods.

We find a third major variation in religion when life presents itself to men as a realm of law. The ultimate power with which they must then reckon is the Law, or the Vindicator or Giver of the Law. The secret of life lies in obedience and the supreme good is the reward of obedience. This is the phase of religion which predominates, though by no means exclusively, in the Old Testament. With it go the appropriate conceptions of sin, atonement, and forgiveness. Sin is the breaking of the divine law. A broken law requires punishment, the repudiation of the offender by the lawgiver or judge and the outward expression of his just anger. So at this stage evil and disaster are interpreted as punishment. The spokesmen of God promise punishment for broken law in the future even though it seems absent in the present. Sinners are rigorously punished by the religious authorities in the name of God in order to protect the community from the just wrath of God. The way of atonement must lie through punishment, through the paying of damages, through all the means by which men who have broken laws achieve good standing again. Conversion from this view-point means turning about from a life of disobedience to a life of obedience. It is in that sense that you will find it in the Old Testament. Forgiveness at this stage very readily comes to have the meaning which we attach to a judicial pardon, that is, the ending of punishment or the remitting of penalty.

It is this type of religion which lies back of Christianity as that out of which it grew. But Christianity represents the emergence of a fourth and higher variation. When we come to Christianity, life is no longer viewed in its fundamental character as a realm of things, nor as a realm of many wilful spirits, nor as a realm of law. Life is seen to be, in its deepest character, a realm of personal relations, of fellowship. The secret of life is found to lie in love. The pearl of great price is the perfect community of selves knit together in God. The reality with which men must ultimately reckon and in which they may wholly trust is the loving and creative will of God. Jesus taught this to His disciples in the terms which must forever be identified with it, the terms of family life at its best. Life is a household. The source and ruler of life is a Father. The way of life, the way that leads to true life, is the way of union with God in love, a love that must realize itself in love for the brethren. In such a view sin takes on a deeper meaning. It is no longer a substantial something that can be washed off with holy water. It is no longer the breaking of an external law of action. It is a state of the will and the affections, a state of self-seeking, of self-satisfaction, of self-dependence, of lovelessness, unappreciative of the supreme preciousness of brothers, quick to judge, slow to forgive. For such a soul the way of reconciliation and atonement cannot centre in ceremonials or sacrifices, in the paying of penalties or in more rigid observance of some external rule of action. What is required is a conversion, a remaking, a rebirth of the heart and will, repentance and faith, the childlike surrender of the life to the love of God in quiet dependence, the renunciation of self-will, the gathering up of all the scattered attachments of the self and the submission of them all to the one rightful Master of Life. And the forgiveness sought and found is not a judicial pardon and remission of penalty, carefully weighing the deserts of the sinner in the light of his acts, but a welcoming love that throughout all the wanderings of the alienated will remains ready to receive the prodigal back and rejoices exceedingly over one sinner that repenteth.

Jesus preached and taught a gospel of reconciliation and at-one-ment. And His ministry was a ministry of reconciliation. He shepherded souls, bringing them out of sin into communion with God, converting them, and established a fellowship of those whom He had shepherded. He uttered the forgiveness of God to men with convincing authority as one in whom the mind of God found utterance. And He died at the hands of His enemies, approaching death as the crowning act in His work of reconciliation.

Out of the ministry of Jesus and the powerful religious experiences that followed it there issued a new religion. There are many ways of characterizing Christianity, all of which are inevitably partial, but for our purposes we might characterize it as the religion which finds religious satisfaction in Christ. And since the ultimate goal of religious satisfaction is reconciliation with God, union with God or at-one-ment, we might define Christianity as the religion of at-one-ment or atonement through Christ.

In considering the ideas of sin, atonement, conversion, and forgiveness within Christianity, it is important to keep in mind a distinction between what we may call historical Christianity and true Christianity. Historical Christianity is that great living historical religious movement which issued out of the influence of Christ, which has expressed itself in manifold forms of institution and worship and thought and way of life, but has been knit together by a common consciousness of being organically joined to the historical Christ as its source and head. But this great complex thing which as historians we must call Christianity, as Christians or as students of Christianity we must judge to be itself not fully Christianized. This we will recognize whatever our notions as to what is true Christianity. The fully convinced Baptist will recognize that historical Christianity has not throughout its length and breadth been true to Baptist principles. The fully convinced Roman Catholic will recognize that it has not always and everywhere been true to Catholic principles. When we say that historical Christianity has not always been true Christianity we do not judge it by some alien, non-Christian standard, we judge it by itself, we judge that Christianity has not been true to itself, to its own deepest nature, its own essential spirit or fundamental standpoint. Historical Christianity, being something that has dwelt within the minds and lives of men like ourselves, has been much like most of our minds and lives, an imperfect fusion or confusion of many different, and more or less conflicting, systems of thought and principles of action.

Nothing illustrates this more clearly than the

history within Christianity of just these ideas that we are considering. I have defined Christianity for our purposes as the religion which finds at-one-ment with God, and so salvation from sin, and so forgiveness and conversion, through Christ. But it holds true of Christianity as it does of religion in general, that men's ideas of what is wrong with them determine their ideas of what is necessary to right them. Consequently Christians, that is, people more or less conscious of having been righted by Christ, have interpreted what He must have done for them according to the prevailing diagnosis of what needed to be done.

We have noted several accounts of what is wrong with men, that have flourished influentially within religion. There is the idea that we are soiled or corrupted because we have come into contact with or are made of bad, corrupt, or unholy stuff. There is the idea that we have broken the divine law, are guilty and liable to punishment. And there is the idea that we are the wrong kind of persons to enter into companionship with the blessed company of true persons, God and the sons of God. All three of these have flourished and mingled within historical Christianity, and have controlled great systems of Christian thought.

Eastern Christianity and the strands of universal Christian thought that have been largely influenced by Greek religious thought, have worked much with the idea that the trouble with man, that which keeps him from God, is in the nature of a corruption of his substance. He has gone bad and, like other things that have gone bad, is liable to change and decay. How, then, must Christ have righted him? It must have been by something like transfusion, by injecting into human nature the cleansing, preserving, life-giving stuff of holiness, of divinity. This transforming fusion is thought of as having been begun in Christ and carried on in the sacraments, where sacred substance is taken into human life to cleanse and preserve and give eternal life. In all distinctly sacramental Christianity you will find marked traces of this form of thought. And you will find another example of it, in a form from which our sensibilities rather recoil, in the idea that we are saved from sin by being washed in the Savior's blood. That is a perfect example of the way in which advanced religion takes up into its own life the metaphors of very early religion. And I would suggest that the right insight in all these rather crude metaphors is the simple one that only the clean can cleanse. You do not take a dirty rag to wash your face. Only the clean can cleanse. Only the strong can make strong. Only the holy can make holy. If Christ makes holy it must be that the stuff of holiness is in Him.

When we turn to Western Christianity, the characteristic notion as to what is wrong with man is that He has broken the divine law, is guilty and liable to punishment. It is in this mental atmosphere that most of the ideas of the atonement with which we are more or less familiar as a part of our religious inheritance, were developed. Man is guilty, guilty not only as an individual, for it was recognized that you cannot neatly isolate individual from social guilt; he is guilty as a race. The first man Adam sinned, that is, broke the laws of God, and in one way or another we inherit his guilt, somewhat as you might inherit your father's debts. So we are born into the world guilty and unless something is done about it the divine punishment is as inevitable as it is just. And to make matters worse, we add to our inherited guilt our own individual infractions of the divine laws. That is the background. Against that background there is the Christian consciousness of being at peace with God, assured of the divine forgiveness. What must Christ have done to secure this result? Somehow He must have taken away our guilt and secured our pardon. And to do that He must have taken upon Himself the penalties of pain and death due to us, have paid our debts, have given God the satisfaction that we cannot give Him. Here again beneath metaphors that repel us and that are false to the true spirit of Christianity in many of their implications, we could find, if there were time for patient and sympathetic examination, truths that remain; that the breaking of the laws of life does bring penalty and suffering, that the death of

Christ was the product of sin, and the greatest condemnation of sin, revealing it as that which slays the best.

But we must pass on. Throughout all historical Christianity there has run another idea of what is wrong with man and what must be done if he is to be righted, the idea that it is our wills that are wrong, our affections, the whole spirit of our lives. The trouble is that we are untrue to our own true nature as children of God, sharing something of His creative power, meant to be masters of nature, masters not slaves, builders and not destroyers, spirits not animals; untrue to our nature as brothers, meant for understanding and love and fellowship, not strife and self-seeking, destined for the aristocracy of true servanthood, not competitive power over one another. If that is what is wrong with us, what we need is a radical change of our wills and our affections, a conversion, a kindling of our love for God and our fellows, an overcoming of the conflict within us between what we are and what we know we were meant to be, the infusion into our lives of a new spirit, a Holy Spirit. If Christ is the one who does this for us it must be by possessing the Love of God, by being the love of God among us. He must possess the Spirit that we need and the power to impart it. He must bring the forgiveness of God, not as a judicial pardon that waits apart until we merit a favorable decision, but as a pursuing love that seeks us out in faith even while we are afar off and merit nothing. He must in His own life and consciousness reconcile, unite, God and man. It is the experience of the truest Christians, of those who stand out in history as the most impressive examples of this religion, that Christ does these things for those who steadfastly walk in His way, commune with His Spirit, and commit their lives in simple trust to His Father. For Christians, then, atonement, conversion, and forgiveness are all aspects of the penetration of our lives by the Christ-life.

MYSTICISM AND PRAYER

CHARLES LEWIS SLATTERY

THE words Mysticism and Prayer defy definition. They belong to the class of supreme words, such as Life, Love, Faith, Truth, God. Each man must by experience discover his own definition, and even when he feels that in his heart he knows the meaning, his best phrasing will leave depths which his definition has not sounded. Nor need he be baffled if certain historic definitions differ entirely from his own. One need read only so condensed an account of Mysticism as that contained in the Encyclopædia Britannica to discover the divers meanings packed into the elusive word, which is a thing of the Spirit and lives with the clouds and the winds.

Bearing all these difficulties in mind, I venture at the start to put down roughly a definition of Mysticism and a definition of Prayer. Let us say that Mysticism is the consciousness of God's immediate presence and of our union with Him. And let us say that Prayer is talking with God.

Now both Mysticism and Prayer lie in that department of life which is beyond reason. Reason can go a considerable distance, and then we know that it can go no farther. Yet there is evidently in that nonrational beyond, a region of immeasurable distances. This region is part of our experience, part of our life. We know it and we can talk about it, but we cannot reduce it to hard, exact terms. It is not irrational; it does not contradict reason: but there is a quality in life, as real as a mathematical demonstration, for which reason is quite inadequate. The faculty by which we understand this quality in life is more than emotion, more than feeling. We cannot dismiss it with an inferior word. It is the land beyond the mountains. It is a land to which some men go, to which all men may go; but no man can make clear to one who has not gone to it what that country beyond the mountains is. The best he may do for his friend, is to take his hand and go with him; as they go forward, the man who is guided discovers that what his guide vaguely intimated is true, because he himself has experienced it. And so he comes to know. The only approximately adequate name for this faculty (by which we know the quality in life beyond reason) is experience.* You can test the prophet's rhapsody by going whither he has gone. If then you experience what he has experienced, deep calls unto deep, and you know what he knows. You have the assurance of a quality in life which is as real for you now as the inevitable conclusion of a logical argument.

* Strictly speaking, this is that part of our experience which philosophers call "numinous experience" in distinction from "sense experience."

Accordingly, what I am aiming to do is simply to set down certain convictions which I have concerning Mysticism and Prayer, and to seek no other verification than that which may be recognized in your experience.

I

The first conviction I have is that every one, consciously or subconsciously, talks with God.

We do many things unconsciously. Millions of people in the world never consider the unwearied function of their existence called the circulation of the blood. They know nothing about it. Breathing also is, for the most part, an unconscious process; only when we climb a hill, or are weak, do we become aware of it. So talking with the Unseen God is for hosts of people subconscious.

When men complain of the weather, of bad fortune, of physical pain, they are talking neither to themselves nor to their neighbors. If questioned, they may say that they are complaining to Fate or to Nature—a something or a Someone outside humanity to which or to whom humanity is subject. However vaguely or crudely defined, God is held responsible, and they cast the blame on Him. They are subconsciously talking with Him.

On the other hand, all men have their moments of exultation. A bright day after rain, the coming of spring, a radiant scene, returning health after illness will start a man smiling and singing: he straightway gives thanks. Just to whom he pours out his gratitude he does not stop to think. Voltaire, one morning, saw the sun rise over his garden, and impulsively exclaimed, *Dieu le Père, je t'adore*—and then added a qualifying phrase, lest anyone who chanced to hear him might think him a believer. Voltaire was subconsciously talking with God, and the recognition of the One to whom he spoke came close to the surface. So Walt Whitman, in his transports, spoke of "caressing life": he too was subconsciously giving thanks in the best words he knew.

Still deeper is the manifestation of our subconscious talking with God when a man says, "I ought," or, "I ought not." "I ought" is a pledge to something or Someone beyond the human level; "I ought not to have done what I did do" is, similarly, a confession of sin. Such an one is in the presence of the heart of moral righteousness. The talk is searching, and out of the unseen come answers. Surely (as it seems to me) the man is subconsciously speaking with God.

I recognize that other interpretations are possible, but they are not possible for me. As I look about, and touch men's lives and hear men's cries, I am convinced that, when the shadows are done away, every man will discover that he has, all unconsciously, talked again and again with God.

II

Another conviction, which I now put before you, is that through Prayer man discovers God.

To the careful observer it seems as if a good many people were going through the form of prayer without really praying. Such people, finding their inherited habit mechanical and bloodless, sometimes, as they say, stop praying. Of course, except subconsciously, it is doubtful if they ever began to pray. So we may put people who have only formally prayed side by side with people for whom prayer is only subconscious. To both, the day is almost sure to come when prayer will become so real, so complete that they will know that they are face to face with God. The vision may fade, or it may become a permanent possession; but, in that great moment, they will have the supreme consciousness that they have discovered God.

In one of his books Josiah Royce describes a man who is passing through the depths. In his agony he cries out. He has no faith that there is any to hear. But an answer comes. The man who has heard the answer can give no name to that voice, except to say, "He who answers the cry from the depths has spoken to me." Obviously (as I think) that man, by his prayer, has discovered God.

The man who, by will or by chance, is quite alone, is also apt to discover God. He is in some wilderness, and the night is shutting down. Unable to sleep in his tent, he wanders forth upon the mountain path. On and on he goes, till he wakes from his reverie to find that he is far from the sights and sounds of humanity. The only light is from the stars; the only sounds, the wind in the trees and the water falling on the rocks. He is thrilled by the solitude; and then, suddenly, he knows that he is not alone, He is wrapped about by the Presence. He has been sub-consciously praying, and in the silences he has dis-covered God.

Again, this discovery may come in the abandon-ment caused by a compelling need. In the book of a friend I find the record of a visit which he one day received from a man who had profaned every sanc-tuary of his soul and in despair came for counsel. My friend heard the piteous story to the end; then he said to the wretch, "I see two endings: one is suicide." "Yes," answered the man, "I had thought of that; what else do you see?" My friend answered, "I see God." "I don't know what you mean," said the man. "Yes, you do," was the reply; "you can, if you will, kneel down here, at once, and ask Him to save you." The man looked into the eyes before him, then slipped down to his knees, and poured forth, in utter abandonment, his cry for help. My friend went on to say that from that moment the man's life was changed. A light was in his face and a power in his goodness which astonished all who had known him. He had, as for the first time, prayed, and he had discovered God.

One more instance I give. One for whom I cared deeply lost by death his little child. I did not see how he could endure the grief. A few days later I saw him, and after we had spoken of various things, each trying to avoid the name with which our hearts were full, he broke off suddenly, saying, "I never loved God as I do now." In the bitterness of his loss, he had prayed, and he had discovered the fatherhood and the love of God.

Genuine prayer breaks up our complacent presuppositions. Sometimes our presuppositions are negative: we say that God is not. Sometimes they are positive: we vainly boast that we know all about Him. Then comes the crash. The need for help is beyond all imagining. The night is black, and we cry one intense word: then the light conquers the darkness—and God is there. Prayer discovers God as He is.

III

My third conviction is that Prayer unites men. Men who turn to God are brought together in Him.

Here again a concrete illustration will admit us quickly to the contemplation of this unity. Two travellers came one night to a rough frontiersman's cabin. Two wild-looking men occupied the two rooms, but they invited the strangers to eat with them, and gave them one of their two rooms for the night. In spite of the hospitality, the guests feared their hosts, and took turns in watching them through a chink in the wall. Presently the watcher saw the unkempt pioneers take down a Bible, read from it, and then kneel to pray. Instantly the suspicion vanished. There was no danger beneath that roof. Where prayer is, there is unity.

When men pray together anywhere, they are bound together. When the saint kneels with the sinner, each acknowledges the weakness of the other as his own, each rises upon the strength of the other's goodness. When two or three say together the opening words of the Lord's Prayer, "Our Father," if they think at all what they are saying, their petty distinctions and separations pass, and they are one in a common ownership. The supreme prayer of the Christian Church is the Lord's Supper, where all sorts of people, out of every walk in life, draw near with faith, and become one body in Christ. Even when death comes, the unity is not broken, for as the beloved who has gone must certainly be speaking with God, so the one surviving and bereft must also be speaking with Him—and in Him they meet and are at one.

"Have I not prayed in heaven?—on earth Lord, Lord, has
    he not prayed?
Are not two prayers a perfect strength? And shall I feel
    afraid?"

That is the assurance of a poet that prayer is the one bond tying the worlds together into one eternal home.

IV

My next conviction is that our prayers mean even more to God than they mean to us. As the clearest name for God is our Loving Father, so we project the human relationship of father and child to its perfect ending, and see, in the joy of a human father over the confidences of his child, the faint reflection of our heavenly Father's joy in the prayers of His earthly children. God, I think, waits for our prayers.

If any one believes in God at all, he is sure that God reveals Himself. Astronomy and geology, biology and botany, chemistry and physics, history and biography, all alike, once you believe in God, tell you about His character and His ways of working in His world. Up, through all human relationship to the workmanship of God, the belief thrusts itself that God so abundantly reveals Himself that we assume that God longs to be known. So it is that the saints of the ages have dared to try to please God: more and more they have felt that they knew what would please Him—and they have been sure in some mysterious way that He did delight in their frail, uneven attempts to do what He would have them do.

From such revelation of God's will to be known,

we reach the thought that He loves us so much that He wills to do for us certain definite things. Prayer, we find, is the necessary medium through which God's will for us becomes effective. Just as there must be atmosphere to receive the light and warmth of the sun, just as there must be the wire or the ether to receive the current of electricity, so, we say confidently, there must be prayer to receive the gracious gifts which God desires to give us. Hence prayer goes beyond all mere asking. It is the opening of our lives to God, that God may rejoice to do for us what he wills to do.

There is an adage of psychology that we can will to do only what we have done before, or what we have seen another do, or have heard that another has done. Prayer oversteps that limitation. When Christ in Gethsemane prayed to His Father, "Thy will be done," He was willing to do what had never been done or imagined. A moment before He had prayed that the cup might be taken from Him. Then He willed to do a new thing in the world: to die that He might live; to fail, that He might succeed; to lose the battle, that He might win the eternal victory, and, in it all, to save a world. So it is quite possible that when we, in our feeble, stammering way, say, "Thy will be done," we too are willing to do what we have never done, have never seen another do, have never heard that another has done. We know not what we ask; but God knows. And He must rejoice,

because through the prayer of one of His children
His will for a new deed in the world has become
effective.

Prayer may thus be looked upon as the satisfying
of God's love for the world. Paradoxical as our freedom may seem, we believe that we are free. God, we
surmise, desires not perfect automatons, but friends,
who, out of free choice with all the risks of failure,
give themselves up to His love. When Christ asked
Simon Peter three times if he loved Him, the question was certainly for only one purpose: the Master
of men wished to hear Simon say the words of his
love. Evidently this expression of love was to Him
as music. Here is a deep revelation of the heart of
God. Prayer is the language through which men tell
God that they love Him, and thereby know and receive God's love. The response for which God perpetually waits is given; and the yearning of God for
His child is satisfied.

V

Quite naturally now, I reach another conviction:
it is this—Prayer accepts the best. From what has
gone before, it seems hardly necessary to say this;
for it is implied in our accepting what God wills to
give us; but let me make it as clear as I can.

Properly prayer begins with asking for things. To
ask for things, the sceptic murmurs, is irrational:

we cannot change God. And it is unnecessary, cries the mystic: He loves us unutterably. Both criticisms are true. But life is not simple. We reach truth and life by strange passageways. We are at our best when we have the ingenuousness of children and say in our prayers to the Lord God whatever we are minded to say. We swiftly run over the list of favors we wish God to do for us; we are far away from Him; we see nothing, we hear nothing. Then, suddenly, we are in His presence. Out of the light and the stillness, God tells us that He cares, that He will do at least whatever we have asked, for He will do what is best. Immediately the things we have asked for drop from our minds, as the toys of childhood are deserted by maturity. We are careless whether these things are given us, or not. We forget them. We see only God our Father, holding out to us the vague unknown, the most glorious, the best.

With this vision filling our hearts, we cry, "Thy will be done." We see the old demands and needs and desires, sliding down and away into the waves of the sea. As they disappear, we say, "Thy will be done:" but we say the words in no mood of resignation. In one sense we do resign them; but resignation is not the sum of our emotion. For we see looming before us the transcendent answer to prayer, the best—not merely the best which the world has known, but the best which God knows. And there it is before us, ours; ours, by the divine gift; ours, by the medium of our prayer. "Thy will be done," after such an experience, can never again be the expression of resignation: it is the joyful acceptance of the best. It is not going down into the mournful valleys, stripped of their light and their gladness; it is climbing to the top of the highest mountain to see, with ineffable expectation, the coming of the Light, the fulfilment of every wildest hope of happiness.

So, in prayer, we rise towards God's will. The commonplace and cautious shrewdness of men is gone. We are not concerned about the little victories men gain after a few years' steady industry. We need not be assured that the victory will be given in this century, in this millennium, or even within the course of this world. That is in the hand of God, to give soon or late; but the victory is certain. Our only duty is to put our hands, in faith, to the task—and to keep on praying that the vision of God's will shall not fade from our sight.

A man sees what he as an individual is to be. The way ahead, if he goes that path, is lonely, dangerous, full of human misunderstanding and censure. But he need not falter. The will of God summons him; and on he goes, deaf to the twitterings of the prudent and the worldly-successful, who proclaim dolefully that he is wasting his life.

A man sees also what the world is to be, if it obey God's will. The man, being part of the world, must let God's will for it speak through him; so he is found pleading for a united Church, for a federation of nations, for universal peace and love, which shall be when the Kingdom of Christ is fully come. A man who has reached up, through prayer, into that beatific vision of the world as God shows it to him, is undaunted, when the so-called wise of the earth cry him down. He knows; for he has talked with the Lord God. He has seen God's face; and lives.

One of my colleagues drove an ambulance in the War. When he told me how he drove to and fro with his precious freight, the bursting shells illuminating the darkness of his rough road, I asked him if he was ever afraid; for he must have appreciated the imminent danger of death. "No," he replied; "it came over me, in those nights, what these men of mine were trying to do; I saw the cause of God in the awful struggle, and then I longed to show God how much I cared. I did not mind whether or not I was killed; I was so eager to show that I would give everything for the cause, that if loyalty to it meant my life, I was ready." In the joyful acceptance of the best by that ambulance driver, you see the meaning of "Thy will be done." When we pray our prayers till we attain the presence of God, our spirits rise beyond all the highest levels of our past achievements, beyond all our highest dreams; we see God; we see, in His loving hand, the best; and, in a flash, we know that we can receive it. And we do receive it. God's best is ours.

VI

I have not said the word Mysticism since the beginning; but I have not once forgotten it. I have been steadily trying to lead up to it. You will not be surprised if I now draw together all the convictions which have gone before into one crowning assurance, and say that I am sure that by prayer we enter into union with God. For when we receive the best, we receive Him; and our wants, just so long as we continue to live in Him, are transfigured into our real needs, then transcended, and, in their highest and best form, fully received.

Mysticism has much to say about silence and meditation and other important words of religious ecstacy. I have thought that I should be more clearly understood if I clung to the inclusive word, prayer. Prayer, you will find, is as varied, as is the expression of love and trust in human relationships. People often say, "Our friendship is established, because we can sit in the same room and utter not one word; yet our communion one with another is constant." Or two people may find their friendship enriched because they are together in some solemn and brilliant scene, or because they are hearing together some overwhelming music, or are sharing in some tremendous crusade for truth, or are stooping together to lift some burden from one who has been grieved or injured. Practically endless are the ways in which human communion one with another binds soul to soul. Even more, essentially endless are the phases of what we indeterminately call prayer. Prayer may be words, familiar and honored; or words, stumbling and confused; or thoughts without words; or deliberate vacancy, awaiting God's thoughts to be given; or meditation, or revery, or fixedness of attention upon one tiny manifestation of God's life in the world, a leaf in one's garden, a passing cloud, the shimmer of light in the roadway after rain.

Only this warning may be given: prayer is exceedingly hard work. It is not, as the vain ones suppose, merely words or merely thoughts or merely contemplation. These little doors are but entrances to an absorbing work. Prayer is the ruthless breaking down of selfishness; it is stiff climbing; it is rising into the majesty of the life of God. Prayer means all that a man has, all that he is, all that he hopes to be: it means his whole heart. Prayer asks everything, but it gives the All-in-all.

Prayer is God's Fatherhood acknowledged; God's Love accepted; God's Life possessed. That is the testimony of Mysticism. We may not at first be convinced that the mystics are right; but we may follow them into the great adventure. Even after we have ventured, and perhaps have at length entered a like experience, we may find it hard to make any one else understand even dimly what we have discovered and what we have won. Often we feel that the news of such divine friendship is too sacred to tell to any one. But if a friend asks us frankly for explanations and reasons, we must do what we can. The most generous friendship can give only one counsel: it is this—"Try really to pray, hoping, at last, to come into the presence of God."

PERSONAL RELIGION

WILLIAM LAWRENCE

Personal religion is natural and simple; as natural and simple as patriotism. The little child born in this country is an American child. Its physical and nervous texture, its stock and traditions are different from those of an Egyptian or a French child. He is an American before he is conscious of the fact. When in two or three years he waves his little flag, he begins to feel that he is an American: later he becomes a more intelligent one. We may speak of personal patriotism in that child.

Our common conception of personal religion is that it begins later in life when one is "converted" or "gets religion." I claim that personal religion, like personal patriotism, may be in the stock and tradition of a child.

Wishing to talk to you in the simplest, most direct way on personal religion, I am going to ask you to pardon my egotism, if I tell you my own experience: for what is my experience of seventy-five years worth, if not to pass it on. To use the language of the law or business school I present myself as a "Case."

I was born of Christian parents. They happened to be communicants of the Protestant Episcopal Church. The stuff that was in me was New England Anglo-Saxon Christian stock. I started off the first day of my life with those characteristics.

Soon after my birth my parents brought me into St. Paul's Church, now the Cathedral on Tremont Street, Boston, for baptism. Did they think of it as a bit of magic whereby my character became Christian? Far from it. The point of it was that in baptism I was formally recognized as a child of God and received into Christ's Church. I knew nothing about it.

Then and there began in an unconscious way my personal religion. As I grew up, maybe when I was two years old, five years old, ten years old, there came a time, just as is the case with the little boy who begins to wave the American flag—when I consciously discovered that I was of Christian stock and of Christ's Church. That no doubt was a crisis in my life.

As I grew older it was as a Christian boy in a Christian home. Here again I want to emphasize the simplicity and the naturalness of personal religion as expressed in the Christian home. It was just as natural for me after I was dressed to go into my father's dressing-room and kneel down with my brother and say a very simple prayer after my father, as it was for me to go down-stairs with him to breakfast. It was just as natural after breakfast that we should ring the bell and call the servants to come to prayers with the family, for our servants all came to prayers with the family. There in a perfectly natural way was developed the personal religion and the corporate religious life of the family.

Twice on Sundays we went to church with my father and mother, just as naturally as we went to school or as we went out to play; there was nothing peculiar about it; nothing exceptional. So that, as I say, religion was woven into the very texture of our habit, of our character.

And yet there are some people who would say, "Is personal religion as simple as that? Isn't that very exceptional?" I think not. The difficulty is that it is made exceptional. "Do you mean to say that that went on until you became an older boy and almost until you went to college?" Yes. "Did your father and your mother pay so much attention to all of you—there were seven of you—in those respects?" Yes. They assumed that the most important thing that they could do was not only to educate their child at school and develop him physically, but to lead him spiritually. They were our common leaders and our companions.

The whole religious life was a part of the family upbringing, very simple, very natural.

To-day many a parent sends his boy off to boarding school and says to himself—or herself, "He is all right; he is fixed; he is at boarding-school; they will see that he has prayers and he will be going to chapel, and we can do as we please."

I am more and more struck with the stupidity of parents as I get older, and the intelligence of the young people; the stupidity of parents in thinking that the standards are going to be created by the school rather than the home. No matter how young, the schoolboy or schoolgirl looks back to the home for his or her ideals, for his or her standards, and any young person is sure to follow the habits and standards of his parents rather than those of his school.

The result is that the boy goes to a church school and in a very nice and dignified and orderly way always goes to chapel. He has to. But when he goes home on a holiday or after he has left school and gone to college, what does he do? Why, he follows his parents, and if they do not go he does not go, because he—intelligently—has discovered how much or how little value they put on religion and religious sanctions. He takes his personal religion at their value.

The point that I am trying to make here is that personal religion was a natural thing to us because our parents went with us. They never sent us to church; they never sent us to Sunday-school; my father always went. And they felt that that was the most valuable part of the education of the boy.

Did my father have nothing else to do, that he gave so much time to the religious care of his children? He happened to be one of the leading business men of Boston. He was treasurer of Harvard University at the same time. He was active in athletic interests also. When the Civil War broke out he rode over here from our home across the river and drilled the students in broadsword and in other exercises preparing them for the war. He recruited the second cavalry regiment, of which Charles Lowell—whose name is on the Soldiers Field stone—was the colonel.

So, we grew up in a religious atmosphere which was calculated to bring us—when we became conscious of the facts of Christ and of the Christian faith and the Church—to enter naturally into those relations and to become boys of Christian character and of Christian interest and standing. We were not prigs or religious enthusiasts but just boys.

What are the processes of thought, habits and character in a boy of simple personal religion? To my mind he should possess a keener sense of duty than others because of his religious standing and faith. The boy has come to the point where he realizes that there is a Heavenly Father, who watches him, who cares for him; he becomes conscientious as to what he may do and what he may not do. The prodigal son and its story bulks big in his life, and he discovers that when he does wrong it is not simply a 'fool thing' that he has done or a mistake that he has made but that he has sinned against God. If overstrained this may make him morbid but if naturally held it makes him strict with himself, conscientious, and of a keener sense of duty.

He reaches a point of hero worship in his life and Jesus is to him a type of chivalry, of heroism, One who sacrificed Himself for others. Then comes that castle-building in his imagination whereby he sees himself as the hero sacrificing himself for others. The emotional, the imaginative spirit of the boy, are all intertwined with Christ, with God, and with what we call religious associations, religious motives. He has one habit, if he is brought up in the right way, of kneeling down to pray morning and evening, it may be for a minute, or three minutes, but in the doing of that he recollects himself as a child of God and a follower of Christ.

I am not sure that we begin to appreciate the persistent, steady and tremendous influence upon boys and young men of the habit of, it may be only for the moment, kneeling and recognizing one's self as a child of God, with responsibilities which he would not otherwise have recollected or appreciated. If the power of suggestion has any force, surely the suggestion that comes from that daily prayer twice a day is something that has its pervasive influence throughout the day.

Then the boy comes to college; his faith, his personal life, his personal religion is very simple, as I have already suggested, but when he has gotten into the intellectual life of the college—and I am all the time thinking of myself—he gets some jars. The first one that I remember was a moral jar. Here were boys that were members of the church, communicants, brought up in church schools, who were a disgrace to the church in the way that they were behaving. And here were other boys of pagan stock, or no particular religion, who had fine, straight characters.

As one came to think of it, those who had been brought up in a religious way were as a whole somewhat superior to the others, but it was the exception—as it often is—that bulked. And I said to myself, "What on earth does this faith amount to? What does membership in the church amount to?" It was a moral jar. Why should I sustain my religious faith when there was so much that was fine in my pagan friends? I was bewildered. Then temptations began to come in. And I went through that process of thought—"You've got to think this thing through. Where are you coming out? Assuming the pagan attitude, the fatalistic or the materialistic attitude, where are you going? Life after all is but an adventure based on some working hypothesis. I cannot demonstrate faith; I cannot demonstrate fatalism. I have got to choose some working hypothesis and I rather think, my stock being what it is, that my best adventure is for faith in God. On that working hypothesis I will live. If

I accept the fatalistic, materialistic point of view, there is not enough moral force to keep me straight. If I am nothing but a bit of dust floating in the air, it is a great deal easier to go slack, to do what I want to, to follow the fast crowd, and take my chances. There may be men who without faith can stand straight and true. I cannot."

My next alternative was to stop thinking and make no decision as to the basis of life. I then said to myself, "If you are going to get anywhere you have got to have some principle in life. If you wobble through college and through life you will have no speed, no action, no progress; something has got to be settled."

And then I came to the third alternative and the final adventure. After all, my stock has been religious. I see nothing inconsistent in a religious life, with science or with philosophy or with anything that stands for the truth. Why shouldn't I go on in just the same way, with a simple faith, and let come what may?

And so I went through college with all kinds of fellows as my friends, belonging to different clubs, left at large liberty by my father.

I have to say frankly that the official college religion did not do much for me. We had to go to chapel and I went. The best part of the college chapel was the character of the Plummer Professor, Doctor Andrew Peabody, who was revered by all.

As I say, the chapel did not mean much but the home meant everything. I was fortunate in being able to go home on Sundays. There the routine went on, of personal religion in the home.

My second jar was on the intellectual side. You have no conception of the force of that in my day. On the first page of the Bible was given the date when the world was made, and of course Adam and Eve, Joshua and the sun, Jonah and the whale were all literally true, and he who did not believe those things was looked upon with some suspicion, if not as a heretic. Well, to jump from that frame of mind into a belief in the theory of evolution, was an immense leap, which overthrew the faiths of a great many young people. Those faiths remained thrown over so long as the religious authorities claimed that young men were untrue to the Christian faith if they believed such things. We had to leave many questions of science and philosophy in abeyance, and throughout life I have learned that a large part of the interests of life and thought have got to be left in abeyance. With a complete confidence in the final victory of the truth, we—I speak for myself—may leave a very large part of the circumference of thought and life outside our purview, and let the philosophers take care of those things. But so long as I am not untrue to myself and untrue to the truth as I see it, I claim that I may hold my religious faith and move on quietly and with serenity. That may not be very philosophical but it is very simple and human and, to my mind, the wise path to take in life and faith.

There was one person who beyond all others helped me though, and that was Phillips Brooks. You all appreciate that young men are moved not so much by institutions as by personalities. When you have left college you will remember two or three or four personalities that have influenced and that have led you. They may not have been the greatest scholars or the greatest teachers but they have been true and attractive men. Phillips Brooks was such a personality, one with enthusiasm for the Christian faith, with the mysticism of the New England mystic; at the same time he had the glow of confidence in the nineteenth century and what is essential in personal religion, the optimism which believes the best and sees the best in others. He lifted the standards of college life because he lifted the standards of the lives of the members of the faculty and of the students. I look back to him as the one force in my life which enabled me to grow steadily in an intelligent faith.

Now, what is personal religion? Personal religion is the binding of God and the soul of man with a living cord in such a way that the man is led on and on and, seeing in Christ the very revelation of God and believing in God's Holy Spirit as the very power of God, he moves on. Freedom in spiritual experience is of the utmost necessity. One may say his prayers sitting in a chair; another with his forehead in the dust. One may pass through life believing that the great sacraments of life are in nature; another that the sacraments of life are in the Church. Each and all of us must have his own method of personal religion but it must be a method persistently and consistently followed through.

From my experience I should say that those who are in a real way religious have as compared with men of no faith a healthier point of view; that they are more optimistic in their outlook, and that they last through life as responsible men whose principles stand true and whom people gradually learn to depend upon. Such a man, being a lover of God, is also a lover of men. He appreciates that the Christian faith means service and that it is his duty as a Christian to pull more than his weight in the boat. This may lead him up to the highest realms of heroism, of chivalry, of charity, of loss of self in behalf of others. It may express itself, on the other hand, in an altruistic spirit recognized in his social and in his business life. This Christian motive makes him the finer and the more unselfish man.

While we know that the religious life is often identified with drabness of thought and dullness of life, I believe that in the long run those who have faith in God have a vision so much larger and higher that in response to it, art, poetry, music, and all that we associate with the highest realms of thought and of emotion are more open to a man or a woman who is religious than to one who is not.

I say this with emphasis because of the common impression that those who are to be poets and musicians and artists and the like, cannot be religious; otherwise they will be confined in their habits of thought. To my mind it is just the other way.

A religious man also is an optimist. As I have gone on in life the great strength of religion has been in a serenity and a courage and a confidence through my faith in God, that leads me to weigh at less and less value the incidents of the world and the passing of things that are considered important, as compared with the great principles of life and with the being of God. He who has a complete faith in God has courage, strength, serenity, and force, which cannot belong to those who have no faith. Think of the benediction, which we hear so frequently that it passes over our ears, and think of the serenity that it may bring—The Peace of God, which passeth all understanding, keep your hearts and minds in the knowledge and love of God.

THE BIBLE, ITS NATURE AND ITS USE

HENRY J. CADBURY

THERE are two ways of attempting to describe what the Bible is. Christian people inherit certain standard terms for application to the Bible and they tend to limit their description to such ready-made terms. Behind those terms is the hypothesis of a personal God who reveals his will to men through chosen instruments. The Bible, then, is such a revelation of the true God, or, in more accurate terms, it is the record of that revelation.

Traditional theology has worked out the logical deductions as to how such a revelation ought to have taken place, and what must be the nature of the resultant record. The method is called inspiration; the result must be an inspired record and one that is consistent, uniform, and inerrant. The record partakes of the divinity of its source. It is morally impeccable, historically accurate, logically harmonious. Its authority is infallible, its revelation of God's will is final.

For the Christian who begins in this way his approach to the Bible, with such preconceived labels and formulas, the problem is simply to make the Bible as he finds it square with his *a priori* definitions, or at least so to deal with the Bible as to notice whatever can be used to confirm such a description and to interpret or even to ignore whatever seems to contradict it. Whenever two passages seem contradictory human ingenuity can usually find some way of reconciling them. For the variant genealogies of Joseph of Nazareth, for example, several different explanations have in fact been proposed from quite early times. Whatever in the Bible seems intrinsically improbable—*i. e.*, in contradiction with experience, can also be explained often by far-fetched analogies. Thus the miracles of the Bible are proved to be natural, or, if supernatural, are found to be appropriate to the unusual circumstances, or are accepted by faith.

The second approach to the Bible attempts to examine the Bible first and to form an opinion about it later. It tries to brush aside preconceived notions and to bring to bear upon the book an open and inquiring mind. This method is a more modern one and in many ways a more difficult one. It requires more real knowledge of the Bible, and, what is harder to acquire than knowledge, a willingness to admit ignorance and to suspend judgment. It does not aim at any sweeping labels or generalizations. It finds the phenomena do not reduce themselves to any simple formula. Its aim is to test and evaluate the several parts of the Bible and to subject to detailed analysis any estimate it makes of the whole.

These two ways of dealing with the Bible differ as

two methods of buying clothes. In one case a suit is made to order; in the other it is ready-made. The old view of the Bible superimposed certain abstract definitions, the new view attempts to make its judgment fit fresh observation. Now I am not denying that ready-made clothes sometimes fit remarkably well. They are cut to the lines of average measurement. So the older view of the Bible had behind it some of this element of experience—the experience of a larger number of persons rather than the experience merely of the latest reader. The new view therefore leads often to conclusions similar to the old one. This is what is meant by the saying: "Read the Bible as an ordinary book and it will prove to be the most extraordinary book." But it makes a great deal of difference from which side you approach the same position.

The development of these two views toward the Bible constitutes two of the most interesting chapters in the history of human thought. We are now living in a period of conflict between them. The so-called Fundamentalist-Modernist controversy is an alignment precisely along these opposing positions and the rival philosophies that underlie them. Given the older view of the Bible, every other plank in the Fundamentalist platform is consistent and justifiable. Without that view of the Bible the Modernist can neither understand nor persuade the Fundamentalist.

But the conflict which we see in groups of persons often exists in the individual also. He starts at both ends at once. The older view of the Bible is inherent in his background. It is subconscious and difficult to outgrow. The newer view is natural to his education and to his common sense, but it is scarcely conscious, articulate, or explicit. As the young person with this dual inheritance goes on his way, he becomes aware of an unresolved contradiction. He is perhaps quite perplexed and in his perplexity he often turns away from the whole difficulty instead of reaching a satisfactory solution.

The most unsatisfactory solution which such a person can reach is that which arrives only at the stage of denying the older view. Often the debate degenerates into such controversy over old definitions—one side affirming that they fit, the other arguing that they do not. There arises "a fight about words to no profit." The man who is still in that stage is unfortunate, whichever side he is on. A true appreciation of the Bible is thereby closed to him.

Suppose the works of Shakespeare were in such a plight—the object of heated debate on a few fixed categories. Suppose students were absorbed in merely affirming or denying the Baconian authorship, the historical accuracy, the logical consistency of every line in that collection of masterpieces. A by-product of such controversy would doubtless be a considerable acquaintance with the content of Shakespeare

but such controversialists would have little opportunity or sympathy for an appreciation of the true
worth of the literature.

Many college men of intelligence are just in that
stage with respect to the Bible. They know it and
think of it just in those matters about which controversy is waged—its miracles, its contradictions, its
unscientific or unethical standpoints, or the "hard
sayings" of the Sermon on the Mount. They know
just where it seems most vulnerable and they attack
it or defend it in those places. Such a state of affairs
is most unfortunate. The Book of Jonah is a case in
point. For every ten thousand persons who are cog-
nizant of the incident of the fish that swallowed the
prophet, scarcely one person in any theological camp
is aware of the sublime lesson of internationalism
that is so effectively taught—and that too in an age
so sorely in need of just this moral message.

When one leaves this controversy behind, the
practical question remains for the layman how he
may study and use the Bible. Several further difficulties confront him. He cannot with all his best resolves quite leave out of mind the prepossessions
about the Bible on controversial matters. He finds
the book exceedingly unhomogeneous, and obscure
in its references to ancient persons, places, and occa-
sions. Every student of literature is familiar with the
difficulties caused by obscure references. The Bible
is no worse in this respect than Pindar, Dante, or

Milton, and the student should know that such ancient literature cannot be understood by a simple
reading in an unannotated text. The Bible needs
editors and teachers just as Homer and Chaucer do.
The student ought not to assume that this alone of
ancient writings can dispense with the ordinary aids
to interpretative and historical understanding.

In many respects, however, the student will find
the main lines of the Bible similar to those of other
literatures. If it is approached as neither a book of
magic nor one of science, but as a monument of the
literature of a nation and of a religious fellowship, it
falls into familiar categories. Much of it aims to be
simple history. As such there is a reality and vivid-
ness about it that speaks for itself. Many scenes in
its pages, *e. g.*, in II Samuel or in Acts, are merely
clear and well told episodes from history. The bio-
graphical element is also readily understood. It
delineates clear-cut personalities, such as Jeremiah
the prophet, against a setting that is often easily
understood. The letters of Paul are a revelation of a
man as well as of a situation and are scarcely ex-
celled in intimacy in the whole range of autobio-
graphical sources. And every page of the Bible presents to the student the ever-present problems of
literature. How came one thus to express his
thoughts? What manner of man was this? What were
the sources, the habits, the processes of his thought,
the background and setting of his life? The literary

approach to the Bible is for college students one of the most interesting and illuminating of experiences. It makes the Bible's meaning much clearer and its difficulties less.

Few will deny the merit of the Bible as literature. Æsthetic appreciation, in spite of excesses, is one of the easiest ways to use the Bible, especially the Old Testament. English-speaking peoples are fortunate in the possession of a tradition of translation, which by its purity of diction and archaic flavor preserves the majesty, earnestness, sublimity, and other literary qualities of the originals. If for no other reason, the Bible deserves study because of its influence on civilization and upon other literature. There are striking evidences that educated men are coming to include a knowledge of the Bible as a necessary constituent of a liberal education.

But what is the religious and moral value of the Bible? Here again probably all will agree that it has merits, that certain passages if they stood by themselves could be unqualifiedly commended as among the purple passages in the world's idealism. Personal religion, ethical ideals, social aspiration, are all well represented between its covers.

This selective use of the Bible is the way in which most men really appreciate it, but for well-trained minds this use of the Bible is not enough. It means that most of its contents are ignored or unused. Many of its good points appear to be neutralized by what can only be stigmatized as bad ethics and bad religion. By our verdict Job's friends are not the only persons in the Bible who speak unrighteously for God. The Bible is as vulnerable in ethical standards as in historic and scientific accuracy. The Christian conscience has long found stumbling-blocks in Scripture which it has sought to moralize by allegory and other methods.

But this moral and religious unevenness in the Bible is just one of the most instructive things about it. We have here the portrayal not of one absolute standard, but of several. When these are arranged in order and compared they give a most romantic picture, not of a stable ideal but of developing and varying religious and moral achievements.

From this viewpoint an enthusiasm for the Bible is easy and natural. One does not have to claim for it abstract perfection. Such excellences as one finds have the advantage of being one's own responsive appreciation. One can speak well of the book without being bound to justify everything within it from every form of criticism. The task of the admirer and lover of the Bible, and even of the apologist, is easier. And as for the reader, it is better, as has been well said, to *feel* the inspiration of the Bible than to construct a theory about it.

In conclusion a few suggestions may be offered to enable one to secure a knowledge of the Bible and to get the benefit of its various values. Something can be done by the old method of reading it through in small sections every day in the Authorized Version. But for its fuller worth other methods are needed.

1. Read a book or long section at a single sitting.

2. Use a modern translation, especially if you are superficially familiar with the Authorized Version by having heard it often read or quoted.

3. Have at hand a simple commentary for reference. There is some truth in the statement that the Bible is the most poorly edited classic.

4. Read books that in an interesting untechnical style give an orientation about the Bible as a whole or about special large phases or subjects in it, at the same time continuing to familiarize yourself with the Bible itself.

5. Strive to approach the Bible with an open mind, cultivating toward it the utmost intellectual curiosity and spiritual sympathy.

ETHICS AND RELIGION

GEORGE HERBERT PALMER

Two weeks ago a very remarkable paper was heard here. It was on substantially the same subject that has been assigned me, on the nature of religion, but it was treated in a peculiarly profound way. It took up not only the psychology of religion, but the ethnology and the archæology of it. That is, after pointing out how religion first appeared in the minds of each one of us and showing the special mental phenomena with which it was connected, it passed on to the history of religion to show how it had grown with increasing civilization and how certain nations had developed special aspects of it.

I had a double satisfaction in this lecture; for not only did I hugely enjoy the great learning apparent in its psychologic ease and its remarkable literary power, but I felt myself discharged from a certain portion of my own work. I had been a little abashed at the immensity of the subject assigned me, and I saw, inasmuch as Doctor Pratt had dealt so fully with portions of it, that I could discharge myself from the metaphysical and historic part of my work. That is, while he has gone over the philosophy of the matter so satisfactorily—and substantially I agreed with him in it all—it has been left to me to deal more with the practical part. The religion of to-day becomes my topic. Of course this must eventually lead to a kind of confession of faith on my part. Therefore, I shall say little in regard to either ethics or religion as an independent science and will merely make a few remarks in regard to each of them.

Ethics! What does it deal with? The means by which we may live together. That is the whole topic of ethics. When several persons are packed together in a fairly contracted world, how can they act so that each one will have the largest opportunity to bring out his powers and at the same time will secure that others have a similar opportunity? But ethics has ordinarily been defined, and to me satisfactorily defined, as the aim at self-realization, that is, the bringing out of the fulness of the powers of each one of us. I do not see how we can imagine any other ultimate aim for ethics. What can there be outside life to justify living? What can a man give in exchange for his life? Nothing. Life is its own justification.

Yet, after all, when I say the moral life is self-realization, such a statement opens the way to grave misconception. There is one word there which is ambiguous—self. You think you know all about it. I wonder if you do. Have you been accustomed to thinking of yourself as a single independent being? If you have, I want to say there is no such being and never was. The single person is a contradiction in terms. The smallest possible unit you can find for a personality is three—father, mother, child. Did you ever know a person who escaped that trinity? I think not. Do not, therefore, indulge yourself in the fancy that you can be a separated individual.

It is true that as you grow up the factors of father and mother fall away largely, occupy a far less important aspect, but that is only because they reappear in so many other relations. That is, a person is an individual being plus his relations, and those relations are what constitute him to be what he is. What would you be if you were not an American, if you were not a Harvard man, if you were not a person who had the friends you have had, if you had not read what you have read? All these relations constitute you to be what you are. What is there that you have not received? Therefore, when I say that the aim of ethics is the fulness of self-realization, you will have to understand that self in a peculiar way. I have often thought it would be most convenient to speak of this true self as the conjunct self, the self plus. Then we can contrast with this the separate self.

No doubt from time to time it is important for us to fix attention on the singleness of our being. Each of us is unique, each different from all the rest; therefore, we do need again and again to speak of ourselves in the single way. What we should always remember is that this is only a temporary mode of utterance. There is no such thing really existing. The real thing is always the conjunct self.

If self-realization, full realization of the conjunct self, is the aim of virtue what is the moral vice? Selfishness. And what is this? Is it acquiring all we can possibly obtain? Whenever a dish of apples is passed to us and to others is it wrong to pick out a good one? Not at all. It is perfectly proper just so long as we do not make our gain the loss of somebody else. That is where selfishness comes in. When I exalt this unique unit of myself to the injury of others, or even do not regard them, there certainly is selfishness. That is, the service of the conjunct self calls upon us, whenever we act, however slight the action may be, to see that more than our unitary personality be involved in the action.

I was walking down one of the paths in the college yard the other day and saw a man in front of me reading a letter. When he had read it he tore it up and threw it on the ground. He had done with it; it was of no more concern to him. He threw it down never asking himself whether it was going to be agreeable to other people. That is the very essence of moral vice. Wherever you trace iniquity you will find it will run up to this, the setting up of the abstract or unitary self against the conjunct self.

The aim of us all then should be to bear in mind steadily this conjunct self and to understand that we are called upon to promote the relations in which the unitary self stands, promoting them to the utmost, feeling ourselves servants of all with whom we are connected.

If this simple explanation will serve well enough for our purpose in tracing the relation of ethics and religion, what is the simplest statement of religion? The sense of a being greater than we. It is expressed in reverence, the bowing of the head, and the acknowledgment that we must serve. In short, it is the sense of dependence. This, I think, is what is fundamental in religion as brought out by Doctor Pratt the other day.

But, being so brought out, how general is it? How largely is this religious emotion acknowledged in our civilization? How far do the men of our time recognize a God? Practically everybody does, just in proportion as he is rational. Of course I understand that many a man goes through life in pretty irrational fashion, and if so, he will not traffic much with God.

But inasmuch as all men, if rational, cannot fail to see that there is a unitary ground of all being, they experience just what we mean by God, the attitude of every one of us toward that ultimate ground of existence. No man can now be a man of science without this, though there has been considerable change in this matter during the last century. Formerly the scientific man was content to take a group of similar phenomena and trace any single event that happened to that group and let it stand there without carrying it farther. This is just what occurred in the early history of our races. That is, we could have gravitation; we could have heat; we could have electricity; we could have chemical affinity, and to say that any one event came under the laws of this group would be sufficient. As the early Greeks used to express it, there would be a god for this group, just what we call polytheism in that early time. It shows a good degree of rationality that no one was contented merely to see an event happen, but felt obliged to see it plausibly connected with something else; and this would be most conveniently accomplished by thinking of a good many different gods. With something like this, science too up to a certain time was satisfied.

But at length the doctrine of the relation and correlation of energy was discovered and we perceived a unity running through all separate groups, so that anything that happens is affected by the whole; that is, there must be a unitary ground with which all things, if fully traced, can be shown to be rationally connected. Therefore, I think we may say to-day that just in proportion as persons are rational, no matter what their occupations are, they recognize the being of God. Not all call it by that name. They frequently speak of it as nature.

There are two questions, however, which immediately arise in regard to this general being or God. Is that God a personal God? What is his character then?

Those two questions I suppose are not always so clearly settled as the fact that there is a God. Personally I can imagine only a single answer to the first; for if we are to conceive of God as the groundwork of all that exists, in whom we live and move and have our being, I do not see how we can rationally leave out of him the element of reason or intelligence. In the great evolutional movement which has gone on throughout the ages, its culmination has been intelligence. This is not only the crown of all creation, but at the same time it is what is most influential over creation; it is the one thing that changes the world, that toward which all creation moves. It would seem to me singularly irrational to leave this out of the compendium of all being. It is more sensible to think of intelligence as the groundwork of all being but only gradually disclosed. The unthinking indeed may be contented to go about the streets where all sorts of things happen and, when they happen, to say, "That is enough. It isn't my business to philosophize. I do not know what these events are connected with. I just take them as they come." That is the case with a large mass of the population, but it means that in such stopping they are irrational. The minute you begin to think things out you certainly must say that in any ground of being, intelligence has a place.

But here let me interpose a few collateral remarks. It is often said there is no use in going off into philosophical and theological discussion, for such doctrines are always changing.

The philosophy of one age is not the philosophy of another, the beliefs about God in one age are not those of another. When then we come upon a department of life which cannot hold its own but is continually changing, what is the use of bothering our heads about it? To which I should reply that doctrines of philosophy do change continually; there is nothing fixed about them. I should only have to add that this is far less true of philosophy and theology than it is of any other human interest. One might say with truth that the only fixed matter in the world is change. Change is a universal law. Nothing is exempt from it. In every department of human life it goes on, in every department of non-human life. But there are two kinds of change. There is one sort which sees that it was mistaken and sets out again, only to have its new point of view pushed aside by the next that comes on. That certainly is a very miserable sort of change, but is not the only kind. There are changes which carry their past on with them, which see a deeper meaning than was seen before and are continually, therefore, evolving it.

Now, when we ask, "What are the changes of religion, theology or philosophy?" I have an idea that they are of this second sort. If you doubt it and think it is not true that the destructive changes are less in these departments than in others, I invite you to go into the college library, into any alcove of physical science, and I believe you will find that any books written fifty years ago on science are entirely superseded to-day. They are dead things. What is asserted in them is not true. It is gone; other doctrines have come up and taken their place. And if you go into the alcoves on philosophy and theology you will find that the speculations and pronouncements of more than two thousand years ago are vital still. They are not completely accurate. They stop far too short, for there was a depth of meaning in them which was not at that time fully understood. But they can be read to-day with large instruction for us all. What we are trying to undertake at present is largely a mere deepening of what is there. They have not been really superseded.

When then I call on you to consider the nature of this ultimate being, this God or ground of all things, and to see that it must include intellect, I want you to remember that it will not be precisely the same God as was conceived two thousand years ago or perhaps even a hundred years ago. It has been changing all the time because it has been deepening its meaning.

I might say further that when any one of us lays hold for himself of that mighty thought, it will appear with a special meaning, different for each one of us. No one of us can comprehend in full anything so large as that. We may look in a certain direction with some assurance that it is the right direction, but our business is chiefly to see how far it can be connected with our own lives, to illuminate them and give them strength. That will undoubtedly differ with different persons, and we ought not to be shocked at finding that the way in which I approach religion is different from the way in which you approach it. Because each of us is but a fragmentary being, we must content ourselves with fragmentary insight.

Shall we not then acknowledge that to comprehend religion in its fulness exceeds the powers of any of us. We may consequently be inclined altogether to reject authority in religion and to content ourselves merely with what we can verify in our own experience. The ultimate test for each of us will then be how largely does it strengthen my being? That is a popular cry in our time; throw aside authority! All authoritative religion is wrong. With that cry I largely sympathize. I should only feel that it was not made quite clear, for it seems to suggest that every one of us must begin at the beginning and think the whole matter out for himself and be uninterfered with by anybody else.

Well, nothing like that occurs in the other departments of human life. I do not see why it should occur in religion. On the contrary I see that something very unlike this occurs with every one of us. That is, we are not brought into the world without a bank-stock; there is a heritage that belongs to each one of us. I have already pointed out that we come into existence not as solitary beings but as conjunct beings, that is, my present existence is tied in with more than my present; it is tied in with the existence of my parents, with the existence of my countrymen, in short with a circle of inheritance. Fortunate indeed it is that we do have what I call a bank-stock of belief at starting. The business of the school, as I understand it, is to put each one of us in as large a possession as possible of this inherited bank-stock. We go to school to learn what is generally agreed upon in our community about the important facts of life. There are then some things that we must take on what we may call authority. I suppose there is no one here who has not inherited a large stock of beliefs in regard to the being of God, possibly inherited, indeed, a belief that there is no such being. At any rate, it has come to him, not through his own exertion at all, but because he is a member of the race, because he was born in Massachusetts, in Boston, and came to Harvard College. All those things start him out in life.

What is the work of a university then? We come to a university to get control of our own minds, to see how far this inherited bank-stock fits our case. What does it mean to me? Nothing is good, we all know, that has not been criticised and criticised continually. As I send my mind back into my earlier years, I see what I inherited. I personally was brought up a Puritan. Thankful indeed I am that I was, and substantially those Puritan beliefs are mine to-day. But I trust they are very largely criticised, readjusted, worked out so as to fit my case and mean something directly to me, to strengthen my life, to carry on that self-realization which I called the highest aim of ethics.

It is plain, accordingly, that any attempt to separate authoritative beliefs from personal beliefs is impossible. The inherited beliefs which are authoritative to us are not really our own until we have passed them through the elaborate criticism which is the business of advanced education. It is again and again said, "Oh, if you send a boy to college he will go to doubting everything." Of course, that is what he is here for. He cannot come to a personally strengthened certainty until he has doubted. I should not agree to the proposition that doubt means casting aside. Criticism should illuminate, should serve to bring out full meanings that were not originally understood. That I believe is commonly the result. All pressure of general authority is taken off during these years. At least we try to take it off here at Harvard.

Have we any aids in this constructive criticism which I speak of as belonging to every one of us in proportion as we are rational? I believe so. Just turn to any other department of life. Take the recognition of beauty. We have not discovered beauty. It is not anything of my individual creation or of yours. It has been in the world a good while and it has affected men profoundly. To ascertain its meaning shall I turn to Leonardo, who not only was a great producer of beauty but who has speculated on its nature? Shall he bid me what I am to admire? Yes and no. I am glad to turn to him or to any other great master of beauty and have him point out to me what he counts beautiful. I shall be much interested in listening to what the masters say in regard to the character of beauty, but I shall not take it on their authority. I shall listen only because I think they have seen farther into beauty than any others that I may happen to know and I want them to open my dull mind and lead me to see what they have seen. I shall then, casting aside authority, decide whether their teaching accords with my experience and tends toward my strength.

Now, precisely that seems to me to be the way in which we shall best grow in our conceptions of religion. I should turn to those who I believe, and who indeed the world believes, to have had the deepest comprehension and experience of religion and to have united it most closely with life; I should like to come under their tuition and have them explain what they have found. Then I shall ask myself, "Has that any meaning for me? Can I connect that with my life?

To-day in our western civilization, taking ourselves as we stand, I think we have two great sources of aid in probing into the nature of religion. They are widely unlike. One of them is a series of pictures describing the experience of a race that is universally recognized as pre-eminent in its understanding of religion, that is, we have the Bible. It gives us a series of pictures of the growth in that marvellous people of the conception of God, beginning in the most elementary way where God appears merely as a tribal deity capable of all sorts of iniquity himself and approving iniquity in others. Then we can trace that people, criticising such conceptions of religion and mounting ever higher through a thousand years, until in some of the psalms we have examples of the most exalted lyric poetry that exists in any language, and all of it impassioned with the experience of God. Here we are taught by a series of pictures, that is through history, the meaning of God.

On the other hand, men have busied themselves with reflecting about these matters, have turned over the thoughts about God and have tried to formulate them into the most graphic and rational doctrines. An institution has been built on this theoretic foundation. We have the church.

To each one of us these two authorities appeal. Each tries to point out what we should think about God. Our business is to get as much illumination from both of these as we possibly can, and then subject it to personal criticism.

Accordingly, as I said at the start, I am obliged

here to pass over into a personal confession of faith. I do not commend it altogether to you. I daresay you will find modes of approach that will be more serviceable to you than mine. But when I come to ask myself where shall I find the deepest insight into the being of God and learn how he can be best connected with personal life, I have no doubt where it can be had. In Jesus of Nazareth. Confessedly his thoughts about the nature of God have shaped all humankind as those of nobody else have. Just the same, therefore, as when I want to find out about beauty I go to the acts and thoughts of men like Leonardo da Vinci, in precisely the same way I turn to Jesus of Nazareth.

As a young person I accepted the authority in which I was brought up and that authority was grounded largely in the two sources of the Bible and the church. Jesus of Nazareth is now for me a superior authority and I turn to him searching every word of his which I find recorded. There are all sorts of stories about him. These were carefully gathered together, sifted and set down according to the best understanding of those who wrote them. This precious deposit I have but I cannot accept every word that is there. I have to verify it in my own experience and say, "Would that strengthen me if I thought in that way?" I am told that Jesus was hungry as he walked across the plain. He saw a fig-tree in the distance and came up to it expecting

something to eat. Not finding anything he cursed the
fig-tree. I am obliged to say the story is out of character for him and for me. A boy angrily strikes the
object that hits him, and in common life that sort of
action is frequent and may easily be reported in our
record. But such stories mean nothing to me. I cannot
say they are all false, for much that originally I
might have called false I now see to be true. Fifty
years ago those of us who tried to accept the New
Testament had a pretty heavy load to carry when we
read continually how Jesus by a word, by a touch,
made sickness cease. Those miracles of healing we
had to say we could not understand; we knew of no
such powers to-day. It seemed as if it would have
been better if they had been omitted from the New
Testament. We now see that if they had been omitted
it would have discredited the record, whereas formerly it demanded credulity to accept them, we now see
it would need credulity to accept the nature of Jesus
without such things. We have discovered powers
which were familiar to him, and we have records of
those powers.

There is no possibility, therefore, either of taking
our text as it stands or of throwing it aside. We have
got to discriminate; we have got to ask ourselves
what parts of this text carry the thought of God most
fully home to us, make it familiar to us and an element of strength in our lives. Well, as I search the
sayings of Jesus to find something of this kind, asking

myself what is the heart of his thought about God, I find that on the whole—I daresay partly on account of my profession and special circumstances—I seem to see that he has one sacred word which completely sums up his whole teaching. That word is "Father," —"God is my Father." Whatever else he is talking about, he is always referring to his Father. His teachings, he tells us, are only valuable so far as they are the words of the Father.

There I seem to have got hold of something that for me illuminates all life and brings strength to me under all circumstances. For what is the business of a father? If he is a true father, if he is working out to the full the functions of a father, it is his business to educate the child, to bring out its powers on every side. He does not, if he is a good father, make the child subservient to his own needs. He makes himself subservient to the needs of the child; he adjusts and limits himself so that the child can understand him and draw strength from him. He has a thousand interests that could not possibly be interests of the child. These he suppresses. But he accepts the level where the child stands and makes it his first business to endear the child to him and himself to the child. He lets the child understand that he is always there as a father, that under all circumstances he can turn to him with assurance of supporting strength. Where there is such a true father the union of the two is complete.

Jesus teaches then that God can only be rightly thought of as a father. Divine relations, he seems to say, are human relations, that is, human relations carried to a point to which we can hardly carry them. This Jesus proclaims as a gospel, good news to the world. Consider it a moment and see if it is not good news. There is no such thing as blind fate. God is your friend. Everything that he allows to happen to you is intended for your good. God gives you an opportunity and he is perpetually furnishing these opportunities to bring out your powers to the utmost.

Suppose you could believe that everything that happens is for your good. Jesus believed it and accepted everything that came to him as for the best; it was all intended kindly and for his enlargement, giving him a wider scope for his powers. What a joy life would be. You never could be lonely again. You would always have an intimate at hand wherever you were.

That is what the mystic has understood by religion, the immediacy of personal connection with God. Could you then regret anything? Nothing. Whatever happened to you, however severe, however seemingly adverse, you would know was for your advantage. If you took it rightly your powers would be increased. "I have come that ye might have life and that ye might have it abundantly." What an abundance of life would be poured upon us if we took this view to heart! What is called disaster falls upon me. Partly it is my own fault, but this hardship has been arranged by my Father for my instruction. But there is good in it. It is my business then to accept it uncomplainingly as if it were good and not evil and to keep my affection for him through all.

And now perhaps I can turn back a moment and ask what is the relation between religion and ethics. I pointed out in the few words I had to say about ethics that it was an exhibit of the way in which we should live together so that each one of us could have his powers carried to the utmost without injury to the development of the powers of others. Now that we have learned what religion is, we see that it is immediately subservient to ethics. It, too, insists on abundance of life. Religion, says Matthew Arnold, is morality touched with emotion. That is true, but it does not define which emotion, whether of hatred or of love. I suppose we shall all understand that love is meant. We want to escape duty oftentimes. But should we if we knew that the demands of duty expressed the affection of the Friend who is dearest to us, our Father? Certainly not. That would change its character. By religion morality would be touched with love, and the whole quality of duty would be changed. Its harshness would disappear; we should see that it was all meant for our advantage and that in that advantage every one was to share.

It will be well then to ask ourselves how far such

a doctrine as I have explained as my own belief is justified by the world around us. Here we have the problem presented of a loving, good God in an evil world. There cannot be any doubt that evil is about us everywhere. We are encountering it every day; encountering it in ourselves particularly. Is that an aspersion on the being of such a God as I have described? I do not see that it is. I have said that a wise father limits himself. He does not take his boy and force him to go through certain acts. He does not impose himself upon the boy. He tries to bring out the boy's own powers as fully as possible. Is a father ever a wise or a true father who does not entrust the management of that boy to himself? He assists him; he suggests what is best, he shows him how he himself lives, and so on. But he expects his boy to grow by experience, even by experience of error. We might expect that an infinite God would be able to stop all evil at once. Our heavenly father does not do so. Does this obvious fact prove him limited in power or in love? In power, I should say, self-limited, because of his love of his children. Perhaps the way in which a loving father has always limited himself for the sake of his children will be best understood by watching the same principle at work in the education of to-day. Any one inspecting Harvard College would find many loafers here, men squandering time and opportunity and forming habits pretty sure to unfit them later for grappling successfully with the world.

How shocking to tolerate such a mass of unintelligent evil! Are the officials here men of limited ability, or do they care nothing for their charges? Why do they not stop this waste? The answer would be, "Their ability is limited, self-limited. They know that a student forced, as the blind education of the past attempted to force him, is no student at all. They therefore limit themselves to offering opportunities, to making these opportunities attractive, and letting the ultimate guidance, even if erroneous, be in the student's own hands. Men of independent intelligence are therefore common here to-day to a degree unknown of old. Now our father in heaven had been using the elective system long before we discovered it.

A wise father, too, gives his boy many difficult problems, such as science has been at work trying to solve for thousands of years. It is far better so than if they had all been solved at the start. We had to find them out for ourselves, and in that intellectual attempt we were to realize our best end. Our Heavenly Father could have given us all that. But how unfortunate for us it would have been. We should not have had our intellectual powers developed as they have been. Hardihood is also an important point. How many boys fail in the attempt to develop it? My father sends me out some morning a mile away, in the cold, to get a can of milk. How cruel! Why, no, he wants to accustom me to meet severities of weather. That hardihood is a necessary element in the training of any child by a wise father.

And then, what takes longer to train in the child and what our Heavenly Father has been especially careful to train us in is overcoming time, teaching us to prefer a future good to an immediate good. He has so arranged it that the rush for the immediate good is apt to defeat itself and in the long run bring injury. He is constantly suggesting to us the directions we had better take, and one of them is frequently this— to learn to wait.

The great aim in the teaching of a father is readiness for self-sacrifice, so-called, that is, the putting away of the notion of a separate self and learning how important the conjunctive elements are, far more important than anything we could reach in our isolated capacity. How he has displayed this in himself, going to his death for us all! "For this purpose came I into the world." However deeply he feels it, he does not desire to shirk it, but rather to suffer for the sake of others so that they shall have life.

Such is the teaching of Jesus, the greatest teaching that a father ever undertakes to introduce into his child's life. Here, then, is a gospel. Here is a new view of the world. Here we are at home in our father's house, a happy place, a place for which we can be the more thankful because we see that the evils of it have not been exterminated by any alien power but must be exterminated through love: we are to Love God and to love our fellow men. Those are the things that will bring out our powers and the powers of all who enter upon the task.

I said at the start that I was well aware that I was biased in approaching the notion of God from the particular point of view of education. I ought to have said perhaps that I recognize that Jesus has not originated this idea. The notion of the Fatherhood of God runs all through Greek thought; it is all through the Hebrew thought of the Old Testament; it is everywhere. It is so fundamental a fact that it cannot be overlooked, but just as we have seen the notion of God growing from the crudest, most elementary thought among the Hebrews up to the magnificent significance it has now attained, just in that way the notion of the Father has grown until on the lips of Jesus of Nazareth its full meaning has been spoken out.

In closing perhaps I ought to comment a little more on the connection of religion and ethics. I think we may say that the contents of religion are in no wise different from those of ethics. There is no act which is an essentially religious act. In religion I am speaking of how it would be viewed by our Father in Heaven. Athletics is the opportunity to get a physical body and learn the care of our health. It is just as religious as going to a prayer meeting. There is no act, in short, that belongs peculiarly to religion. All upright acts are religious. The Psalms express this profoundly. Here is one of them, the 15th:

> Lord, who shall abide in Thy tabernacle?
> Who shall dwell in Thy holy hill?
> He that walketh uprightly, and worketh righteousness, and speaketh the truth in his heart.
> He that backbiteth not with his tongue, nor doeth evil to his neighbor, nor taketh up a reproach against his neighbor.
> In whose eyes a vile person is contemned; but he honoreth them that fear the Lord. He that sweareth to his own hurt, and changeth not.
> He that putteth not out his money to usury, nor taketh reward against the innocent. He that doeth these things shall never be moved.

Such are the commands of both religion and morality. Only the inner attitude is different. Instead of thinking of the command of duty any longer in abstract, as "It," we now think of it as personal, a "He"; "It" was changed to "He" by passing from ethics to religion, and that "He" can be a much-loved friend.

Question: Will you please explain more fully why the record of Jesus' life is easier to believe with the miracles than without them?

Professor Palmer: Because we now know that a powerful personality has an effect on other personalities. How far that goes, we do not yet know, but we see multitudes of cases where it does occur; so that that which formerly looked exceptional and almost contradictory, through recent experience we see to be a matter of frequent occurrence.

Question: What is your idea of Buddha as a religious teacher?

Professor Palmer: I should rule out all questions on racial religions. Those were fully discussed by Doctor Pratt. I have wanted to confine my attention to religion as it now exists among us and to asking what are its practical applications.

Question: Is your theory that "Everything happens to us for the best," the same as fatalism?

Professor Palmer: In fatalism all happens because of an "it," an unintended "it." In my theory it happens through a kind intention. I do not feel therefore that we can longer use such phrases as "good events" and "bad events." They become good or bad as they are used. Good and bad are terms that apply to our treatment of them, and I hold that whatever occurs in the world is a kindly-intentioned event. If accepted as such, it will bring me a blessing, and when I say "me" I must not think of myself in a separate way but in a conjunct way.

Question: Is not the Fatherhood of God rather the expression of a hope and a yearning than the actual fulfilment of a need?

Professor Palmer: I pointed out that it would seem to me to be irrational to take any event that occurred in a disjointed way, as if there were nothing behind it. Whatever occurs is connected. We find connection everywhere. How far back shall that connection go? Shall it go only to a detached group of phenomena, or shall it go still further to an ultimate ground, and in that ultimate ground must we not include intelligence? What sort of intelligence, I ask?

Then, in trying to find out what sort of intelligence it is, I go to those who seem to have fathomed it most fully and into whose life it has brought the greatest strength. I know of no better way of finding that strength than through Jesus of Nazareth. But I do not take his mere dicta as I find them, I take them only as verifiable in my own experience. Experience is the ultimate test everywhere. Authoritative teaching is good, and we may be thankful for the education of that sort we have had. But as we grow more intelligent it becomes imperative for us to scrutinize our own experiences and see how far they justify the earlier teachings.

Question: The Gospel of John says: "No man cometh unto the Father but by me." On that ground what does this seeming exclusiveness of the Gospel mean to those who never heard of Jesus or Jehovah?

Professor Palmer: Exclusiveness is banished by the Gospel of Jesus which declares that God is no alien force but a loving father in whose image we are made. Divine relations are comprehensible only through a deeper understanding of those of mankind.

Jesus is therefore frankly an anthropomorphist, an ugly word announcing something generally condemned. Among the Greeks of the seventh century B. C., Xenophanis denounced it, saying "it was no more sensible for men to imagine gods in their own image than it would be for oxen or horses to imagine gods like themselves." Yet if oxen and horses had reflection, though their conceptions would be incomplete, how could they think of God more wisely than by attributing to him the power, patience, and affections found in themselves? Anthropomorphism becomes foolish only when we attribute to an infinite being those characteristics of ours which are essentially adapted to time and space.

If then the gospel of Jesus is true and in human fatherhood God's character is best reached, the case of the heathen is less forlorn than it is often assumed. Family relations are everywhere. Each household has within it an outline representative of the Most High. Let this be studied and lived up to, and Jesus' way of redemption will be accomplished. However superior our advantage is in beholding the great exemplar, no home has been left altogether desolate.

Question: Some of your remarks seem to border upon foreordination. Do you believe in foreordination as it is in Calvin's system?

Professor Palmer: Not as it is in Calvin's system, though I think it is important to recognize that God is concerned with our future as well as with our present. I think he is concerned with it by offering us opportunities pointing in a certain direction rather than in forcing those opportunities upon us. I pointed out that it seemed to me that every wise father led his child but did not oblige him to go. His discipline was not that of a state prison but that of companionship, affection, love.

Question: Are there not religious men, as, for example, the mystics, who have had little or no ethical interest?

Professor Palmer: They allowed elements to enter into ethics which I should not allow, and pretty generally, too, they failed to grasp the notion of the conjunct self. They sought to come into intimacy with God by removing themselves from their fellow men, going into a cloister, stripping off fleshly powers, making themselves as miserable as possible, with the fancy that that helped them with God. All those seem to me directly contrary to the teachings of Jesus and his understanding of the Fatherhood of God.

Question: Since things are changing constantly, is there anything really we can call ultimate?

Professor Palmer: Not ultimate in the sense that the future will disclose no larger meaning than we have now. There is no such thing as a final settlement all round. The world is an infinite world, and we can go on continually finding more and more in it. I believe I said the only thing we can call constant in the world is change.

Question: What is your definition of a miracle?

Professor Palmer: An alteration in the physical world at the dictation of the mental world. There is a miracle (extending right forearm and hand). I thought about my arm being in the air before it was there, and that is what made the arm go up. The arm was influenced by physical change. Into that world of physical change my thought entered and became a power. Precisely how that connection is made between the physical and the mental world we are continually trying to explain. We have never got the matter clear. But it is no more difficult for a religious person to explain than it is for a scientific person. It is one of the mysteries of the world, how matter and mind can connect. Wherever at the instance of mind, physical things change, there we have a miracle.

Question: Discipline and training of one's children are reasonable, but would a good and all-powerful father allow the total destruction and wreckage of his children?

Professor Palmer: If he were limiting his interference I can conceive that that might go on. How it would be adjusted thereafter, I do not explain; I did not mean that through this gospel which Jesus seems to me to have proclaimed he has enabled us to perceive and understand all the mysteries of the world. When an earthquake occurs and destroys a city and thousands of innocent persons it is to me a blank. I cannot explain it. I do see what is the fundamental groundwork of the world—love, the development of every one of us. If I could explain how that particular case is connected with that groundwork, I should have to be in the place of God himself.

Question: Is not organized worship artificial, and a superstructure that obscures genuine communion with God?

Professor Palmer: If it is uncriticised I think it is. If it remains there as a deposit, something brought over to enrich every one of us when we begin poor, I think it is an enormous blessing. Indeed I should say that every one of us in the work we do ought to aim not merely at benefiting individuals, but our work is never first-rate until we are building up some institution. To merge ourselves with some institution and be lost with its advance seems to me the glorious aim for every one of us.

Question: If God is good, how can we explain the fact that there are irrational people, not realizing the aim of life, having no comprehension or need of morality and religion? They do not see evil as an opportunity to gain character. Is that good?

Professor Palmer: I think God has counted it so. He has allowed them to go to wreck if they wished to go. He has offered them every opportunity not to go, and that is the utmost any kind father will do; he will not enforce righteousness on his son; he will give him opportunity for it.

Question: What justification is there for the way of Providence in permitting idiots and others unfit to partake in the religious life to be born? If this is a benefit to others, what do the unfit get out of it?

Professor Palmer: Idiots get no more than trees or stones. But others should. That we shall take part in each other's limitations is an essential, it seems to me, of the religious life, as it is indeed of the moral life. We must bear each other's burdens. I cannot separate myself from you. You and I belong together. What a great statement of these things that sermon of Doctor Brown's was last Sunday on the Good Samaritan. There were three persons involved there—the robber, the ecclesiastic, and the Samaritan. Now, the robber, according to Doctor Brown, had for his instinctive principle, "Yours is mine, and I can take it." The ecclesiastic had for his motto, "Mine is mine, and I will keep it." The Samaritan had as his motto, "Mine is yours and we will share it." I do not know how the whole groundwork of ethics and religion can be better summed up than in those statements.

Question: Does tne content of religion include more than the content of ethics, or are the two contents coextensive?

Professor Palmer: The two contents seem to me to be coextensive. As I said, there is no essentially religious act. All religious acts are moral acts and cannot be otherwise. What doth the Lord thy God require of thee but to fear the Lord thy God, to walk in all his ways and to love him, to serve the Lord thy God with all thy mind and with all thy soul?

Question: Isn't the view of the conjunct self a product of the practical reason? How much religion is at its basis?

Professor Palmer: It must be worked out in a scientific way and so be connected with the rest of life. If our life does proceed on this amity with God, thought must enter into it, and the conjunct self will then be seen to be something for us to use and verify in our moral life.

Question: How do you reconcile the conjunct self with the Emersonian philosophy of self-reliance?

Professor Palmer: I do not know any other way of getting self-reliance than to see how we are linked in with God. If we feel, we do not feel merely for ourselves but we feel for others. Our business is to go on with them, not alone but with them. It seems to me Emerson has stated the truth here admirably.

WHAT IS THE GOOD OF RELIGION?

RALPH BARTON PERRY

THE things of greatest value are often the things whose value is most obscure. As being coeval with human life, such things have not been needed first and invented afterward, so as consciously to associate the achievement with the need; but their very indispensableness has led to their being ignored. Thus, for example, man has never been without some form of domestic life and some form of political life. The family and the state being universal and perennial, or the need for them having always been in some measure met, men do not naturally ascribe value to them, as they do to remedies or tools which supply a "long-felt want." Men take them for granted, and profit by them without prizing them. Presently, however, owing to disputes between the advocates of different *forms* of domestic and political life, or owing to their *abuses*, some one challenges the institutions themselves. He asks in effect, "Since we are in doubt as to how the family or state should be constituted, and since it is admitted that they do harm, why have any family or state at all?" Then for the first time it becomes necessary to bring to light the underlying purposes or uses of these things, or the fundamental needs for the sake of which they exist. The challenge of the sceptic has to be met, and in the course of meeting it men come to see that if they did not have these institutions it would be necessary to invent them.

So it is with religion. Humanly speaking it is ubiquitous, or nearly so. Men have never had to get on without it, and have therefore had no occasion to prize it. They have attacked other people's religions, and have even sought to reform their own, but that there should be some religion has been taken for granted. It is only the sceptic who raises this question and insists upon an answer. Sooner or later, however, this sceptic is bound to arise and to put his question: "In view of the conflicts and abuses of religion, why *have* any religion? *What is the good of it?*" This challenge is the late product of civilization and of sophistication, but once raised, it compels the friends of religion to go below the questions of doctrine or worship or ecclesiastical polity that divide them, to the deeper question, "Is some religion better than no religion, and, if so, why?" In answering this question they will be forced to bring to light the underlying needs which religion satisfies, and which would make it imperative for men, if they had no religion, to invent one.

This sceptical challenge has in modern times commonly assumed one of two forms. It has been held that religion is pernicious, or that religion is gratuitous. Thus Mr. Salomon Reinach is said to have defined religion as "a body of scruples that thwart the free exercise of our faculties." * This harsh judgment of religion is a characteristic product of the age of science, during which the "believers," who constitute the great majority of mankind, have not changed their minds as frequently or as quickly as the scientist. Religion became, in the last century, the chief symbol of that resistance which the stable and uniform convictions of a cult offer to the more eccentric novelties of theoretical and experimental inquiry.

That religion is gratuitous is suggested by the exclamation of Jean Christophe: "As if a healthy, generous creature, overflowing with strength and love, had not a thousand more worthy things to do than to worry as to whether God exists or no!" † This might be taken to imply that the best way to find God is to forget him, but it also expresses the feeling that religion as commonly conceived in Christendom is a sort of *pis-aller*, or measure of last resort. It is a medicine for sick souls, a compensation for weakness: in short, a confession of failure.

Both of these views of religion are characteristic of modern European and American civilization. They both regard religion as a symptom of defect. They affirm that men need religion only in so far as

* Quoted in Paul Sabatier, *France To-day*, trans. by H. B. Binns, 1913, p. 14.

† Romain Rolland, *Jean Christophe*, trans. by G. Cannon, pp. 231–232.

their development and education are incomplete. If men's minds were emancipated and well-informed, they would regard all religion as outlived superstition. As men enter into full possession of their faculties they will discard religion, as the restored cripple throws away his crutch.

Such a challenge raises the question whether religion has its roots in something permanent and universal, or is a transient episode in human life. That religion yields satisfaction of some sort, no one would dispute. But are its satisfactions of the type that spring from those deeper demands of human life which it is the business of a progressive civilization to awaken and fulfil? Or are they the illusory and provisional satisfactions of a primitive culture? Is religion something to be grown out of, or something to be grown up to? Is it a symptom of maturity? Or is it a symptom of childhood—of the naïveté of the first childhood, and the decay of the second?

Our inquiry into the values of religion is circumscribed in a second way. We limit ourselves to the profounder and more abiding values of religion, but we also limit ourselves to the *peculiar* values of religion. We are not, in other words, concerned with those uses which religion serves but which could equally well be served by some other instrument. A book can be used to fill a vacant space on a shelf, but this is not precisely what a book is for. Another object similar in size and shape would do equally well. An occasion of worship can be used for barter or employment, as in the churches of rural Quebec, but this is a use which could be, and usually is, supplied by secular agencies. Compulsory college chapel is said to conduce to college spirit and to victory in football, but mass-meetings would do as well. In some communities the church sociable provides the opportunity for neighborly gossip which in more advanced communities is supplied by the *thé dansant*. Church music gratifies the ear, altar paintings the eye, and incense the nostrils; but these are needs that can be met by concert-halls, art-galleries, and smelling-bottles. The church can suppress violence and deal justice, but these are functions which are commonly supplied by the state. In other words, where there is comparatively little division of labor religion attaches to itself many uses which in more complex societies it proves possible and expedient to provide for in other ways. In so far as it is social, religion may be put to social uses, and in so far as it is art, it may be put to artistic uses; but since these uses may be supplied by agencies that are not religious, we know them to be accidental rather than essential. Religion, once existing, may be the most convenient way of supplying them, but religion is not required for them. They are not the uses of religion *qua* religion. They do not relate to that which is *religious* in religion.

Such, then, is our problem: to discover what are

these permanent values which attach to religion, and which attach to nothing else.

Having set ourselves this problem, we are compelled, whether we like it or not, to define religion. This will doubtless seem to many to be a highly improbable achievement. It is, no doubt, a somewhat notorious philosophical pastime, like the squaring of the circle and the invention of *perpetuum mobile;* but with this important difference, that no one has yet proved the achievement to be impossible. I am sustained, also, by the reflection that only the definitions that it is difficult to make are worth making. This is probably due to the fact that the value lies not so much in the definition as in the effort to make it.

Religion appears to arise from and to rest upon two distinctions, and its universality is due to the fact that these distinctions are constant features of human experience. The one lies within the realm of fact and the other within the realm of morals. Let us, for the sake of simplicity, call the first the distinction between the "natural" and the "supernatural," and the other the distinction between the "worldly" and the "unworldly."

The first of these basic distinctions has been well described in a recent book by Professor John Dewey:

When he [Herbert Spencer] says that every fact has two opposite sides, "the one its near or visible side and the other its remote or invisible side," he expresses a persistent trait of every object in experience. The visible is set in the invisible; and in the end what is unseen decides what happens in the seen; the tangible rests precariously upon the untouched and ungrasped. The contrast and the potential maladjustment of the immediate, the conspicuous and focal phase of things, with those indirect and hidden factors which determine the origin and career of what is present, are indestructible features of any and every experience. We may term the way in which our ancestors dealt with the contrast superstitious, but the contrast is no superstition. It is a primary datum in any experience.*

In further clarification of this distinction I may be permitted to repeat an earlier statement of my own:

Man is periodically reminded, if he is not perpetually mindful, of the great residual environment that is beyond his control. Man proposes, but after all something beyond him disposes. Floods, droughts, pestilence, rigors of climate, subjection, error, failure—these are the facts that teach and drive home the lesson of dependence. The most impressive and unanswerable fact is death. The whole fabric of personal achievement, woven by innumerable painstaking acts, all the fruits of struggle and of growth—possessions, power, friendship—are apparently annihilated in an instant, and with an ease that would be ridiculous if it were not so deeply tragic.†

When I refer to this duality as that between the natural and the supernatural I do not mean to imply that the supernatural *violates* the natural, as is commonly supposed when we use the terms "miracle" and "law." Such a case, if it has any meaning at all,

* *Experience and Nature*, 1925, pp. 43–44.
† *Lectures on Doctor Eliot's Five-Foot Shelf of Books: Religion,* 1914, p. 9.

would be only a special case of that feature of experience to which I allude. The natural, as I interpret it, is that field of existence which has assumed the aspect of a familiar and dependable routine, where the connection of events is so stabilized that a man can count upon producing one event by another, or can anticipate one event upon the occurrence of another; while the supernatural is that outlying and underlying field which is the source of the unpredictable and catastrophic, or of the great tidal movements of evolution and history. The line between these two fields is, it is true, a movable line; and as science advances this line moves out in all directions like an enlarging horizon. But movement does not obliterate the line, and it is doubtful if the contrast is any less poignantly felt. Whatever its area, even when it is expanded to include electrons and spiral nebulæ, the cosmos continues to have boundaries, and man continues to gaze fearfully and hopefully beyond them.

The second distinction, which I have called the distinction between the "worldly" and the "unworldly," arises within the moral field, as the tension between inclination and duty, or the opposition between the drag of moral inertia and the flight of moral aspiration. Here, as in the first case, the distinction may appear upon different levels, as the antithesis of appetite and prudence, or of prudence and loyalty, or of narrower and wider loyalties, or of humanity and saintliness. Moral attainment is always a limited attainment, and whatever the elevation on which man stands, he always feels the beckoning call or the more exigeant demands of a greater perfection. Above that moral level on which one moves with a sense of competence and success, —the level of instinct, habit, or average attainment, there is always some higher level which induces a sense of inferiority and moral strain. Where one lives at ease is never Zion.

Having separated these two distinctions, the factual distinction between the natural and the supernatural, and the moral distinction between the worldly and the unworldly, we may now, without confusing or losing sight of them, understand the ways in which they may be combined. And first let us consider what would usually be regarded as complete religion. This would be the case in which the idea of the supernatural was combined with the idea of the unworldly, or in which devotion to the highest ideal was founded upon a conception of ultimate causes. A special case of this would be that case which is most familiar to those reared in the Christian tradition, the case, namely, in which the ultimate cause is itself supposed to be the embodiment or guarantee of the highest ideal.

But while it is no doubt in a certain sense true that religion tends thus to unite the deeper things and the higher things, it is in accordance with prevailing usage to regard as religious any attitude which involves either factor. When a man has adopted a cause with fervor and self-sacrifice, we say that he has "made a religion" of it. A devotee of "the cause of righteousness" may be religious in Arnold's sense of "morality tinged with emotion," even though he should invoke only natural causes, such as sanitation or a League of Nations, in its support. Similarly, when a man takes account of deeper forces that he believes to be moving behind the scenes, he is said to be religious even though in his reckoning with these forces he is concerned only with his immediate temporal ends. If he prays for victory in football or battle, or for recovery from sickness, he invokes the supernatural, but he is not dedicating himself to the ideal. In short, while religion in the full sense may be said to involve both supernaturalism and unworldliness, it may in a partial sense be either a worldly supernaturalism or an unworldly naturalism.

All three of these possibilities, however, bring to light a central feature of religion which our analysis has hitherto neglected. Viewed subjectively religion is a state of practical and emotional conviction, in which one accepts a view of ultimate causes for the purposes of life, or adopts an ideal as his moving end. The man whose prayer takes the form, "Oh! God, if there be a God, save my soul, if I have a soul!" is rightly held to be lacking in religion, not because he is without the necessary ideas, but because he has not committed himself to them. Charles A. Dana is said to have denied that he believed in ghosts, though admitting that he had always been afraid of them. In religion it is more important that one should fear God than that one should believe in him, if by belief one means an act of cold intellectual assent. Religion must touch the heart, and enlist the will; it is essentially a faith, a hope, a surrender, a struggle, or a consecration.

If in this analysis I have hitherto made little or no use of the conception of God, it is because we can learn more about God from religion than we can learn about religion from God. God, in the only universal sense in which this word can be used, is *the object of the religious attitude*, that is to say, of *worship*. But this attitude, as we have seen, is analyzable into two components, so that God may be defined as the object of the one, or of the other, or of both. God is the supernatural worshipped with fear and hope, viewed with solicitude, and reckoned with as the ultimate arbiter of fortune; or, God is the unworldly, the supreme ideal, worshipped with praise, with loyalty, and with love; or God is at one and the same time both the chief corner stone of the universe and the acme of perfection. Project the line of insight in the direction of ulterior causes, the line of aspiration in the direction of ulterior goods, and God is the culminating point in which these two lines converge.

Having found a reasonably just conception of what religion is, we may now return to our original question of the values of religion. We have first to affirm explicitly what might, perhaps, be taken for granted, that it is *religion* which we are judging, and not its *objects*. We do not ask, what is the good of the supernatural, or what is the good of the unworldly, but what is the good of *taking account* of the supernatural, or of *devoting* oneself to the unworldly. Religion does not consist in the fact that "God's in his heaven, all's right with the world," but in the fact that Pippa feels so. The value of religion, therefore, is not the all-rightness of the world, but the song in Pippa's heart.

Recognizing that the seat of religion and of its values is in the worshipping mind, we may now see that its values are three: the value of taking account of ultimate causes; the value of directing the will to the supremely good; and the value of a state of ardent conviction founded on one or both of these ideas. The first is the value of control and adaptation. To live successfully, whatever be one's purpose in life, requires a knowledge of the causes by which events may be produced or anticipated. Religion merely extends this principle to the knowledge of ultimate causes, and judges him to be a "fool" who has said in his heart "there is no God." The second is the value of preferring the greater to the lesser good. Religion extends this principle to the greatest good and puts the very sobering question, "what doth it profit a man to gain the whole world and forfeit his soul?" The third value is that joy and concord which spring from the dissolving of doubt or of internal conflict—that "peace of God which passeth all understanding."

Let me amplify each of these in turn. The knowledge of causes is doubly useful. If one can produce the cause one can then produce the effect, or, if not, one can at least make ready for the effect. This is taken for granted within the sphere that I have called the natural sphere, where the causes, or at least the sequences, of events are well understood. It is useful to know that water is a cause of growth, because being able to obtain water, one can then by irrigation produce the crop; and it is useful to know that night follows day because although one cannot prevent the night one can at least prepare one's bed. But there are causes which upset one's calculations, and make the future both uncontrollable and unpredictable. One cannot know these causes in ordinary ways, and since it is needful to know them, one tries to know them in extraordinary ways. The need being great, one takes what knowledge one can get, a guess, a speculation, an imperfectly verified opinion; and, having taken it, one believes it or acts on it, for otherwise it would not be of any use. Religious belief of this sort usually takes two forms, the one aiming at control, the other at adaptation. Since the ultimate causes cannot be controlled by physical means, it is thought that they may be controlled as a weaker man controls a stronger man, by importunity or by propitiation. It is conceived that the ultimate causes, being themselves governed by appetites or emotions, can be wheedled, or tempted, or flattered, or otherwise moved to indulgence. This is one of the meanings of worship throughout all its wide range, from the cruder forms of magic and burnt offerings, to those higher forms in which the worshipper seeks by pleading to arouse and exploit a divine parental tenderness, or by consecration to draw the divine power into the circuit of his own will. Where there is no hope of control there remains the value of adaptation. Though impotent to influence him, one may prepare to meet one's God; or, being assured that the future, whatever it be, is in the hands of a father who knows and supplies the needs of his children, one may "take no thought of the morrow."

It is important to note that religious value of this type is dependent on factual truth. Though it might be irreverent or distressing, it would not be *foolish* to say in one's heart that "there is no God," unless there *were* a God. Provided there were no God of the sort supposed, a benevolent Creator, for example, one could safely ignore him, as one can safely ignore Santa Claus. Whether it would be safe to take him on faith or on insufficient evidence, would depend on how completely one accepted the teaching that God helps him who helps himself. It is commonly supposed that although the margin of error is greater in the case of religious truth, the risk attaching to error is less. The penalty is, it is true, usually remote; and the difficulty of obtaining the truth encourages a speculative or gambling spirit. But it would seem, nevertheless, to be true that the danger of religious error must be proportional to the importance of religious truth. A mistake about ultimate causes is the most serious mistake a man could make. What he thinks about ultimate causes would most profoundly affect the whole course of his life. Could there, for example, be a more fatal blunder than to have neglected all of the opportunities afforded by this life, owing to a mistaken expectation of a life to come; or to have neglected every prudent calculation, owing to an unfounded trust in a divine caretaker; or to have wasted one's years in the use of ineffectual methods of salvation, based on a misunderstanding of God's intentions? There is a shrewd recognition of this risk in the common practice of keeping one's powder dry at the same time that one puts one's trust in God; or of judiciously dividing one's investment between the corruptible treasures of earth, and the incorruptible treasures of heaven.

At any rate, it is clear that in principle this first value of religion, the promotion of one's fortunes through control and adaptation, is conditioned by truth. Religion is in this respect of use or value, in so far as in accord with the fact; harmful, in so far as contrary to fact.

When we turn to the second value of religion, that of unworldliness, we find that this value, too, is conditioned by truth, although it is truth of a different sort. It is a good thing to worship a supreme good with one's whole heart, provided that which one worships *is* supremely good. I do not believe that any of us would be disposed to say that provided only one *has* an ideal and is true to it, it does not matter *what* the ideal is. Or, if we are disposed to praise the having of an ideal, without specifying what the ideal shall be, it is because when we use the term "ideal" we *assume* that it shall possess superior goodness. It is possible to devote oneself to that which is unworthy of devotion. The Puritan who accounts it a virtue to be willing to be damned for the glory of God, believes that the glory of God, because God is justice and love, is a greater good than the salvation of his creatures. One does not account it a virtue to be willing to be damned for the glory of Cæsar Borgia. Even the loyalist who submits to the whim of his king, ascribes kingly virtues to him, and calls him the father of his people. Divested of such worthiness to be obeyed, God or king assumes the aspect of a tyrant, and to worship him is slavishness.

This second value of religion consists, then, in

moral enlightenment—in the orientation of the will and the emotions toward what is truly best. God, so conceived, is the representation of the best, or the symbol of perfection. There is a way of criticizing religion which rests wholly on this interpretation of God. Epicurus said, "The impious man is not he who rejects the gods of the vulgar, but he who ascribes to the gods the things which the vulgar believe of them." * Impiety, in other words, consists in attributing to the object of worship that which is not really worshipful. Christianity may in this sense be defined as the religion which has taught men to esteem love above all things, or the religion whose God is the symbol of perfect benevolence. If this be the Christian standard, then notable Christians have failed to be Christian. The following incident is narrated of The Blessed Angela of Foligno, one of the most celebrated of the Franciscan saints:

On her conversion to God she "mourned to be bound by obedience to a husband, by reverence to a mother, and by the care of her children," and prayed earnestly to be released from these impediments. Her prayer was heard, and "soon her mother, then her husband, and presently all her children departed this life."†

It can scarcely be consistent with the cult of tender compassion that it should have the effect of hardening the hearts of its saints. Recognizing this cult as

* A. E. Taylor, *Epicurus*, Philosophies, Ancient and Modern, p. 77.
† G. G. Coulton, *From St. Francis to Dante*, 1906, p. 58.

the essence of Christianity, Nietzsche, the greatest of its opponents, has condemned it as giving vogue to "one of the most corrupt concepts of God ever arrived at on earth," because "everything strong, brave, domineering, and proud has been eliminated out of it." Nietzsche, in other words, believed that a hard heart was better than a soft one, and that a religion which idealized compassion was therefore morally false.

The third value of religion is to be found in the subjective effect of the belief upon the believer. Plato speaks in the *Republic* of the effects of music upon the will and emotions, and distinguishes between the Ionian and Lydian harmonies, which are soft and relaxing, and the Dorian and Phrygian, which are the strains of courage and of temperance.* Similarly, it might be said that there are Ionian, Lydian, Dorian, and Phrygian beliefs—beliefs that are enervating, and beliefs that are bracing. Applying this standard of *morale* or mental hygiene, there is a pathology of belief which classifies certain beliefs as depressing or toxic; and a therapy of belief which classifies them as palliative, anæsthetic, stimulating, and nutritive. It is entirely conceivable that at some future day there should be developed an elaborate *materia medica*, or pharmacology, of the mind; or that the soul-sick should be able to choose their diet of beliefs in accordance with its content of spiritual

* *Republic*, III, 398–399.

calories. The healing of the sick, whether in body or in soul, has always been a recognized office of the Christian church, and to-day it is explicitly referred to as "faith-cure," or "Christian science," or "religio-therapeutics." It is probable that in the long run more converts are made to religion by the experience of feeling better after taking it, than by any other sort of evidence; which is neither surprising nor discreditable.

There is a value of this subjective sort correlated with each of the modes of religious belief. There is an access of hope and confidence that comes from the belief in an invisible but powerful ally; and there is a whole-heartedness that comes from the focussing of all one's energies upon a single supreme end. These are the most important conditions of happiness,—the sense of having the upper hand, and the sense of being at peace with oneself. Religion has, therefore, a peculiar relation to happiness, as giving men both the courage to live and also something to live for.

We have, then, three values in religion, the value of metaphysical truth, the value of moral truth, and the subjective value of metaphysical or moral conviction. I am inclined to think that the value of every religion may be judged on all three grounds. Does it truly reveal the ultimate causes of things, and so bring the believer into fruitful relations with his environment ? Does it direct the believer's aspiration to that which is truly best? Does it bring him joy and peace, and make life worth living?

Having distinguished these three values the next step is to consider whether they are independent, or are so interdependent that a religion which has one will necessarily have the other two. In my opinion they are independent, and for reasons which I shall now endeavor briefly to set forth.

Let us consider, first, the relation between the first and second of these values. Is that which is metaphysically most real also morally the best? Not *necessarily*. Christianity teaches that this is actually the case, or that God conceived as the author and finisher of human destiny, and God conceived as perfect love, are one and the same. But let us imagine the universe to be ruled by a malicious despot, Satan having usurped the throne of God. It would be folly to ignore such a usurper. He would, in fact, be the most important force to reckon with, whatever purpose one might adopt. To come to terms with the Evil One, whether by joining his party or by opposing him, would now be one's religion in the first, or metaphysical sense. It would remain just as true as before, however, that the best thing in the world was love, and if one followed the dictates of moral enlightenment one would be obliged to worship a God of love, however low his fortunes might have fallen. It does not necessarily discredit the cause of Sisera that the stars in their courses should have fought against it.

Those who identify religion altogether with the second or moral value express this independence by saying that it is a matter of indifference whether God exists or not. If the God one worships is truly the best, then one's religion is in this sense justified; whether such a being operates as a cause in the world, or is only a fiction of the imagination. In other words, the question whether it is or is not love that makes the world go round, is irrelevant to the truth that love is the highest quality of life. In so far as we insist that religion shall express both metaphysical and moral insight we must recognize at least the logical possibility of two Gods: one, the ultimate cause, to be reckoned with; and the other, the highest good, to be the goal of aspiration. It is only when the power and the goodness of God are distinguished, or when one recognizes that as being powerful he is not necessarily good, nor as good necessarily powerful, that one can realize the full significance of bestowing both of these attributes upon him. To identify these values, or to assume that where the one is the other must be present also, will lead commonly to one or the other of two errors, the error of accepting as good whatever is real and powerful, or the error of accepting as real whatever is good and admirable.

Next, let us consider the relation between the first and third values, or between the value of control or adaptation and that of subjective happiness. The independence is in this case even clearer than in the case above. The truth about the world we live in may, for any logical reason to the contrary, be disquieting and depressing. Metaphysical news may, like any other news, be bad news. In any case, there is no reason at all to suppose that the actual situation is of more hopeful augury than any imaginable situation. The most true account of the world is not necessarily the most assuring. This independence is even more striking when one considers that the inspiring effect of a belief has nothing whatsoever to do with its truth. If one were to ask oneself, "What belief about the world would make one most eager and confident," and constructed a belief accordingly, there would be no presumption whatever in favor of its truth. And if one were to adopt a false belief on this subjective ground, then one would inevitably forfeit those values of control and adaptation which are conditioned on truth. To underestimate the enemy's forces may be good for morale, but it does not conduce to victory. To live in a world conceived after one's heart's desires is, as we say, to live in a "fool's paradise;" a *paradise* because it makes him hopeful and happy, a *fool's* paradise because there will sooner or later be a rude awakening for which his belief has ill prepared him.

It is of first importance to note that while the third, or hygienic, value of religion is independent of truth, it does imply belief. The peace and joy of religion do not arise from make-believe, or from pretending what one knows is not so. That which is, in truth, no more than a fiction, may have the psychological effect of inducing happiness, but only in the man to whom it wears the aspect of reality. The agencies employed in religious conversion are designed, not to stimulate the play of the imagination, but to induce a settled conviction. Religion does not save unless it is *accepted*, any more than medicine cures unless it is *taken*.

The emphasis upon the hygienic value of religion to the exclusion of its truth, often has ugly consequences, which have done much to multiply the enemies of religion. It may lead emancipated minds, whether benevolently or selfishly, to propagate beliefs which they know to be false: the augurs wink to one another, and lie to the uninitiated. Or, it may lead to the shock of disillusionment in those who have been deceived by the augurs, or who have deceived themselves. The cult of deception in the interest of happiness is both mendacious and precarious. This does not mean that one should believe only what one can prove—which would make all humanly important beliefs impossible. It means that one should not wilfully close one's eyes to relevant evidence, or withhold it from others;—that one's "over-beliefs" should be shaped and reshaped in accordance with the available evidence, and in an atmosphere of candor.

Here again, the importance of distinguishing two values lies in the hope of attaining both. A religion which is either false to the facts or depressing to the will is something less than a religion should seek to be. It is the function of religion both to make the truth palatable and to expose happiness to the light of truth.

The independence of the second and third values is not so clear. It is, I suppose, fairly clear that the belief which would work a miracle, and cure a cripple or a blind man, would not necessarily be morally enlightened. I mean that in the very use of the term "miracle" it is admitted that there is no intelligible connection between the content of the belief and the physical effect. It would also, I think, be admitted that insomnia, neurasthenia, apathy, irresolution, or internal conflict might be cured by some sort of mis-guided fanaticism; as they are, in fact, cured by the warlike passions, even when these are aroused by motives of personal or national aggrandizement. If, on the other hand, we mean by the peace of religion that spiritual wholeness, in which the total person-ality is harmoniously integrated and which is the condition of deep and lasting happiness, then I should concede at once that any ideal which can achieve this result is thereby proved and justified. I concede this because I believe that it is just this integrating power which constitutes the meaning of a "high" ideal.

But even so, the power of an ideal to integrate a

personality is relative to the constituents of that personality. In particular it makes the very greatest difference whether a person does or does not possess a strong social passion. The man who is indifferent to the misery of others, or to the state of mankind generally, has relatively little difficulty in being happy. If one were thinking of inward joy and peace, and of nothing else, then there would be good reason to recommend on grounds of mental hygiene that a man close his eyes and harden his heart, lest he be too heavily burdened with "the heavy and the weary weight of all this unintelligible world." E. L. Godkin once said:

> There is no country in the world to-day in which you can be very happy if you care about politics and the progress of mankind, while there are many in which you can be very comfortable, if you occupy yourself simply with gardening, lawn tennis, and true religion.

The writer of these words evidently did not construe the love of God to embrace the love of man, and held religion to be a comparatively cheap and irresponsible way of securing happiness. If, however, one insists upon a joy and peace that shall both feel and transcend the poignant tragedy of human existence, or upon that rarer and more difficult happiness which shall embrace sympathy and compassion, then one has conceded the point which I am at pains to make. One has virtually affirmed that happiness is one thing and moral elevation another, and that personal happiness in itself is not a sufficient proof of moral elevation. In other words, that a religion should cure would not in itself prove that it was a true religion, in the moral any more than in the metaphysical sense. If one seeks a religion that shall be both a cure of unhappiness and also a moral chart and compass, then one must test it by both standards independently, and not assume that because it will serve the one of these uses it can safely be trusted to serve the other.

There are, in short, a good many ways of being happy. There is a fool's way, and a wise man's way; there is a noble way, and a base way. A religion will be all that a religion ought to be, only when it enables a man to be happy in the presence of unvarnished facts, and with the most soaring aspiration; or to be at the same time realistic, idealistic, and joyful. The devotee of such a religion will be like the skilful swordsman, who fights with *élan*, with a sustained vision of his distant goal, and with a swift and correct judgment of the situation that confronts him.

RELIGION AND HEALTH

RICHARD C. CABOT

I

Certain assumptions or presuppositions underlie what I have to say about healing, physical, chemical, or spiritual. I find it convenient to use the metaphor of the trolley-car and its trolley. The human being in relation to the physical world is something like the trolley-car and its trolley. He can be in such relation to the physical world that he maintains his health, or in such relation that he loses it. When he is in relations that are successful he is propelled along his way by physical forces much as the energy generated in the power-house propels the car through its trolley. The average man does not often think of this connection. He doesn't realize the degree of his dependence on the regular functions of eating and drinking and sleeping because he is too busy. He thinks of himself as an independent going concern. But obviously enough he cannot go any distance without food, water, sleep. He cannot go more than a minute or two without respiration. Physical forces, through the air, through water, through food, pass into his body from moment to moment. Without these he is stranded, sick, and soon dies. He has, of course, his own power of independent self-guidance so long as he is not detached from connection with these physical forces. In that respect he is unlike the trolley-car, which does not guide itself at all. Nevertheless he is dependent at every point upon the physical world whose currents of energy pass into him, through him, and out.

On the mental side he is not less dependent on a world of facts and a world of motives which come to him, on which he depends, by which he lives. And as he can get "off his trolley" physically so he can get off his trolley mentally, get out of relation with the world of fact, until he is, as we say, insane. He can also get off his trolley in relation to his energies; he can run down like a clock till he feels no motive.

These two systems of energies entering man, partially controlled by his individual wishes and ideals but nevertheless supporting him from without— these two systems depend upon each other, as everyone knows. We call them "body and mind," and the "interrelations of body and mind" are familiar facts to everybody. What the body does to the mind we all know, when we are out of health and notice the forgetfulness, irritability, or depression that result. What the mind does to the health of the body is not so familiar. I will discuss it later.

II

Given these two systems of forces passing into each individuality and out again, we have next to notice the extraordinary *tendency to self-maintenance* on the part of both the mind and the body of man, the extraordinary power of maintaining and regaining health. That is a fact of which very few persons except physicians have any adequate conception. At least three-fourths of all illnesses cure themselves without anybody's finding out that they exist. The proof of that we find in the examination of the human body after death, showing as it does the history of very numerous diseases which it has suffered, overcome, and never known the existence of. This power of self-cure, of self-maintenance, shows itself not only in the milder illnesses that we are not conscious of, but also in the severer diseases that we usually are aware of, for instance in typhoid fever. Typhoid fever has a ten per cent mortality. That means that in ninety per cent it cures itself, for we do nothing really curative in that disease. Pneumonia has a twenty-five per cent mortality; that means that seventy-five per cent of all cases cure themselves. So we can go on through the diseases. One lists about two hundred and fifteen diseases* known to medical science, and of these there are about eight or nine which we can cure by drugs. Surgery cures a few more. I will not try to state the number. The rest cure themselves or are not cured. The vast majority

* Uncertainties as to whether we should count certain illnesses as one disease or as two make it impossible to-day to give exact figures.

cure themselves. But this tremendous accumulation of energy of the favorable side, the self-curing side, of disease is in contrast and in co-operation with what man does for cure, and it should be in clear recognition of this that any attempt, spiritual or physical, is made to aid these extraordinary powers, the forces of self-healing which we find in the human body.

I do not think that these self-curing energies are any less powerful in the human soul. The vast majority of people who get into trouble, as I have seen trouble during many years, get out of it themselves, without important help from any human source. The number who are helped by some one who interests himself or herself in their affairs is almost infinitesimal compared to those who get on their own feet and maintain themselves without help of this sort.

But this great power of self-maintenance, of self-cure, which we can attribute to "nature" if we know what we mean by that word, or which we can leave unexplained, does not go on unless our normal contacts with the physical forces outside us are maintained. The ninety per cent of spontaneous recoveries from typhoid fever do not occur unless the patients are properly fed, properly nursed, unless everything is done that we know how to do to maintain the ordinary currents of energy which pass into the body in health. Without these, the potent self-maintaining powers of the body do not work.

Sometimes there is need not merely of maintaining the ordinary supply of energy through the food, sleep, and air which go into the human body but of increasing this supply. What we call the "cure" of tuberculosis, for instance, means making more out of the energies of the universe, such as food, fresh air, and the changes that the body undergoes in rest, getting more good than usual from those, in order that with this help the body may overcome its disease, as in seventy to seventy-five per cent of consumptives, taken early, it will.

Generalizing from what I have said, we can say that the body and the mind—but I am speaking of the body now—the body maintains itself in two main ways: First by getting into connection or into better connection with the great physical forces of its origin, and second, by borrowing energy from other parts of creation. What we call eating is borrowing energy from other parts of the world, from the bodies of plants or animals in which solar energy has been stored. When we come to the cure of disease we borrow from the minerals in the mines, we borrow from the plants and the trees, we borrow from many animals, and in late years we have begun to borrow from other human beings in that often life-saving operation the transfusion of blood. (1) By getting into connection or into better connection with the great forces of the universe, and (2) by borrowing energy from other parts of creation, we get what we call our health, the maintenance of health or the recovery of health in disease.

It is commonplace that bodily health is affected by thought and by emotion. Take first the field of industry. When a man who is out of a job gets a job, or when one who has a job gets "a rise," it does not affect his mind alone. Anybody who looks carefully can often see a demonstrable effect on his body. His tissues often show themselves better. And so recreation, the pleasure we get in games, the delight that we get in beauty, has its demonstrable and recordable effects on the body. Every doctor sees human affection, our affectionate relations to our friends and families, recorded in a better state of the organs and tissues as well as in a happier state of mind.

We know more now than we did twenty years ago about how this is brought about. One of our fellow townsmen, Professor Walter B. Cannon, has done more than anybody else in the world to make clear the connection between emotion and bodily changes, the changes made in the body chemistry by the emotions of fear and rage which happen to be easily studied in animals and are of great interest. The mobilization of stores of energy from the liver, for instance, where they are stored, into the blood where they are needed by the animal in his moment of fear or rage; the changes in the coagulation of the blood, so that if the animal is injured his wounded blood vessels will close more quickly; the changes in the action of the heart—all proved to result from emotion.

If such every-day matters as work, play, love, rage, fear, have these wide-spread and demonstrable effects on the body, it seems natural that a quickening of that central energy to which I give the name of religion would affect the health. Starting from the centre it would radiate out, and one would recognize it to be central, and I should say religious, by the fact that it changed a man not in one respect, but in all respects, in his ability to enjoy himself, in his ability to enjoy beauty, in his ability to enjoy his friends. If a change comes over a man's life which radiated in all these directions, why, let us say it has made better connections with the central energy of his life, his religion.

I define a man's religion, as whatever is at the centre of his thought and energy. The path which I described a moment ago, the path between a psychical event like emotion and a physical fact like a fight or running away, is not the only path between a psychical event and a bodily change. I can illustrate another path by taking the case of a man in the Cook County Hospital in Chicago, whose physician told me of him. He had the disease we often bring up when we want to make it perfectly clear that we mean "organic" disease—he had a broken leg. He had been carried straight to the hospital from the scene of his accident and the surgeons had done what they usually do in such cases—they had "set the bone" as we say; that is, they had put the two ends into proper apposition to each other. Then they waited, as we must always wait, for nature to do the rest of the work, namely, the union of those broken bones. We generally forget when the surgeon has set the bone that he then must wait for nature to do the healing. But nature does not always do it. Then we have "ununited" or "non-united" fractures. That is what happened with this man. He lay there and was given the ordinary care but his bone did not unite. About that time somebody had the thought of looking a little into his mental life. He had been thought of hitherto as "a thigh fracture," which he was, but he was also a human being. They found that as he had been carried straight to the hospital from his accident he was out of the way of knowing what had become of his family. He did not know whether he, the principal breadwinner, was being missed by his family at home to the extent of serious want, perhaps starvation. Because of that uncertainty he was losing sleep; because of losing sleep he was losing appetite; because he was losing appetite and sleep he was losing nutrition, and because nutrition was not going on as it should, those chemical and physical changes which unite a bone when it is broken were not taking place. Have we the right to say this? Yes; because when the Cook County Hospital people investigated the state of his home—found that his family were well and happy, were being well taken care of and were in no want—and supplied him with that information, he began to sleep and to eat and to gain in nutrition, and *then his bone began to knit.*

That is a perfectly familiar chain of causes and effects, but it is worth while to reflect for a moment on the fact that it carries us from a purely psychical event, worry, to a purely physical event, the knitting of a bone. When we maintain, as any one familiar with the facts must maintain, that psychical events may have a decisive effect on disease, we can support our belief by this little chain of causes and effects.

Consider how the case that I have just described carries out the general principles with which I began. This man was out of connection with the ordinary facts and forces of the universe which through nutrition would have maintained his health if he had been well and were now counted on to restore his health by knitting his broken bone. We managed to bring about a better connection with these energies so that he was less isolated from his proper place in the world. Then he was healed.

If religious life is defined, as I have tried to define it, as the centre of any man's energies, whether he calls himself an atheist or a theist, then it is obvious that any enrichment or development of his religious life will show itself in an increased curiosity and search for knowledge, in an increased interest in the world around him and in his fellow beings, in an increased organization of his own life which may be in disorder, and in addition one would naturally expect that it would improve his health. I referred a moment ago, in speaking of the scientific researches of Professor Cannon, mostly to the negative emotions, some of which have a depressing effect on the body. There has been so far as I know no similar study of the positive emotions, happiness, joy, gratitude, love. But it seems to me that, on the basis of the observations that we can any of us make, it is safe to say that there must be a physical and chemical effect on the body from anything which produces these positive emotions. Religion then would tend to improve any man's health, first by removing conflicts, worries, remorse (and their bad effects on the tissues), and secondly by the influence of these positive emotions which we have every reason to think have an effect upon the nutrition of the body and so upon any disease that may be there present.

III

But when we speak of religion in this general way, classing it with all sorts of psychic forces, one neglects an important point, namely the difference between true religion and false. If we speak of religion merely as a powerful psychic influence on health we neglect this distinction. Supposing that a faith comes to a man and gives him strength; supposing that faith does not stand criticism, does not wear well in the ordinary vicissitudes of life, it is obvious that any good effects that it has on his health will not be permanent.

We saw this, not in the religious field but in a most extraordinary way akin to it, in the year 1890, which I think the physicians old enough to have passed through it will not forget. In the year 1890 Robert Koch, the discoverer of the tubercle bacillus and probably the leading scientific physician of his time, announced that he had a cure for tuberculosis. Our professor of bacteriology at Harvard went over to Germany and brought home that cure, the efficiency of which he had witnessed in Germany. So consumptive people began to be inoculated with tuberculin. We all of us know now that it turned out to be a failure, but we forget that *for a time* it had an extraordinary success. So long as we had faith in Koch's tuberculin the patients got extraordinarily better. They gained in weight, they ceased to cough, they lost their fever—obvious and undeniable signs of improvement. Then some four or five months after this, it gradually began to leak out that tuberculin was not a cure, in fact that in the doses we were giving it was a dangerous thing to give. It makes our hair stand on end now to think of the doses we used to give. I gave them myself. And the patients improved, improved tremendously under them. But

Koch was this time a false prophet. Our faith and our patients' faith in him would not stand the test. And when the faith oozed out of the doctors the health oozed out of the patients.

When one says that any strong psychical influence can affect health and disease, one neglects this essential difference between truth which can stand fire and will stay true, and fake which will make a great impression, an enormous temporary impression, but won't last.

IV

With all this in the way of general introduction, with these presuppositions as to the forces underlying physical or psychical cures and as to the relation of these two, I go on to speak of some of the particular religious cures referred to in the title of this paper.

Ordinary *"faith-cure"* I suppose is best exemplified in the pilgrimages and cures at Lourdes. You know that to this little town in France there come every year hundreds of sick people from various parts of the world. You know probably that there are physicians there to examine and record carefully what their troubles are. You know that many pilgrims go through there a profound religious experience which I will not try to describe. Then what? Well, the vast majority of them go away no better at all. That is agreed upon by all who have been there. The vast majority are not cured or even improved physically. But it must also be admitted by any one who consults the facts, that a small, perfectly demonstrable number are cured, and cured not merely of hysteria or nervous troubles, but sometimes of organic disease. If one asks how that is possible, the answer is: it *may* be possible by just such a train of events as I described in the man in the Chicago hospital with the broken leg.

How can a religious experience make an ulcer heal? Well, in the same way that that man's freedom from worry made his leg heal. It is not in the least inconceivable, it is not contrary to any known laws of medicine, that a person who suddenly got the central motive of his life enormously increased, who seemed to see light on all the problems that had been dark, whose central happiness was multiplied a hundred times—it is not at all strange that his organic lesions should sometimes heal. There is every evidence that they do, just as it is evident that in the vast majority they do not.

Or take another case, the work of the Reverend Mr. Hickson, known to many of you by his services held here in Boston a few years ago. Since he was here in Boston he has made a journey around the world, holding the same sort of services in almost every country on this planet. In a recent book he tells the story of that journey. It is essentially the same story as that of Lourdes: an enormous number of people come to his services in which there is prayer and the laying on of hands. Most of those people go away no better; a small proportion go away cured. It is interesting, if one is trying to make comparisons with the New Testament, that Mr. Hickson's cures are of very much the same sort as those in scripture. They are cures of blindness, deafness, and various defects of locomotion, not typhoid fever, pneumonia, or blood poisoning, but defects of hearing, of eyesight, and of walking. Those cures come again and again, in Asia, in Africa, in Australia, in every continent that he visits.

Are we to call this miracle? That depends on your definition. If you define miracle as St. Augustine has, as *that which is contrary to the behavior of things as we have hitherto known it,* then of course some of these might well be put down as miracles. We do not need to define it in the sense that Thomas Aquinas defined it, as not only contrary to nature as we have thus far known it, but to the laws of nature itself. There is equally good authority from the ecclesiastical and more appeal from the scientific point of view in the Augustinian definition of miracle as that which is contrary to the ordinary course of things as we know it. Miracle in that sense is really around us all the time. Anything that is really *new,* is miracle in that sense. Anything that we cannot explain by what has preceded it is a miracle in that sense. When a man composes a new song it is a miracle. You cannot explain it. When a child is born into the world, if he is new and unique as every child is, you cannot explain that child. He is different from anything that went before; he is in that sense a miracle. In that sense these cures can be called miraculous because they take place more quickly than we are accustomed to see them. The healing of an ulcer ordinarily takes weeks or months. If that process could be speeded up, as it perfectly well could be by some chemical stimulus so as to close the ulcer in a few minutes, then it would be so different from what we have seen that it might be called a miracle.

Have we any reason to call this thing divine, to use religious or theological terms about it? I use the word divine to mean that which suddenly shows us more than we have known before about the central nature of things. I recognize that to any one who has a religion and believes in the divine government of the world anything and everything may be called divine. But we usually call an event divine which shows us quickly more of the essential nature of the universe than we had seen before. Now that might easily be true of the events I am speaking of. Miracles always seem to me comparable to deeds of heroism. They show us more about the nature of man than we knew, more about the nature of the world out of which this man came, than we knew before. Every heroic act as I see it is a miracle. Miracles, like heroism, are born out of the sense of a supreme need. It is often said that they come out of the faith of the sufferer. That is the other half of it; we have the sense of supreme need plus the awareness, the trust, that some help is possible. We are accustomed to say that "necessity is the mother of invention." Out of the sense of necessity—the sense that this thing *must* be, some new idea, some new strength comes. So I think miraculous powers come out of a man when he suddenly feels that he must do what ordinarily he cannot, and in some way manages to draw into himself strength enough to do it.

Christian Science believes, as I have been stating that I believe, in the healing of disease by spiritual means. But there is a negative side to Christian Science which carries it a little away from agreement with what I have been saying. It does not believe in cure through drugs and through surgery. It is opposed to the use of drugs and surgery. Well, what is to be said of that?

The first thing is that *so are we all* most of the time. Most of us who are patients do not want to take drugs or to be operated on, and most of us who are physicians know that those are the means which we should come to only when we cannot get along without them. We know that most healing takes place without them and that in most diseases we do not know enough to avail ourselves of these resources at all. The only question is, have they *sometimes* a place? On just the same kind of evidence that I believe we can and should get help out of food, I believe that we can and should get help in eight or nine diseases from drugs.

When I was in France with the army we had an epidemic of meningitis and we had an antitoxin for it worked out by Doctor Flexner of the Rockefeller Institute in New York. Treating the patients with that antitoxin seventy-five per cent of them got well. We were feeding them according to a certain standard, they were in a certain ward, and had certain air and light. Then we ran out of that antitoxin, and the epidemic continued. We sent for more and they sent us more said to be as good as what we had been using. We injected it in the same way, under exactly the same conditions, and seventy-five per cent died instead of seventy-five per cent getting well as they did before. It was one of the most terrible experiences I have ever gone through. Then one of our officers went on a mission around France to try if he could not beg, steal, or borrow some of the original antitoxin, which we had in the beginning. He did get some, and then we went back to exactly the same seventy-five per cent of cures. Nobody can say that that was a psychical cure. It was a laboratory experiment. It was carried out under conditions as exact as for a laboratory experiment only at a terrible expense of human life. That is the sort of experience which makes me sure that under certain conditions drugs save life.

The action of drugs and surgery is not any different in principle from the action of food and sunlight. We know that we cannot live without sunlight in its direct and indirect effects, and we have the same reason to believe that we can be benefited by certain drugs. Currents of nutrition, air, thought, inspiration, come to us out of the world around us, through other men, through animals and plants. They maintain and heal us. In ordinary medical work human beings, doctors, do something to mediate these influences. They are not all as spontaneously absorbed as we absorb the air. We have to have the help of other men to get the good of them. So the spiritual help of Christian Science is mediated through the healer. Shall we admit that healing which always comes, as I see it, from the central force of the world, from God, can come to us through food and sunlight but *not* by drugs and by surgery? I do not see any reason to think so, and that is my difference with Christian Science.

I was talking in Holland this summer with a very intelligent Roman Catholic nun. She asked me if I could give her any help on a matter that was troubling her. She found to her dismay that her spiritual life was sometimes definitely enhanced by taking a cup of tea! This troubled her. I suggested to her that there was no reason that the power of God could not come to her through a cup of tea, just as well as through prayer. She took the idea at once and was comforted.

I see no reason why we should admit only *one* of

the different ways through which healing comes to our bodies. I want to take them all, and in that I disagree with Christian Science, the good effects of which I see on all sides. I have not the slightest doubt that it does good, that it cures disease, organic as well as functional, only I do not want anybody to say, "And nothing else cures." I do not want to see anybody trust all his salvation to any single channel of communication with God.

I have been asked to say something about the Emmanuel Movement, which means the co-operation of physicians and clergymen to help people in trouble and in sickness. In this country we owe this attempt to the Reverend Elwood Worcester of Emmanuel Church in Boston. Doctor Worcester always wanted to avail himself of all methods of healing. He differed wholly from the Christian Science point of view in welcoming any help coming through drugs or through surgery, and he himself only wanted to treat some of the patients for whom—and it is a large majority—there was no aid available through drugs or through surgery. So it came about that he treated in particular the people who have what we call "nervous" troubles, which means that we do not know what their source is and that we find no change in the physical tissues. I went over my records recently to see what proportion they make up in a general practice like mine, and I found that they made up almost the same percentage from year to year—forty per cent. Those are the people whom Doctor Worcester wanted to try to treat through the influence of religion. For the treatment of these people most physicians have no special skill. They have no preparation for it in their training. Some of them have just the same skill that any other sensible, warm-hearted person who wants to help people has. The clergyman is just as fit, *provided* the physician has first seen the case, as was always so with Doctor Worcester, and has certified that there is nothing particular to be done by medical care or by surgery. This was a ministry of common sense, of good habits, of tranquillity, and of religion.

I want to say a word, before I close, on certain terms that are often used in the discussion of this subject. In the first place, the term *organic* disease as contrasted with *functional*. We used to mean by "organic" disease one that shows a change in the tissues, in the organs of the body, and by "functional" one that does not. But that definition does not hold. Diabetes, one of the most stubborn and fatal diseases, sometimes shows at autopsy no change in the tissues. In other words, it is a chemical and not a physical disease, and there are many others. Epilepsy is sometimes a chemical disease. And yet diabetes and epilepsy are as stubborn and in many cases as incurable as any others. All we can mean, then, by organic disease is a stubborn disease, a disease hard to cure.

No scientific man when he is in a scientific mood uses the word *incurable*. We often hear that word. "Do you mean to say that Christian Science or radium or any other particular agency can cure an incurable disease?" Well naturally no, but there is no reason ever to use that word. What can it mean? It cannot mean anything more than that the person who uses it has never known of a cure. We ordinarily speak of cancer as a disease which untreated, unoperated, is incurable. But that is quite false. Anybody may read an article in which a German writer has collected a large group of unoperated cases of cancer which got well of themselves. Of course these are but a few *out of many millions*, but they are well attested. No person can name an incurable disease, but only one that has not been cured in his experience. No one can keep up with medical literature. In some Japanese medical journal a disease that I have never known cured may have been reported as cured last week. And so we must say "not yet cured" and must add "subject to my limitations in keeping up."

Finally, I should say that this problem resolves itself into the question, can we get a grip or a better grip on the world forces out of which we came and which maintain us as we are? And by getting a grip or a better grip can we get more help than we usually do, something new, something original? I have tried to answer that by saying yes, we can in three essential ways. (1) We can get a better grip upon the ordinary forces than we usually have, by drawing back, away from the surface of things, as the painter steps back from his toil in order to get a better view, as the man lost in the woods does when he stops to climb a tree in order to see where he is. Getting away from the surface of things we may get a better grip of the truth by which we can orient our life. (2) We may get a better connection by an obstinate, persistent seeking, what is called in the New Testament "knocking," that is pushing, seeking a great deal harder than we ordinarily do, which is the essence of scientific discovery. The scientific man uses the same senses and intellect as we do, only he pushes harder and more persistently till he gets a better grip on the energies outside him and in him for the solution of his problem. What I have been describing is what is ordinarily called prayer. Prayer is an attempt to rise up above the surface of our ordinary life in order to see it better, to see where we are and where we go next. Or it is an attempt to burrow and penetrate into the sources of truth and hope and faith by which we live.

(3) We get this better grip by *borrowing from others*. I spoke of the physical healings for which we borrow from every part of physical creation. But most of us who have any consciousness at all of our spiritual life know what a continual borrowing *that* is too, and how, in so far as we are wise and humble, we are al-

ways borrowing from the wisest and best people we can find. We can say perhaps that this borrowing from others can be achieved in two ways: first by what Schauffler calls *"creative listening,"* where we hear more than most people do by listening to the wise and also to those who are not very wise, and secondly by contact with the sort of person who works miracles. That is how we can raise ourselves higher.

In the Christian religion we think that the Founder was such a person, and if we follow Christian history we see that there came down all through history a type of person who had been in contact with the Founder or had been in contact with those who had, and who still had, as I believe many people to-day have, the power of working miracles in the sense in which I use the word. In relation to Christ we have often used very violent metaphors: "the blood of Christ," and "being saved by the blood of Christ." But when we think of that familiar and life-saving medical device, the transfusion of blood, it does not seem to me after all that this metaphor is too violent.

RELIGION IN EDUCATION

HENRY W. HOLMES

THE most important thing about any human being is his general purpose in life. Men and women are distinguished from one another, to be sure, by all sorts of characteristics; and their abilities, both natural and acquired, vary endlessly. Individuality, therefore, as we commonly understand it, is largely a matter of the inherited stuff of human personality as this is affected by experience, including education. But the heart of *selfhood* is purpose—what a man intends to do with himself in the onward moving course of life, with all its complexities. And the chief task of education, accordingly, is to help the individual to understand himself and his world in order that he may put himself wisely and effectively at the tasks wherein he can be happiest and most useful.

This view of life and of education has never been better expressed than by Josiah Royce in his *Philosophy of Loyalty*. I quote the following sentences from that "golden book" of modern ethical analysis (page 171):

. . . a self is a life in so far as it is unified by a single purpose. Our loyalties furnish such purposes, and hence make of us conscious and unified moral persons. Where

[213]

loyalty has not yet come to any sort of definiteness, there is so far present only a kind of inarticulate striving to be an individual self. This very search for one's true self is already a sort of life-purpose, which, as far as it goes, individuates the life of the person in question, and gives him a task. But loyalty brings the individual to full moral self-consciousness. It is devoting the self to a cause that, after all, first makes it a rational and unified self, instead of what the life of too many a man remains—namely, a cauldron of seething and bubbling efforts to be somebody, a cauldron which boils dry when life ends.

There are many problems and questions involved in such a statement, but this is not the place to raise them. Nor is this the place for proving the validity of these sweeping generalizations. Perhaps such views are not susceptible of proof except in the long process of putting them to the test in life. Their final verification may have to wait until those who hold them have made the fatal experiment of living in the light of them. Meanwhile, however, a minor verification is possible: one can test a central theory by thinking it through to its practical consequences and asking whether the conclusions thus arrived at are consistent, profitable, and inspiring. The complete test of truth lies in the whole of life; but our universals may be checked in the meantime by the views they lead us to adopt on particular problems and special issues. Such checking is, of course, a test not only of the universals themselves but of the correctness of our application of those universals to any particular issue in question. In any case, I propose now to apply the general view of life and education I have just set forth to certain special problems of religion in education. My theory itself and my reasoning as to the application of it may be commended or condemned by the practical conclusions I shall draw.

If selfhood lies in purpose and if education finds its end in the definition of purposes and in the constructive effort to carry them into effect, what is the place of religion in education?

Religion itself may be stated in terms of purpose, and such statement is familiar to modern ears. To be religious is to do the will of God—which implies belief that God exists and that he has purposes in life in which we may participate, with which our own purposes may be in accord. Persons who differ widely in theology (that is, in their theories as to the nature of God, his relation to the world and to human beings) and persons who differ widely in their views about religious institutions and practices (about the church, and sacraments, and the Bible, and prayer, and numberless questions of detail) may yet agree that the essence of religion is the dedication of one's life to purposes chosen because they appear as those of a "Power not ourselves that makes for righteousness." To lead a life of religion means, then, to work with God.

I find in Professor Kirsopp Lake's *The Religion of Yesterday and Tomorrow* a passage which expresses this idea of religion with fuller insight and more adequate analysis than I can myself command. He says (pp. 64 and 65):

> . . . there are two great experiments in life which are the basis of religion. The first is positive or active; it is made when a man is conscious that there is a purpose in life of which he is only a part, but with which he can co-operate if he choose, *and he does choose*. It is the subordination of the individual self-seeking will to the great purpose of which he discovers some part by this experiment, though it stretches away far beyond his ken. . . .
>
> The second experiment comes when the first seems to be beyond his strength. It is negative or passive, or appears so in comparison with the first. It is made when a man is conscious that there is a source of life which imparts help to him when he is weak, comfort when he is in sorrow, and purification when he has sinned. He turns to it when the first experiment seems on the point of breaking down, not because it was a mistake, but because of the human weakness of the experimenter. . . .

In both these "experiments," as Professor Lake calls them, religion enters life to help in the choice and the execution of purposes.

In this choice of purpose and in conduct based on purpose, of course the possibilities of error are infinite, and no increase of knowledge can save us from mistakes; but the meaning of religion when stated in terms of purpose is clear enough and the task of education for religion as so stated is also clear. So far as education helps us to define our purposes wisely or to carry them out effectively, it is in all its parts a help toward religious living. The special task of religious education, as such, is to help us to think as clearly as we can about God and his purposes and to relate our own plans of life to those of God as nearly as we can understand and grasp them.

This makes religion essentially a practical and an individual thing. It becomes a matter of judgment. All our theoretical conclusions bear on it, and all the influences which mould our thought and help to determine our plans of life enter into it; but we cannot escape the final and personal responsibility of choosing a way of life which shall express whatever views we hold.

To educate children for religious living means, therefore, to help them to face a fundamental and universal problem of life, to face it on their own responsibility and in the light of their own knowledge and their own experience. To *make* a child religious is a contradiction in terms. Indoctrination, habituation, predetermination of any sort whatever, is only avoidance of the issue and may become the worst sort of obstruction to genuine religion. It would be absurd, of course, to give up teaching doctrines, but the only *religious* way to teach doctrine, dogma, form, or ceremony, is to teach it as the answer to a problem. And we may waste our effort and do waste it in teaching children *about* religion without helping them in any sense to be religious.

I can face the practical issues of religious education in our own time only in terms of these more general views.

Let me begin by dealing with a question I used as the title of an address in a series of lectures similar to the present series, here in Phillips Brooks House, in 1923. Must a teacher, I asked, be religious? In attempting an answer to that question, one may well traverse most of the controversial issues of religious education as we face them in America.

Taken literally, this question can have but one answer—*No*. There is no legal or moral compulsion upon teachers in general to be religious in any accepted meaning of the term. In certain institutions, to be sure, the teachers are expected not only to be religious, but to profess a particular faith; some schools, as we all know, are conducted entirely by members of ecclesiastical orders; and in many schools there is a more or less explicit requirement of religious profession and religious practice. It is true, also, that the public at large expects a teacher to be at least respectful of religion and is suspicious of one who flouts it or is openly antagonistic to it. But in our public schools generally and in many of our private schools no questions are asked as to the teacher's religious beliefs and no requirements set as to his observance of religious forms and customs. The teacher, merely because he is a teacher, is under no greater obligation with respect to religion than is any other citizen.

I regard this situation as essentially sound. I believe it to be advantageous both for religion and for education. Yet I protest against the statement that our public schools are Godless, believing them in fact not to be Godless and having no desire to make them Godless. I believe in religion and in religious education. I do not believe in laws to prohibit sectarian schools. Although I am unconvinced as to the practical value or desirability of any scheme I have so far studied for the introduction of religious teaching into public schools, I am not antagonistic to experiment in that direction. And I believe that all teachers should be sensible of a certain obligation toward the religious development of their pupils.

These opinions, stated thus dogmatically, may seem inconsistent. But there is a single idea which can be said to lie behind them all, the idea of the purposeful character of human selfhood. To see life and education in terms of purpose means to commit oneself in education and in religion to a policy of liberty. In education and religion alike, liberty implies the development of individual responsibility. Education of every kind and grade ought to help the individual toward command of his own life, toward possession of himself. The religion of every man should be his own religion; integrated into his own purposes; understood, so far as it can be rationalized at all, by his own mind; felt in his own heart. Therefore, the position of teacher should be based on no religious test. Therefore, the atmosphere of our schools should be favorable to religion in general, but specific religious education should be left in the hands of the churches, as voluntary organizations.

Every effort to force religion upon men has ended in failure. If the experience of the world can teach us any lesson with finality, it is the lesson of religious toleration. No effort to stifle freedom of thought in religion, freedom of worship, freedom not to worship at all, can possibly succeed. It is in its very essence an effort to deprive a man of what is most precious to him—the right to find himself in his own world. We may give up for the common good, without complaint, the fruits of our hardest labor; taxes, or required service, or imposed restraints, all are tolerable; but to give up our right to think for ourselves, interpret for ourselves our own relation to the whole of things and the meaning of our own lives—that is intolerable. Whatever the risk, religion must be free, just because it stands at the centre of the last citadel of freedom, the conscience of the individual, his own mind and heart. "Stone walls do not a prison make, Nor iron bars a cage. . . ."

But to assert that religion must be free is to assert that it must be free not only from external compulsion but free also in its growth. I mean just this, that religion ought not to be fastened on children any more than it is forced on adults. To use in religious education methods that bind children to a predetermined doctrine or to prescribed observances through fear or through blind habit is as false to the nature of religion and of education as the legal prescription of doctrine or observance is false to the ideal of liberty in adult life. I recognize the importance of habit-formation in education. I admit that it would be absurd, indeed that it would be wrong—and of course it would also be impossible— to keep children ignorant of the ideas and practices of religion. They must be exposed to religion, just as they are exposed to politics. It is right to organize worship for children and make them attend it, even when they don't want to. It is right to make them study the Bible, observe the Sabbath, learn prayers. But it is not right to fix their minds on the great problems of religious thought before they are old enough to think for themselves; it is not right to use authority, appeal to fear, or take advantage of immaturity to win an allegiance to a given creed or given forms which cannot later be reviewed by reason or renewed or shifted under new insight or new emotional response.

In religious education, as in so many other problems of life, there is an apparent dilemma in the application of the principle of freedom. To let children grow up in ignorance of religion is not to grant them religious freedom. And it is practically impossible to spread before them all religions and let them choose; nor would such a procedure have any desirable result. But this dilemma, like many another, is theoretical rather than practical. The spirit in which a child is taught to be a Baptist, a Unitarian, or a Catholic can be the spirit of freedom; the trend of all instruction and training, even if it be denominational, can be toward understanding and the larger and more generous attitudes of feeling and of will. Actually, there is a difference between education that is prescriptive, narrowing, and arresting, and education that enlarges and develops. Any one who has seen how the details of instruction and administration in education may be permeated by one spirit or the other knows that the Gordian knot of this dilemma may be cut.

One way to cut it is to refrain from insisting that religion shall dominate education. There was a time, a time prolonged through many centuries, when the church was the sole guardian of learning and practically the sole agent in teaching. The good done by the church during those centuries was incalculable. But it is clear that education could not become general or efficient or liberating under church control. Education could not thrive under the domination of any institution less inclusive or less disinterested than the state itself. Wherever the schools have been taken from the church and made public, education has improved. Wherever they are still under church control, education languishes. Witness the experience of France, the more recent experience of England, the present situation in the Province of Quebec. This is not a denominational issue. No matter which denominational organization is in charge of education, it is bound to serve education for ends less liberal than the end for which all public education strives—freedom for all men to direct their own lives as members of society, "to make the most of themselves for the common good."

Even in the forward-looking educational enactments of Colonial days, with all their insistence on public responsibility for education, the domination of the church was evident. Puritan ministers who should not be deceived by "the false glosses of saint-seeming deceivers" nor deficient in learning "when our present ministers shall lie in the dust" were the end of all educational endeavor. "The leaders of the colony of Massachusetts Bay 'were fully agreed that the main object of the colony should be to uphold the Puritan faith and form a society in harmony therewith.'" Teachers were not to be hired who had "manifested ymselves unsound in the fayth, or scandelous in their lives, & not giveing due satisfaction according to the rules of Christ." As late as 1701 ministers were empowered and required to approve, "by certificate under their hands," the teachers in the town schools. Roxbury hired its earliest teachers to "instruct in all scholastical, moral, and *theological* discipline, ABCdarians excepted." It required generations to free the schools from religious domination under the Puritan faith. Do we want to go back to any such condition, even with due recognition of the rights of different denominations? Do we want to use education to uphold any faith in order to establish "a society in harmony therewith" which shall dominate or be superior to the society to which we all belong, irrespective of faith? The state stands above denominations, as it stands above the schools; and education should serve primarily the interests of the state. This is the fundamental reason for the separation of church and state in education. That separation has cost years of effort and sacrifice. It should never be imperilled.

Was Oregon justified, then, in its law (now declared unconstitutional by the Federal Supreme Court) requiring all children to attend the public schools and thus in effect prohibiting sectarian schools? Would the same law have been justified in Michigan, if its Michigan promoters had succeeded in passing it? Much as I believe in public education, desirous as I am to see it promoted by every proper means, I cannot agree to the principle of the Oregon law. Although the interests of the state should be predominant in education, there is no reason why they should be exclusive. To prohibit private education, directly or indirectly, is an invasion of the rights of individuals and minorities which is directly contrary to the spirit of American democracy. It is directly contrary to the final interests of the state itself.

There are practical arguments for favoring the continuance of private schools, such as the argument that private schools provide desirable competition for public schools. They have greater freedom to experiment and they may also remain as centres of conservative influence. It may also be said that there is no reason why those who can afford to secure for their children a better education than can be provided at public expense should not proceed to do so. The graduates of certain private schools are better educated than the general run of graduates from public schools, and this may prove, in the end, an advantage to society, for whatever disadvantage may accrue from the development of snobbish attitudes is likely to "come out in the wash" of our democratic life. Private schools in general have advantages in equipment, and particularly in the provision for physical education, which the public schools seldom match, although they ought to. But such arguments as these are not conclusive and might well be swept aside. The good which might come from educating all our children in the common public schools might outweigh any practical disadvantages arising from the abolishment of private schools if it were not for the fundamental evil in the denial of liberty which such abolishment would create. And if, in prohibiting private schools, the state would be˙asserting its authority beyond the bounds of reason, then private schools conducted primarily for the sake of religious teaching must be permitted to carry on their work as fully and as freely as other private schools.

But the matter cannot be settled with an assertion, on the one hand, of the right and duty of the state to provide universal education without denominational control nor with the assertion, on the other hand, of the rights of individuals and groups, including ecclesiastical groups, to carry on their own schools. The duty of the state to provide education implies that the state has also the duty and the right of maintaining standards in education in any private schools that may be conducted within its borders. The state should inspect private schools and should certify the teachers of private schools. With the development of exact standards in education and the professional training of teachers, the state can perform this duty more fully and more profitably and without fear of interference with any valuable right of private educational foundations.

Furthermore, no one, because of his belief in any particular form of education, should be freed from his obligation to pay taxes for the maintenance of public education. State money should never be turned over to private educational institutions nor granted for the maintenance of private systems of education. Those who seek special forms of education for their children should realize that they are seeking what is over and above the general need and that they ought to pay for what they secure as a matter of privilege. If the public schools are really Godless, they ought to be abolished. To claim relief from taxes for public education, because public education does not involve the teaching of any particular form of religion, is to claim too much. In the final analysis such a claim can rest only on the ground that everybody ought to be trained in the particular religion in question. As a matter of fact, the public schools are not Godless; they are in general favorable to religion in their atmosphere and in much of the content of their teaching.

To those who think that religious education demands a complete system of schools under the control of any given church, one might well ask this question: "Why should any sect want more than education in our public schools with the opportunity for religious education as it is provided in churches, Sunday-schools, and homes?" Is it not possible to present a religious interpretation of life with sufficient force and attractiveness outside of the ordinary school hours? It seems to me unreasonable to object to simple religious services in schools, general in form, on a voluntary basis, and without opportunity for any direct religious instruction that could be attacked as being denominational. Our law in Massachusetts permits the reading of passages of the Bible, the singing of hymns, and the repetition of the Lord's Prayer, but forbids "comment." This seems to work out satisfactorily and helps to make the atmosphere of our public schools favorable to the development of the religious attitude. Does not the desire for continuous religious *discipline*, day in and day out, argue a desire to go beyond the limits of religion into the indoctrination of special religious views, the inculcation of strictly denominational attachments? The church that cannot stand without such means might be suspected of being afraid of education. There is ample opportunity, out of school hours, for providing every essential help in the development of religion in the individual life.

There has been much effort in recent years to work out a satisfactory plan of teaching religion on public-school time with public-school co-operation, and there is some promise in such experiments. For my own part, however, I agree with Professor George A. Coe of Columbia University in his conclusion that we ought first really to try the Sunday-school. The most effective agent in developing a sense of the reality of God in human life is not teaching, but worship. We need less of instruction and more of worship in the Sunday-school, fewer lessons and more songs, responses, and prayers that are suitable

for children of various ages. Above all, we need presentation of the Bible and of doctrine in the free
spirit of inquiry rather than in the Fundamentalist
spirit of compulsion.

The development of the liberal study of the Bible
in colleges, and particularly the work of the National
Council on Religion in Education (a movement for
the establishment of liberal religious instruction in
the universities of the country, especially the state
universities) holds great promise for the future. No
obstruction should be put in the way of any experiment in the teaching of religion, and certainly the
state ought never to interfere with any effort to secure a wider knowledge of the Bible or of religious
problems on the part of any group, either denominational or interdenominational. It would be far wiser
to permit the teaching of the Bible in the schools,
although that would have to be done at present on a
denominational basis, than to risk the development
of extended opposition to the progress of public education on the ground that it contains no religious
elements. What one may rightly fear is that the
development of sectarian systems of schools may result in such an opposition to the progress of the
public schools that a sharp and fundamental conflict will arise between those who want the schools
carried on under public auspices and those who want
them handed over to the churches. It would be a
fatal thing, both for education and for religion, for

such a division to arise between public education and sectarian education. If any sect is so committed to the policy of conducting the entire education of its own children as to stand continuously and openly against the progress of public education, it is facing a controversy in which the advocates of American institutions can never give up their beliefs. Free public education is a fundamental of Americanism.

It can easily be seen that the whole trend of the argument I have been presenting is toward Liberalism in education and in religion. No one could hold the views which I have here set forth if he were an adherent of authority in religion or of conformity as a guiding principle in education. No reasonable man can deny that there is a use in life for compulsion and that every man must take some things on authority and every child be required to accept some things on faith and submit in certain respects to discipline. But the general end of education is freedom; its general object the development of purpose. The only way to keep education from becoming again what it once was, a process of discipline in conformity to predetermined types of thought and action, is to leave it in the hands of the state. For religious education, freedom depends on the ultimate victory of liberal forces in the churches. Where reactionary forces rule, religious education becomes a binding of the law upon the brow; it becomes essentially ecclesiastical rather than genuinely religious.

And there are dangers, of course, even in the state control of education. Professor Lake, in the book from which I have already quoted says (p. 160):

Education, which, at least in the United States, in the public schools is largely controlled by political agencies, may possibly pass into Fundamentalist hands, and be retarded for generations. This effect on education may easily be brought about by political action, especially in America, even though the majority of the people do not really wish it. It is not difficult for any large group, who have set their hearts on some one thing, to obtain a Legislature almost unanimous in their favor, if they steadfastly refuse to vote for any candidate who is not pledged to their support. They can even bring it about so that it will be scarcely respectable to differ openly from them; though in private it may appear obvious that a majority is not really on that side. If the votes of an organized Fundamentalist party could ever turn the scale in a close contest, it could almost certainly secure the election of a majority pledged to the prohibition of "unbiblical" teaching in any public school. It would to some degree be poetic justice if this happened, for the rapid growth of Fundamentalism is largely due to the fact that a generation ago Liberals thought it right to exclude the teaching of the Bible from these schools. Had they done the more difficult but wiser thing, and insisted that the Bible should be taught properly, as it is in Universities, there would have been no Fundamentalism to-day.

There is also a more sinister cause which may enormously help Fundamentalism. It may appear to large financial interests that industrial stability can be safeguarded by Fundamentalists who can be trusted to teach "anti-revolutionary" doctrine in politics and economics as well as in theology. This consideration gained much support in Holland for the Calvinist party in the first decades of this century. It is a policy which however successful for a time is likely in the end to produce a real revolution. To suppress discussion is always easier than to promulgate truth, though in the end it is safer to try the more difficult task.

These paragraphs present a discouraging picture, both for education and for religion. Education seeks freedom of the intellect and the spirit, and it must resist all effort to restrict the growth of freedom even in the name of religion. If what Professor Lake calls "the present tendency to make the churches intolerable for those who wish to think clearly" goes on unchecked; if there is no hope of church unity based on the broadest toleration and the recognition of the fact that religion is a way of life whereas doctrines are speculative answers to problems which every generation and every individual must solve for himself; if variety of religious thought and religious practice cannot find place in our civilization without a constant effort on the part of ecclesiastical groups to dominate the religious life of the entire people; then those who believe that the hope of the world lies in freedom must fall back upon the public schools as a last line of defense and steadily decline to admit into the public-school programme any religious teaching whatever.

A hopeful and forward-looking programme may be defined, as I see it, in these terms: first, insistence on the importance of public education and such progressive support of public schools as shall make them good enough for all children, anywhere; second, experiment in co-operation between the public schools and the churches in the introduction of religious instruction into our educational system; third, efforts within the churches to make genuinely educative use of their present opportunities for religious instruction and worship for the young; fourth, freedom for the conduct of private sectarian schools, with the most open and plain-spoken recognition of the fact that such freedom, pressed to the point of danger to public education, may lead to a conflict of disastrous character; finally, unceasing opposition to denominational control of public education, to obstructive denominational influence on its progress, and to all claims for freedom of sectarian education from public inspection or for state support of sectarian schools or for the relief of any sect or group from taxation for the public schools.

RELIGION: ITS PRODUCTIVE VALUE

T. N. CARVER

Economics is concerned largely, though not exclusively, with problems of value. True, it is generally with the value of merchantable commodities and productive agents, but there is no reason why the economist might not be interested in the value of anything that has a bearing upon the general problem of prosperity—whether it be national prosperity, world prosperity, or even the prosperity of special groups or classes within the nation. If religion is a factor in prosperity in any of its forms, the economist could scarcely ignore it. In order to focus attention upon this question, I should like to present it in some such form as this: Is religion worth what it costs?—that is, does it add to, more than it subtracts from, the prosperity of those who come under its influence?

I doubt if there is very much that can be said for or against religion as such from the economic or from any other point of view. It is always necessary to specify which religion we are talking about. I do not believe that any one can even name the function of religion as such. There are so many different kinds of religion in the world that there is really very little that can be said that applies to all of them. These religions differ so much among themselves in such fundamental particulars that it is almost impossible to define religion in such a way as to include them all. If some one should succeed in framing such a definition, it would mean so little as to be of very little use. Many so-called definitions of religion, however, make no pretense of being inclusive. Such definitions are very likely to describe what their authors think religion ought to be, or what it is at its best. "Pure religion and undefiled before God and the Father is this, To visit the fatherless and widows in their affliction, and to keep himself unspotted from the world," which seems to imply that all religions that do not come under this definition are false religions, or at least, not pure religion.

After all, it seems to me that this is a more fruitful theme for discussion than the more general one. What is the difference between a good religion and a bad one? If we can find an answer to this question, it will be of immeasurable value to us and to the rest of the world—if the rest of the world can be convinced of it. It may not be possible to formulate a complete definition that will cover every possible point of difference between a good and a bad religion, but if we can even specify some distinguishing characteristics of a good religion or some characteristic that will help us to choose among different religions, even that will be of immense value.

The first and most general statement, I think, that can be made regarding a good religion is that it must help to meet the actual conditions of life; it must possess survival value; it must help those who profess it to survive in the struggle to live. By reason of their possession of this religion they must be able to live together on a higher scale and in larger numbers than would be possible without it. It must help them to economize their energies and apply them to the solution of the problems of living. If it should prove a hindrance rather than a help in these fundamental problems of life, it becomes *per se* bad. If it is a help rather than a hindrance, it becomes *per se* good.

This lays emphasis upon the question, What is religion doing for its people? rather than upon its historical origin or the scientific accuracy of its cosmogony. It may have originated in superstition and ignorance, its theory of the universe may be childish and irrational; and yet its influence upon its people may be, on the whole, good. It may cultivate a teachable spirit, and because of that teachable spirit, its people may rise out of the ignorance and superstition in which they began. It may stimulate the economic virtues of industry, sobriety, thrift, honesty, and mutual helpfulness, and because of these virtues its people may rise out of the state of poverty and misery in which it found them. It may train its people in the simple and fundamental rules of health and thus lower the death-rate, increase the birth-rate, and cause its people to flourish and multiply where others decay. The religion that does these things is a good religion, however ignoble its origin.

In origin and early history there is probably not much that can be said in favor of one religion as against another, yet there may be a wide difference in their influence upon their devotees. Hawthorne, commenting upon the pond lilies that grew along the margin of the Concord River, said:

It is a marvel whence this perfect flower derives its loveliness and perfume, springing as it does from the black mud over which the river sleeps, and where lurk the slimy eel and speckled frog and the mud turtle, whom continual washing cannot cleanse. It is the very same black mud out of which the yellow lily sucks its obscene life and noisome odor. (*Mosses from an Old Manse*, p. 15. Houghton Mifflin Co., Riverside Edition, 1897.)

I do not deny the genuineness of an antiquarian interest. Scientific curiosity, the desire to learn something new, without much regard to the probable usefulness of the knowledge, has been an important factor in modern progress. Even when this scientific curiosity exercises itself by probing into the historical or psychological origin of religion it is to be commended. Nevertheless, we must not expect that this kind of research will throw much light on the value of any religion. "By their fruits ye shall know them" rather than by their origins. This applies to institutions as well as to individuals.

A parallel case is found in our study of government. If government were judged on the basis of its origin, we should all be compelled to think rather poorly of it. It probably originated, not in the consent of the governed nor in the general desire for order, but rather in the desire of some bully for power. By the strength of his arm, or the weight of his club, he subjugated those around him and compelled them to obey his will. There is nothing attractive or commendable about this, yet in the process of time those bullies that governed their groups in such ways as to economize their energies or direct their man-power economically and productively, succeeded in building up great and powerful groups. The disorganized horde without a governor could not compete with these well-organized groups; nor could those groups that were governed by bullies who did not govern wisely. In course of time, through the process of selection—those groups that were well governed growing, and those that were badly governed dwindling—governments improved until to-day we are warranted in saying that government— at least the kind of government that we ordinarily have in mind—is one of the most powerful agencies in human progress. By means of a wise government the people's energies are economized and directed productively, and larger numbers are enabled to live and to live very much better than they could if there were no such thing as government. Instead of judging government, therefore, by its historical and psychological origins, we must judge it by what it is now doing.

It is my contention that we must apply the same test to religion. Whatever its origin, it is a good religion if it now possesses survival value, if it fortifies its people against the evils and the dangers that surround them, if it enables them to prosper, to live together in larger numbers and to live better than they could without it. It is a bad religion which fails in this respect.

Perhaps one of the best ways of approaching this subject is to apply this test to some specific religion, preferably the one we know most about, namely, Christianity. To what extent has it proved a help and to what extent has it proved a hindrance to those who profess it, in facing the issues of life and meeting its problems, and in triumphing over its difficulties?

Some years ago a book was published entitled *The Social Basis of Religion* which contained probably the most unique argument ever written in favor of Christian missions.* The argument may be briefly

* "There are many analogies between the present situation and that which Christianity faced at its birth. The present crisis, although of another character, is fully as grave as that of the first century. Disease, famine, war, and failing resources made impossible an advance in civilization in the Southern regions, then its centre. A new region must be opened up and new races must be

paraphrased as follows: Christianity tends to make Christians prosperous. Prosperity tends to destroy them through race suicide and other similar tendencies. Therefore we must hasten to Christianize other races to take our place after we are destroyed, for if we do not, Christianity will perish with us and cease to exist as a religion. There is not much doubt as to the first proposition. Christianity, at least in its purer forms, by stimulating and encouraging the economic virtues of industry, simple living, mutual helpfulness and the development of all the faculties, has tended to lift people out of poverty and put them in a condition of prosperity. It is safe to say that any influence whatsoever that encourages these economic virtues is a factor in prosperity. To work hard, both with mind and body; to look forward and plan for the future, not only for one's self but

elevated from barbarism into the position of standard-bearers of culture. To-day, we have no fear of war, famine, disease, or failing resources. The advance in knowledge has guarded men against these evils; but it is none the less true that civilization must be extended to other regions and races, or it will go down as it did at Rome. Prosperity checks the birth-rate and promotes race suicide to such a degree that if new races cannot be raised to take the place of those dying out, there will be a decline in civilization to the level existing before the rise of Christianity. All of the earlier missionary efforts will be in vain unless methods are devised to arouse new classes, races, and nations with the same success with which our ancestors were awakened in earlier epochs by the prevailing forms of religious propagation. If laborers remain outside the church, if immigrants are not assimilated into our national life, or if we fail to do for Africa, India, and China what the early Christian missions did for our German ancestors, a slow but certain death awaits the church, no matter what may be its success in other fields." From Simon N. Patten's *The Social Basis of Religion*, pp. 210–211. The Macmillan Company, 1911.

for one's children; to develop the family virtues, and the marrying habit; to discourage luxury and extravagance and keep alive the ideal of the simple life; to sacrifice the impulse of the moment for the larger plans of the future; to do these things is to become prosperous. Nothing but a geological cataclysm or conquest by a foreign enemy can keep in a state of poverty people who are guided and influenced in these ways.

There is not much doubt that Christianity has, on the whole, influenced people in these ways. It has been a positive and not a negative religion. It has tended to stiffen the courage and increase the fortitude of those who were in conditions of adversity. It has contained none of the elements of that cult of incompetence and self-pity which is being affected by the dilettanti. It has not encouraged people to make excuses for themselves. It has always said to the individual, "You can" instead of "You can't." It has not said to the erring, "Poor fellows, you couldn't help yourselves; you are the victims of a bad environment." It has told them that they could rise above a bad environment and keep themselves unspotted from the world, while living in the world. In short, Christianity has given people the kind of discipline they needed in poverty and suffering. It has fortified them against the demoralizing influences of adversity. By so doing, it has enabled them to conquer these conditions and to rise out of them.

In taking this attitude, I think that the influence of the Christian religion has been more nearly in harmony with scientific fact than has the influence of some of those environmentalists who to-day are posing as ultrascientific. It is a pure assumption, made without any evidence whatsoever, that they who succumb to temptation or who are said to be demoralized by environment have more severe temptations or a worse environment than those who do not. No one has even taken the trouble to find out whether, on the average, those who become criminal have been subjected to more severe temptations than those who have not become criminal. Their whole argument is *a priori*. They assume that it must necessarily be true that they who yield to temptation are subjected to more severe temptations from the outside than those who do not; that the reason some manage to live conventionally good lives is because they have never been put to a severe strain. I submit that nobody really knows anything about the facts as yet. There is quite as much reason for believing that they who manage to behave themselves have been subjected to more severe temptations than those who have not, as there is for the opposite hypothesis. Whatever the facts may be, the general influence of Christianity has been directed toward increasing the power of resistance of the individual, toward the strengthening of his moral inhibitions, in order that he may be able to throw off the contagion of bad example, or resist the influences of bad environment.

There are elements both of good and of bad in every environment. There are incidents and examples of nobility and generosity, of loyalty, courage, and fortitude in the worst of the slum environments. There are incidents and examples of selfishness, meanness, deceit, and cruelty even in the best of environments. It is never possible to find an environment in which there are not incidents and examples that would tend to the demoralization of the individual. Every state of society and every condition of life will leave its mark on the individual who is capable of being marked for evil—who is the kind of wax that will easily take an evil impression. And every state of society and every condition of life will leave its mark also on those who are capable of being marked for good—who are the kind of wax that is capable of receiving good impressions.

Christianity, like many other religions, began and spread first among the poor. It gave them the kind of discipline which they needed in their condition of life. It made them into the kind of wax that could be marked for good, or that would take on, from their environment, good impressions. It built up their powers of resistance to the peculiar dangers to which they were subjected. By reason of the very fact that it accomplished this result, it enabled its people to triumph over these conditions and to rise out of them. It lifted them, as it were, out of the reach of adversity and poverty. It put them into a condition of well-being and prosperity. It would not have been much of a religion—certainly not a good religion, if it had not accomplished this result. It would not have met their needs. It would have been of no real use to them. Any religion that is worth anything to anybody derives its value from the fact that it helps him to meet the peculiar conditions which he has to face. It gives him power to resist the peculiar evils which surround him. A religion for the poor is of no use to them if it fails to fortify them against their peculiar temptations, however successful it might have been in fortifying other people against other kinds of temptation. A religion that is good for the sick and the afflicted must enable them to meet their peculiar conditions and to triumph over disease and affliction. In short, it must improve their health in some way or other. The religion, however, that merely does this and little else is of little use to the robust and the healthy.

> "The devil was sick, the devil a monk would be;
> The devil was well, the devil a monk was he."

The facts of health and robustness bring their own temptations and dangers. What these healthy and robust people need is the ability to meet their own peculiar temptations, or to fortify them against the evils that attack them rather than the kind that enables the sick and the afflicted to resist their peculiar temptations. Similarly, what prosperous people need is not the power to resist the peculiar temptations of poverty, but the power to resist the peculiar temptations of prosperity.

Here we find the crisis of Christianity. It has already developed a discipline that was admirably adapted to the peculiar needs of the poor and the afflicted among whom it had its beginnings. It has not yet developed a discipline that will help the prosperous and the comfortable to meet the peculiar temptations that come to them. In a sense, Christianity has created its own problems and may possibly have produced the poisons that will destroy it. This seems to be the implication in the work of Professor Patten that has already been cited. At any rate it seems to have solved its original problem in that it has developed the kind of inspiration and the kind of discipline that lifts people out of the condition of poverty and adversity into a condition of prosperity and comfort. By so doing it has subjected its own people to a group of new dangers against which it has not yet succeeded in fortifying them. Unless it does, Professor Patten's prophecy that it tends to destroy the race will come true. If Christianity is to be preserved, it will be through the Christianization of new races to take our place after we are gone.

However, it is of doubtful benefit to any of those new races to be Christianized, if this is true. It will, of course, lift them out of their present conditions of poverty and adversity into a temporary period of prosperity and comfort, but prosperity and comfort will then destroy these races as they seem to be in process of destroying our own. What is the use of preserving Christianity if its ultimate result is the destruction of every race that comes under its influence? Is Christianity really worth preserving if that is its ultimate result?

I should be inclined to answer this question in the negative; but is it necessarily true that Christianity must ultimately destroy every race through the prosperity and comfort that it brings? The answer is implied in what has already been said. If it is possible for Christianity to develop a kind of inspiration and discipline that will fortify prosperous and comfortable people against the demoralizing tendencies of prosperity and comfort as well as it has, in the past, fortified the poor and miserable against the peculiar temptations of poverty and misery, then Christianity will be worth preserving, and, what is more to the point, it will preserve itself because it will not destroy the races that accept it. It will continue to lift the mass of the people out of poverty and misery into prosperity and comfort, and at the same time will preserve them against their own prosperity and comfort. Can such a result be accomplished?

I see no inherent or physical difficulty in the way.

On general *a priori* grounds one might say that it is no more inconceivable that men should be enabled by some means to withstand prosperity than that they should be enabled to withstand poverty. If we were looking at the two problems in advance, without any previous experience to guide us, I suppose most of us would say that, so far as we could tell, it ought to be quite as easy to train men to stand prosperity as to train them to stand adversity. However, this is not a positive argument. Its only value is to counteract the feeling of helplessness or the conviction of impossibility. It must be freely admitted that, so far as actual experience goes, there is not much that can be quoted. We have a good deal of historical experience to show that it is actually possible to discipline a good many people—at least enough to form a saving remnant from which to breed future generations and keep the race alive in spite of the depredations of poverty, adversity, misery, and disease. We have no experience as yet to show that we can preserve even a saving remnant from the devastations of prosperity and comfort. It remains for the future to determine whether that can be accomplished or not. We must attack it as a new problem. We have no traditions or historical examples to follow. No religion, so far as I have any information, has ever solved this problem of saving people from prosperity or preserving them in spite of it.

One of the principal reasons is that very few persons want to be saved from the results of their good fortune, whether in the form of buoyant health, ample prosperity, or wide social esteem. In adversity every one is likely to realize his need of help and is therefore more likely to lay hold upon any means of help. In good fortune he feels quite competent to take care of himself.

Moreover, the evil consequences of adversity attack the individual himself. The evil consequences of good fortune frequently skip the individual and attack society at large, or future generations. It is a somewhat unusual individual who is willing to modify his conduct with a view to these larger interests or to those interests that require a longer look than the span of his own individual life. He is very likely to say: "What has posterity ever done for me that I should go out of my way to do anything for posterity?"

If one has no emotional interest in posterity, there is probably no answer to that question; at least it would be impossible to present an argument that would convince such a person. The individual is either susceptible to such an appeal or he is not. If he is susceptible to such an appeal, the appeal will be effective; if not, it will be ineffective. There is nothing that can be said in the way of a logical argument that will convince him, because he will not accept the fundamental postulates on which the argument would have to be based.

Instead of appealing by any kind of a logical argument to such an individual—at least to his own self-interest—we can only say to him: They who have an emotional interest to which appeal can be made and who, on this basis, are willing to sacrifice some personal comforts and conveniences in the interest of family building, will build families and leave posterity. They who lack all such interests will go their own way, pursuing their own whims, gratifying their own personal impulses, and will leave no posterity, or at most a dwindling posterity. If there is among the prosperous and well-to-do a saving remnant who still possess the ambition of the family-builder, who are willing to express themselves in this form rather than in some other, they will be the progenitors of future generations and they will preserve the standards and the ideals of the intellectual class. The others, who do not care to express themselves through family-building but prefer those forms of self-expression that interfere with family-building, will continue to do so, but they and their kind will eventually be eliminated. If, on the other hand, there should be no saving remnant among the intellectual classes, no considerable fraction who are willing to choose family-building as their peculiar form of self-expression, then the intellectual classes will continue to die out, and in the course of time, especially in a democratic society, the race will degenerate.

In a democratic society where every individual is encouraged to make the most of himself, to rise into the intellectual classes and ply the intellectual occupations, if it is possible for him to do so, the tendency will be, more and more, toward the elimination of the more intellectual and the preservation of the less intellectual, if the intellectual classes fail to multiply. They who persist, generation after generation, in the doing of non-intellectual work will be the kind of people to whom intellectual opportunities do not appeal. If they alone are the progenitors of future generations, in the course of time the whole population will be of the kind and quality to which intellectual opportunities make no appeal. When there is no considerable element in the entire population who can respond to such stimuli, there will be no intellectual work done, and our branch of the human race will be another example of a worn-out or a burnt-out race, while our civilization will be a decaying civilization.

The religion which I have tried to picture—the one that can make such an appeal to the intellectual classes as will lead them—at least a saving remnant of them—to regard family-building as the principal field of achievement or the principal opportunity for self-expression will be a factor in the preservation of the race and of the civilization which it has developed. Such a religion will be worth what it costs; It will be worth spreading; it will have shown itself to possess survival value, not merely during a temporary period of poverty and adversity, but also through an endless period of prosperity and progress.

FUNDAMENTALS OF PROSPERITY

ROGER W. BABSON

During the past twenty years some two hundred of us in Wellesley have been making a study of the rise and fall of business. During the past year we spent upon this study, and in interesting others therein, over a million dollars. During this study most of us have had our eyes opened to the reality of great truths which we have been told but which we never realized, because there is a great difference, friends, between knowledge and realization. It is regarding these simple things that your committee has asked me to speak to you this afternoon.

My father and mother live in Gloucester, Mass., and I go down to see them as often as I can. In the summer time, not far from our home, Mr. John Hays Hammond lives. There I have had the pleasure of sitting with him on his veranda, listening to the experiences and investigations of America's greatest mining engineer. But whatever the subject we would start to talk about, we always ended by talking about Africa. He would tell me of wonderful undeveloped water powers, of tremendous forests; of gold deposits, iron deposits, and copper deposits—all of the tremendous mineral resources of that continent.

Then I would say to him: "Why is it that Africa does not amount to more?" and he would answer: "Because Africa is still the 'Dark Continent.'" Although the continent which possesses the greatest amount of undeveloped raw materials, and although the oldest of continents, for in the northern portion we find the sphinx and the pyramids, yet it is still the continent which is the most void of Christianity." Practically the only part of Africa which is developed to-day is the little portion south and one or two points on the coast, where Christianity has touched.

If statistics teach anything, it is that raw materials are not one of the fundamentals of prosperity. The greatest prosperity in Europe to-day, from a statistical standpoint, is found in the little country of Belgium, which is the most destitute of all countries of Europe in natural resources.

*　　　*　　　*

I was interested to notice a while ago that the Russian dollar-bonds, which have been selling around ten for a number of months, or perhaps two or three years, had suddenly jumped up to twenty. Having some friends at the Russian Embassy, I went in there and asked about the Russian situation and whether there was any particular reason for these bonds doubling in price. I was fortunate to meet there three engineers who had just come from Russia. While we were talking over the situation I began naturally to argue for Russia. However, they were very pessimistic, and as I argued for Russia I referred to Russia's great natural resources, and then to her inexhaustible available labor supply—two hundred million men—strong, capable, of tremendous industrial energy. These engineers, however, just shook their heads as if in utter despair. I finally said to them, "Tell me what is the real difficulty." They replied, "Mr. Babson, the real difficulty is that our people have lost their faith in God. They have lost the motives, the ambition, the faith, the inspiration, the desire to be of service, which they once had. It makes absolutely no difference what are the natural resources of a country, or the available labor supply, unless the people are actuated by the right motives and the right purposes—unless they are grounded in the fundamentals of religion, there is no prosperity in that country." I had never seen those engineers before, I do not know what are their ideas of religion or their theology. I know nothing about them, but the three men bore that testimony at the Russian Embassy on 16th Street, in Washington. Available labor is not a fundamental of prosperity.

*   *   *

Let us discuss capital as a fundamental of prosperity. Countries as they have accumulated capital, through thrift and service, have become prosperous. But capital itself is merely a tool, like natural resources and labor, and can be used either to up-built or to destroy. Capital can be used to build houses of ill fame and ruin the lives of our young people, or it can be used for the building of hospitals and homes, and other agencies for the protection and development of life. Capital can be used to upbuild or to destroy. During the last few weeks a member of my organization has been making a study of the New England railroad situation. I could preach a sermon on that, using it as a text—showing how those railroads were built originally for service. They were built by people in the neighborhood and of the towns and cities through which they went, in order to get their goods to market and transport their families. They were built economically and honestly. The conductors, station agents, and other employees were all filled with the same pride regarding their system. I well remember, as a boy, taking my first trip on the railroad train from Gloucester to Boston—how the conductor sat down with me and told me about the cities along the road, told me the history of the road—just as proud of it as if he owned it all himself. Then bankers came along and those people were bought out. The control of New England's railroad systems went over to Wall Street. The railroads of New England ceased being operated with the idea of service, but rather with the idea of giving as little as they could and getting as much as they could—the anti-Christ principle. The disastrous result you all know.

This applies all through business to-day. Take our

great newspapers as an illustration. Most of our great newspapers were built up around some one personality who was filled with the desire to put forth a message. The paper grew naturally and developed. Then it passed into new hands and became a business proposition to make as much money as possible. We complain about the cost of living, and discuss the causes of the high cost of living. I have that especially on my mind this afternoon because I have been asked by the Department of Justice this week some questions regarding it. My mind goes back to the little butcher shop in my country town, the town where I was brought up when a boy, Gloucester, Mass. There was a great fat butcher (I do not know why they were always fat butchers in those days) in a big blue coat. There was a great big block, almost as big as a pulpit. I would be sent there to get some steak, and he would take a piece of meat from this place or that place, and cut off the steak. Then he would roll it up in some brown paper, and I would leave the store, having paid him twenty cents a pound, carrying it home under my arm dripping with juice.

When I now go to Gloucester to visit my father and mother I go down to the same shop, for it is operated by the son of the old butcher. I find an entirely different situation, although Gloucester has a smaller population to-day than it did when I was a boy. Twenty-four thousand it used to have and now it has only sixteen to twenty thousand. That butcher shop has no more business than it had then, but is that boy standing by the block as his father did? No. He may be in the shop; but if it is in the afternoon he is out riding in his car, taking his friends on a trip. There is one girl who stands by the cash register and another girl somewhere else, and two or three men are scattered around the store—every one wanting some one else to do the work. As a result I pay sixty cents for a steak, the same as I used to get for twenty cents, from the same block in the same shop in the same city.

The point is that capital, when it means thrift and when it is held and used in the spirit of service, brings prosperity; but when the second and third generation get it, it becomes merely a tool for pleasure. So capital is not a fundamental of prosperity.

*   *   *

Some one asks, "What about our educational institutions?" Well, whether or not Germany in 1914 led the world in intelligence, I do not know. If she did not, she certainly had good publicity agents, for she made us all think so until she committed that crime against civilization. Intelligence is merely a tool. We send our young men to college and we give them diplomas, but we never know whether they are to use their education to upbuild or to destroy; whether they are going to use that knowledge of chemistry to make disinfectants or gas bombs.

[257]

We train men in our law schools—law schools which were established by Christian people and endowed with the money of hard-working, thrifty New Englanders. One boy comes out of that school and helps men enforce law, while another boy, with the same education and the same marks, comes out to help men evade laws. The greatest legal minds in America can be employed to-day either for the purpose of making laws or for the purpose of evading laws, according to who comes to them first. No, even intelligence is not a fundamental of prosperity. It is a mere tool which can be used either to upbuild or to destroy.

Yet—of the four big tools—raw materials, available labor, capital, and intelligence—the educational institutions have stood the test best of all. Let me illustrate that. If you will study the one hundred leading business firms of New England of one hundred years ago, you will find that only one-tenth of them are surviving to-day. But if you will study the one hundred leading educational institutions of that same period you will find that nine-tenths of them are existing to-day. This means that New England of a century ago, with the one hundred great commercial houses and the one hundred struggling educational institutions, has only ten of the commercial houses in existence to-day, and ninety of the educational institutions. In endeavoring to find the reason for this I asked many men their opinions, and this was the consensus of the answers: As the commercial houses became more prosperous, the founders who had the vision of service passed beyond, and this prosperity drew to them men who wanted money and were keen for money. The more prosperous those houses were, the greater the temptation, and the more worldly-minded men were drawn to them. The prosperity of those firms was their downfall. But how was it with thee ducational institutions—poverty-stricken, struggling? There was no opportunity for profit. The salaries paid were very low, and as a result only men and women came into those educational institutions as leaders and teachers who were filled with the spirit of service. The low salaries which our educational institutions have been compelled to pay have served as a screen, keeping out the money-seeker. This has been their salvation. This is the reason why they exist after this hundred and more years of effort.

Fundamentals of prosperity are not raw materials, are not available labor, or intelligence, or capital, or any of those things which you people have been commonly brought up to think. Those are mere tools, just as much tools as a knife. You can put a knife into the hands of your boy and he can use it to sharpen a pencil or he can use it to cut off his finger. And so it is with all of these things. This is why Jesus held them so lightly and told us to beware! These are mere tools, absolutely valueless

in themselves and a source of strength or a source
of danger in accordance with how they are used,
or according to the religion of the men or women who
possess them. So, when you have the opportunity, I
beg of you people to talk to educators about the
fundamentals of prosperity, and to have them get
the minds of our young men and our young women
more focused on those fundamentals of integrity,
justice, charity, self-control, faith, and inspiration.
Upon those religious qualities our prosperity absolutely depends.

*   *   *

Now what are the real fundamentals of prosperity?
The last time I was in New York I was sitting down
with the president of a very large institution, going
over some of the assets of that bank, and we spoke
about the different loans held by the bank. He said
that this one is secured and that one not secured, and
so on and so on, and then he stood up and said, "Mr.
Babson, do you know that practically all of our losses
during the past two years have been in connection
with our *secured* loans?" I said, "How does that
happen?" "Why," he said, "with the *unsecured*
loans we are always very particular to loan only to
a man who stands for the fundamentals such as truth,
integrity, and justice. Those, Mr. Babson, are the
real assets. The records of this bank show most conclusively that whenever we loan money to a man
grounded in integrity, that loan always is good. Our

losses come through those men and corporations who come to us presenting fine statements offering attractive collateral, so attractive that we loan on it without considering the *character* of the man or the corporation behind the note, and that is how we make our losses." Yes, the first fundamental of prosperity is integrity.

I was present at an interesting debate once as to what was the beginning of civilization. One speaker took the position that modern civilization began with the use of the horse—when man found that he could get an animal to do some of his work. He claimed that man then graduated from the stage of the aborigine, or whatever you want to call it, into another or industrial stage, and that was the beginning of civilization. Another debater took the position that industry and commerce started with the discovery of the wheel, that the first man who used a wheel was really the father of our present complicated industrial and commercial life. The wheel was first used in the form of a log upon which great stones of granite were rolled; then the log was cut up and made into chariot wheels, and then these wheels were put on carts, then on stage coaches, railway trains, and automobiles. He showed how the wheel had been the basis of all water-power development, machinery, steam-engines, and the like. Then a third man arose and took the position that modern industry started with that moment when one man found he could trust another, that is, with the invention of credit. When the first loan and the first partnership was formed, in the most humble way, that was the beginning of our great industrial and commercial civilization. Do you know that the group gave the verdict to that man? Thus integrity, which is the product of religion, is a real fundamental of prosperity.

*   *   *

Some of the men here heard me speak the other night before the Men's Club, when I showed a chart of business conditions. I explained how business will run along normal for a given length of time and then something develops which causes it to shoot up. We have a period of great prosperity which continues a certain length of time and then something happens and we run into a decline and have what is known as a period of depression. This depression continues for a certain length of time and we again have a period of prosperity. During the periods above normal there is a shortage of labor, underproduction, etc., and during the periods below normal there is unemployment, overproduction and the like. The bankers call the periods above normal "periods of inflation," and the periods below normal "periods of deflation."

What do statistics show to be the cause of these various hills and valleys of business activity? Statistics show this: During the latter half of every period of prosperity there develop selfishness, extravagance, indifference, and the like. These anti-Christian forces, developing in the latter half of every period of prosperity, cause the period of depression which follows. When that period of depression has continued a sufficient length of time to make people see the error of their ways and quit some of their selfishness and extravagance and begin to develop self-control, thrift, service, and industry, then prosperity returns. The religious forces of thrift, service, and self-sacrifice, that develop in the latter half of every period of depression, lay the foundation and give us the period of prosperity that follows. Statistics show clearly that there never was yet a period of unemployment that was not due to a demand to cast aside either the Multiplication Table or the Ten Commandments. Self-control, charity, thinking of the other fellow—these are the products of religion and the second fundamental of prosperity.

*   *   *

Another fundamental of prosperity is that spirit, whatever it is, which is represented by the words faith and inspiration. Friends, if you want to study the fundamentals of prosperity, read the history of Europe for those years preceding the Renaissance, and the years following. When we go to Europe to-day and see those wonderful works of art, do we stop to think of the purpose for which they were made? We go to art exhibits in this country where most all

[263]

of the pictures were painted for commercial purposes and sold to the highest bidder, but not so in Europe. The pictures seen there were painted by men who were inspired with the spirit of Jesus. They were painted by men who could express themselves only with the brush, and they made masterpieces which have stood for centuries. Were the great cathedrals that we go over there to see built for commercial purposes? No, they were built by people inspired with the spirit of Jesus who wanted to erect something in his memory. They were the Crusaders—filled with the Crusaders' spirit! Ah, it is that inspiration that comes from religion—that faith which comes from religion—which has built those cathedrals, which has carved that statuary, which has painted the great masterpieces—which has made civilization.

The printing-press, as you all know, was known and used in a small way in China two or three thousand years ago, but the printing industry never started until a small group of people in Germany wanted to spread the Bible throughout Europe. They then procured the movable type and set up that Book. It was the desire, the inspiration, the spirit to put that Bible over Europe that built up our great printing industry. An interesting corollary to that is the fact that the first book and the first newspaper printed on the American continent were printed in Mexico City; but it died there, and we had to wait until a band of Pilgrims came over from the other side, filled with the spirit of God, before a newspaper and a publishing business was found that would survive.

Yes, inspiration, faith, that is one of the great fundamentals of prosperity, and without it we have no prosperity. Without vision the people perish. The school and college may be a haven for study, but the church is a rallying point for action. When you come to study industries, I care not what that industry is, you will find that it started in a monastery. Practically all of our sciences, and the original investigations of practically all of our industries, have been developed in monasteries, not by people filled with the commercial sense, but by men working without salary, desiring to be of service and to do something worth while.

*   *   *

Now I tell you, friends, we want to stand fearlessly on these questions. People do not realize the real and great importance of this power of religion. We think too much of the tools, and too little of the hands into which we are going to put those tools. The natural resources, the available labor, and the capital—all of these things are secondary. The most important thing for us to watch is the character of the hands that are going to hold these resources, that are going to control that labor. Are they hands directed by religion? Are they hands controlled by the right spirit? This is the important question, and it is a question which we should emphasize continually.

Somebody asked me the other day why it is that school bonds and municipal bonds in general are so much safer than other kinds of bonds. The answer is simple. Because these bonds are used for good purposes—to render real service. This is the fundamental reason why such securities are better than those of corporations operated simply for profit. When you analyze corporation securities, ranging them in lists according to their ratings, you will find every time the best rated are those that have been used for the building of water-plants or other things worth while, and the poorest rated are those at the other end of the line, used for building moving-picture houses, theatres, and the like.

Just a quotation from Ambassador Harvey—from an address which he gave in London a few months ago: "The real strength of a country is not measured by armies and navies. A schoolhouse at the crossroads is more potent ultimately than a dreadnaught on the sea. One church on the hill is worth a score of regiments. All mankind will some day realize that there is more power and glory in 'Lead Kindly Light' than in all the fighting anthems in the world." Friends, you think that your children, and that your liberty are safe here in Cambridge because of the policemen and the courts. But let me tell you, the real reason why your sister can go out on the streets of Cambridge at night and come back home safely is because of the work of your preachers, your priests, and your rabbis. They are the real protectors of Cambridge, and every other city.

*　　　*　　　*

My first job after graduating from the Institute of Technology in Boston was with a bond house, for which I was statistician, and after being with that house in Boston some six or eight months I went to New York. I had a position in New York that didn't pay very much, and I lived in a simple hall bedroom on the fourth story of a boarding-house on 17th Street, very near Third Avenue. It was a pretty rough neighborhood for a young chap twenty-two to be thrown adrift in, and yet I learned some tremendous lessons there. I remember especially a mission, O God bless those missions! In the slums of every city—yes, while we are here this afternoon—there are those missions, in old stores. I can see that one. It was formerly an old rum-shop and they had simply cleared out the bars and put some sawdust on the floor and put in fifty or sixty chairs, and they had a stove at one end. Lots of them are working throughout this country to-day. When you are asked to help them, help them.

I remember especially that one, and I remember the men who used to go in there, and the women who

used to go in there. There is where the real miracles
are performed—not in the churches on Fifth Avenue
—but in those dingy, hot, smelly missions! And as I
think back on those evenings that I used to spend in
there, this whole subject is crystallized in my mind.
One case well illustrates them all. He was a dis-
reputable prize-fighter, and when he was converted
at the mission he joined the traffic squad of the city
of New York, and lost his life saving the lives of
others. I remember a woman—a little bit of a woman
—who, before being converted, was connected with
the white-slave industry of that city. She now has an
important position with the tuberculosis work of
New York. I remember a man who, previous to his
conversion, was arrested for forgery. He served his
sentence and came out. I recall, one evening, his
standing up and giving his testimony, telling what
he had done and how he was arrested for it and how
he had served his ten years in prison. After he was
won by the Spirit of God he became interested in
art, and he is now a famous etcher. I have seen
hundreds of cases where men were using their powers to destroy, to kill, to steal, to ruin human life;
and after they had come up to that altar they were
changed. Both before and after conversion they had
the same ability, the same powers, the same education, the same natural resources; but they were
moved by a different purpose and a different motive
after conversion and then became great factors in

upbuilding the prosperity of our country. So I say, when discussing this great question of prosperity, that the great need of the hour is not more railroads or steamships, not more banks or factories, but rather, more religion.

THE CHURCH AND BUSINESS

A. LINCOLN FILENE

THE greatest good which the church can do to business is to assist business men to think straight—ethically straight—regarding their own problems.

I understand that a large majority of my audience are students. Many of you are going into business, and I am sure will be anxious to face the problems which will confront you from the standpoint of doing the thing that is fair and just. The church should be able to assist you in this task by making plain that one of the greatest dangers to a young person's mind is that it will become warped through failure to keep in tune with the attitude of people outside the group or class with which he is naturally associated. In order to see human problems squarely, and business problems are fundamentally human problems, the business man should control his environment so that he is thrown in with many different sorts of groups. Only in this way can he hope to keep his point of view from prejudice.

I recall, a good many years ago, an occasion when I was enabled to play some part in the bringing about of the settlement of a strike which was taking place in one of our big industries. Those disinterested outsiders who had been trying to assist both sides to find an equitable way out of their difficulties had been instrumental in bringing the executives most concerned to the point where they were ready to accept a compromise with their employees which our advisory group believed was just. We finally parted one afternoon with the understanding that when we reassembled, the proposed compromise would be accepted.

The next day the atmosphere had entirely changed. We felt that the programme of peace which had been so near consummation had received a severe setback. It was evident in the looks and manner of the industry's executives. We were considerably puzzled as to what had happened in the interval, but one of the members of our group had an inspiration. "I know what has caused you to look so differently at things to-day," he told them. "It is because you spent last evening at the Blank Club" (naming a club the membership of which was almost entirely business men). His guess proved to be correct. The speaker went on to point out that when, after the meeting of the day before, these men had once more been surrounded by men whose positions in life were similar to theirs and who held an ultra-conservative point of view on labor matters, their newly adopted attitude of willingness to meet their employees half-way had been undermined.

Wherever capital and labor are in relation, there

are always two vital attitudes to be understood before we can arrive at the ethics of the situation.

In the conduct of almost every strike we usually find two "rights" in conflict—the right of the employees to quit, and the right of the employer to carry on his business without unreasonable interference.

Company union or trade union is a major question affecting industrial relations in our generation, and may loom even larger in the next generation. Without a great deal of knowledge of how industrial relations work in practice, without a very careful checking up of the attitude of the workers concerned, one should be cautious in assuming that because an industrial concern has set up a company union of its own, it is fulfilling the legitimate demands of its workers for representation in decisions affecting their welfare, or is justified in refusing to treat with the workers' trade-union. Investigation might show that the practices of the concern were such that no effective voice in representation was given to the workers by the company union.

I am not undertaking here to point out the relative merits of company unions and trade-unions. There are shop councils or company unions which are accomplishing much good toward sound relations. I am merely making the plea to the younger members of my audience that, when they come up against problems of labor relations in their business career, they face them not on the say-so of what some other individual or concern has done, not on the basis of propaganda, but on the basis of sober and sympathetic investigation of the important facts which should control their decision.

The church has two major problems in respect to members of the business community. First, to make business men want to do the ethical thing in business, and second, to help show the way to this accomplishment.

In order to do the ethical thing toward his employees, the modern business man must study, as one of his most important tasks as a business administrator, the complicated facts which have determined the attitude of his workers. As the business man of large affairs has grown away from close contact with his employees, their motives have become more obscure to him. Too many times he has ascribed to a spirit of hostility or of stupidity actions of his employees which would present themselves in quite a different light if he had taken the trouble to make an historical investigation into industrial relations in his industry. Let me illustrate.

An authoritative writer on labor matters in a recent article entitled "The Way to Industrial Peace" comments on the testimony given before the Lockwood Investigating Committee of the New York legislature that the Bakers' Union was imposing harsh conditions on the master bakers. Some of the things the Bakers' Union was charged with aiding and abetting were these:

No bakery workman could be discharged without the consent of the union.

Hours of labor were six or seven a day, and $75.00 the minimum wage per week. Most bakers would not accept the minimum and employers had to pay $100.00 a week or more.

The custom in bakeries is to allow workers to take home bread for family use. The New York bakers, even when earning such high wages, used to have their wives make large bags, so it was alleged, and carry home all the bread they could take.

The reaction of the average business man on hearing this testimony would be to believe that the unions were stimulating a spirit of reprehensible selfishness among the bakers. The author of the article, however, calls attention to an earlier period in the relations of bakers and master bakers in New York, which shows a different picture. At the time when Theodore Roosevelt was Governor of New York, an investigation into the New York bakeries revealed that many men were working fourteen to sixteen hours a day in basement bakeries, sleeping at their working-places, and getting very low wages. Unsanitary conditions prevailed. A law was passed establishing ten hours as the legal work-day in bakeries in order to protect the workers' health, but the courts declared the law unconstitutional. The alleged attempt of the bakers, not so many years later, to abuse their temporary advantage over their employers becomes much more understandable in view of preceding events.

The employer who knows that his workers have probably many times in their industrial experience suffered from unfair conditions is in a much better strategic position to persuade his workers to the point of view which he believes just than is the employer who sincerely believes that his workers are in a conspiracy to advance their selfish interests at any cost to himself.

The factor which most strongly operates to prevent straight thinking and ethical behavior in industrial relations is the conflict of group attitudes which lead many employers and employees to accept a hardly concealed warfare as the natural relationship between capital and labor. These group attitudes are largely founded on emotions of fear and selfishness that have become traditional. They can be broken down by the light of a sympathetic understanding, and they must be broken down if harmonious and efficient relations between employers and employees are to develop.

The "group consciousness" of employers in respect to industrial relations has been fostered by the removal of the business head from personal contact with his workers, and by the natural close association of thought and emotion that has grown up among business men. The business head who no longer knows his workers by name or even by sight can be easily led to think the worst of them when he finds their views in opposition to his own. When he finds his attitude reinforced by that of other business men, there is a cumulative emotional effect which makes it very difficult indeed for him to look upon his workers' demands with a cool and critical eye.

James Harvey Robinson says, "Most of our so-called thinking consists in finding arguments for going on believing as we already do." No doubt many a business man, over-partial to the traditions of his group, whose conscience has been troubled when charges were made against him that by low wages, unsanitary conditions, etc., he was working his employees a serious injury, has neglected the main issue and has been led to compensate his injured self-respect by gifts to libraries, philanthropies, religious causes, etc.

In the past the church did not try very hard to stimulate a different attitude in the business man who was following such a course. The church was too easily satisfied that gifts of money indicated a Christian spirit, and attendance at church a desire to travel the Christian path. We need not assume that the church was hypocritical in this; its applied ethics had not broadened sufficiently to cope with the peculiar difficulties in the relations of human beings in industry that have accompanied the rise of our modern industrial era.

When we turn to relations between one business man and another, between the seller of goods and the buyer of goods, or when we look at the relations of the business man to the public we find, as in the relations of employer and employee, crystallized group attitudes, conventional reactions, failure to grasp the significance of present actions in terms of their past origins—all operating to promote relationships which the church, desirous of seeing the spirit of brotherhood and the ethics of fair play prevail, must regard with a good deal of dismay.

In the field of trade relations, that is, the field of dealings between buyers and sellers, abuses such as cancellations of orders, returns of goods, substitution of merchandise of inferior quality to what was ordered, taking of unauthorized discounts, etc., are all practices which have grown up because producers and distributors have adopted the group attitude of looking at each other not as partners, but as antagonists. This again is because producers and distributors are separated from one another—do not know one another, and have lost confidence in one another's intentions.

What both producers and distributors frequently lose sight of is that both sides are committing unethical practices not because these practices are economic or necessary, but because they have lost the habit of co-operation. Manufacturers and distributors need, first, to cut their way through the mesh of the group attitude which holds inactive their potentially generous emotions toward one another. If producer and distributor could be brought to acknowledge something like an equality of blame for the conditions which produce bad trade relations, they would be in a position to begin a new slate on a basis of mutual confidence which will make possible greater justice and substantial economic saving for both.

The public is prone to suspect business of profiteering, false advertising, and other anti-social behavior. Business men frequently think that the public, as represented by the actions of legislative bodies, is ready to yield to any demagogic pleader who persuades it to strike a blow at "big business."

These group attitudes of distrust are only possible because few people take sufficient trouble to clear up misunderstandings regarding facts and motives. When business undertakes to instruct the public as to how business is run, when it is willing to do away with a lot of the unnecessary secrecy which now shrouds business practices, then it can expect to receive from the public through its legislative representatives the sort of treatment to which it sincerely believes its behavior entitles it.

The intellectual task of thinking through the problems of modern industrial relations, not only in their historical origin but their present significance, is one to test the calibre of the hardiest brain. James Harvey Robinson, considering the complex factors which present themselves to the person who would think out human problems in their relation to the modern world, says, "We have . . . first to create an unprecedented attitude of mind to cope with unprecedented conditions and to utilize unprecedented knowledge." And again, "We should proceed to the thorough reconstruction of our mind with a view to understanding actual human conduct and organization."

Unhealthy relations between business men and their employees, between business men and other business men, and between business men and the public not only are economically costly to all concerned, but they directly promote social ills which the business man pays money to overcome, and which the church is obliged to fight against. Students are more and more realizing that to a large degree, sickness, insanity, domestic unhappiness, delinquency, and most social evils owe their origin more or less directly to economic difficulties. Economic difficulties owe their origin very largely to warped human relationships in the economic field.

As a guardian of social morality, the church has a distinct responsibility for assisting business men, workers, and the public in thinking through the problems which lie back of group hostilities in the economic field. The problems which have commanded the greatest popular interest and sympathy are those which have arisen in the relationships of employers and employees. The attitude of antagonism and of group distrust which so often marks questions affecting industrial relations to-day is a direct descendant of industrial practices of the past. I believe it is not unfair to state that the church, generally speaking, did not make the effort to understand the evil social effects of many industrial practices in our past history which have fostered present distrust and waste in industrial relations. It is probably too much to expect that the church, surveying our earlier industrial history, would have seen the evils of the future in the evils of the present. Until we had accumulated a good deal of evidence as to the mental, moral, and physical consequences of certain industrial practices, it would not have been possible to condemn them outright. But there is little evidence that the church was alert to note the development of social evils of this sort.

Speaking of early industrial life in this country, which was marked by long hours of labor and disregard for a healthful working environment, William Chenery in his book *Industry and Human Welfare* says, "Beyond the vague suspicion that factory life made for loose morals, there was hardly a trace of uneasiness concerning the effects of industry upon the welfare of the people. No question of health or fatigue, of compensation for accidents or unemployment, of control, of a possible rift between classes, seems to have occurred to the inaugurators of the industrial system."

There are factors in our industrial life to-day, less harsh though it is than that of the nineteenth century, which may be piling up future social evils which the church must take cognizance of. Possibly the effect of repetitive industry on the mentality of the workers is such a danger.

Intelligent business men, like churchmen, really desire that the relationships among the various elements in our economic life should be freed of friction and waste. The need is to develop a more sympathetic understanding of motives, leading to the demolition of group distrust and the erecting of confidence and mutual service between groups. What part can the church play in such a programme ?

To be effective in the task of making business men or any group develop an increasingly ethical conduct of their affairs, the church must first clean house as far as its own group attitudes are concerned. The church will always be in a rather difficult position in preaching the brotherhood of man as long as it allows itself to tolerate an attitude of suspicion between itself and other religions and between one Christian sect and another. Until the Christian church can attain to greater harmony within its own ranks, it must expect to be censored for permitting the continuance of socially unhealthy group antagonisms.

The ministers of the gospel of brotherhood should certainly devote themselves to the elimination of these barriers that frequently seem to the lay public to be promoting most unbrotherly relationships. What the church's problem may be in overcoming its own group misunderstandings, it is not for me to state. Until it has done so, however, it cannot expect to receive from thoughtful men the measure of respect which its advocacy of more wholesome relationships in human affairs really warrants.

In order to understand what the moral problems are in connection with business, the church must obviously learn more about business itself. It should draw up a list of questions affecting our economic life in which group distrusts play a prominent part. Lack of mutual understanding prevents mutual adjustment. This is a challenge to the minister to urge each side to understand the point of view of the other, and to assist them to this understanding.

I happen to have been among the first group of American business men who recognized the valuable contribution that education had to make to the business world. To make the contact between the business system and the educational system effective, business men must see the need of studying educational problems and taking an active part in the educational movement. The analogy to the church's relationship with business is obvious.

I would suggest as practical steps toward becoming acquainted with the problems of business that ministers should join local chambers of commerce or other organizations of business men. Also, I approve an idea advanced by Mr. Henry Dennison that ministers should make it a practice to talk each week to two or three business men in their congregation on problems of human relations in business. Merely by sitting in at such discussions the minister will much more quickly learn about the nature of the disputes that arise in industrial life and their causes than he would by reading text-books on the subject. The researches of the Federal Council of Churches into social problems, and conferences on social problems carried on by local church federations, are important indications of progress in the church's broadened crusade for applied righteousness.

Ministers should not be expected to take a course in business administration or to become technically trained business men. It is necessary for ministers to study enough in the business field to be able to assure business men that they are not presuming to give guidance on ethical conduct in business without knowledge of the diverse considerations that surround business operations.

Armed then with knowledge and inspired with the

Christian satisfaction of having demonstrated within itself the possibilities of brotherhood and co-operation, the church may well expect to become a continuous influence in helping to direct business into channels where social good is a factor co-ordinate with private gain in charting the course.

Perhaps I can advantageously summarize the thought I have been trying to develop:

1. The church must establish the brotherhood of man among the churches themselves.

2. The church should make it a point to know the causes for unethical practices prevailing in business relationships.

3. The church can assist business men to a similar understanding of the causes of these unethical practices.

4. The aim of the church will be to break down the hostile attitudes of groups by assisting each group to understand the other's point of view. This can be accomplished only by a historical survey which shows how, through misunderstanding and separation, hostile attitudes have been built up.

5. With the establishment of mutual confidence between employers and employees, between one business and another, and between business and the public, it will follow that each group instead of being on the defensive against the other will feel the impulse to state its case frankly and fairly, with the expectation of receiving assistance instead of suspi-

cion or hostility. By indicating the advantages, spiritual and economic, which come from an atmosphere of confidence and co-operation, the church can do much in getting each side to want to understand the other.

I do not wish to criticise the church for what it has attempted to do in industry, because, to the best of my belief, when it has concerned itself in industrial problems it has done so in an ethical, constructive way. I do feel, however, that it is only now beginning to realize the extent of its opportunity for good in the field of business relations, and that it cannot too soon identify itself even more closely with those problems of business the proper solution of which would aid immensely in social and individual betterment.

BUSINESS AND RELIGION

WALLACE B. DONHAM

I HAVE been somewhat puzzled to know what is expected of me in a course of lectures designed to enable Harvard men to understand the main religious systems and concepts, particularly those involved in the present controversy in the churches. It is quite clear that you will not expect from me a discussion of metaphysics, because there are many other people in this vicinity who are equipped to discuss topics of that sort, while I am clearly not equipped to do so. It is evident, also, that you do not expect a discussion of any particular religious dogma, nor do you expect me to make an effort—although this seems implied in my topic—to define religion. It will be necessary, however, to place before you my own concept of religion, not by a complete definition, but by stating some things which it seems to me are clearly not included within the word, and some other things which ordinarily must be included.

I shall speak from the assumption that religion is neither a dogma nor a rule of conduct. I shall not attempt to define affirmatively everything involved in a concept of religion, because I am hopelessly unable to formulate an answer to that question in my own mind and always have been. It must include belief in some fundamental purpose in life, in existence; and it connotes certain types of interest which, while not exclusively held by religious men, if they exist in other groups are in a sense adventitious. These types of interest include a desire to contribute to the orderly evolution of human society toward better things; they connote certain ethical intents and moral purposes, not necessarily coupled with the ability to define ethical standards or moral objectives. Certainly and more specifically, religion connotes an interest in the welfare of others.

In fact, the social value of religion lies largely in its promotion of an affirmative interest in others, in its arousing of a desire to contribute to better joint living and to the progressive but reasonably stable evolution of human society and in its relative freedom from selfishness and self-seeking. I realize I take long chances when in an academic community I attempt to state this point of view, but without making some such effort I do not see how to approach this talk.

The historic foundations of our national life are largely rooted in the religions, interests, beliefs, and points of view of this community about here, this old New England community. With many others— including, for example, Bryce—I have queried what would be the effect on the social organization of our community if the foundations of American religion should be as completely swept away or weakened generally as they have been in particular groups within the community.

This may seem a long way from my topic of business and religion, but I am obliged to go even further afield before I can define to you what seems to me to be the significance of the contacts between religion and business. I must give brief consideration to the forces which have so seriously weakened the hold of religion on the community—particularly for the better-trained and on the average more intellectual groups. This change goes back largely to the effect of the extraordinary scientific thinking of the last two hundred and fifty years, with the marvellous physical results following from that scientific think-ing. The materialistic working hypotheses of the sci-entific group have to an extraordinary extent upset the psychology of the better-trained and more in-telligent part of our civilization.

They have done that by bringing about an appar-ent conflict—Stevenson refers to the truly quaint materialism of our view of life—between these work-ing hypotheses of science, properly adopted as work-ing hypotheses, and the religious aspirations and ideals of the world in which we live.

One of the interesting things to me in reading, as well as a lay reader can, Professor Whitehead's *Science and the Modern World,* was the implication running through that volume that in the best inter-ests of science itself there must be a redefinition of fundamental working hypotheses; a recognition of their limitations and a questioning of their ultimate verity.

The trouble with that conflict is that the articulate philosophy of the scientific group, the part of what the scientist says that is understood by the ordinary educated man who is not a scientist, combines with the extraordinary effectiveness of the working hypotheses to give a false semblance of materialistic verity and finality.

When you add to the upset in the psychology of the more intelligent group resulting from these hypotheses, the effect, especially on that group, of the luxurious surroundings which have come from the applications of science and the materialistic temptations which follow in the wake of that mechanical luxury, the upset psychologically becomes even more serious.

Then add a third fact—that there is nothing in the biological history of the human race which prepares it for a rapidity in change of environment at all comparable with the changes in environment that have been taking place in the last one hundred years, in the last fifty years, or even in the last decade. There have been changes coming from the applications of power, the development of factories, mass production of commodities desired by large numbers of men, the development of fast mail, of fast transportation, the telephone, telegraph, and radio, indeed the whole gamut of things that surround our daily living with an entirely different physical and intellectual background than has ever existed before. All these changes have literally taken place within less than a century and there is nothing in our biological history that enables us to deal with that kind of rapidity in change.

Yet one still sees statements to the effect that these materialistic, mechanistic, working hypotheses are all that is needed for the maintenance and development of civilization in an orderly evolution. It is only just now that men are waking up to that truly naïve quality possessed by such a materialistic view of civilization. With all this mechanistic development, the masses of people are not happier than they were in a simpler type of community. These additions to human knowledge have not brought content, they have not only weakened the force of our religion, but they have strengthened the forces of discontent in all sorts and conditions of ways.

The curious fact is that the scientific group, composed of men idealistic to a degree when compared with other groups in our community, have let loose on the world powerful and revolutionary forces which were from the start, are now, and always will be, outside the control of the scientific group.

The amazing current of creative thinking in the scientific group in the last two hundred and fifty years has placed on other groups social responsibilities such as did not exist before in anything like the present intensity. Defining the present situation as a conflict between science and religion is far away from the constructive substance of things that must be done to bring the forces of religion back into touch with the community, with something of its old power and its old effectiveness. If we persist in considering the situation as a conflict with science, religion is doomed to failure, because evidences of superficial truth in the working hypotheses of science and of their real significance are easy to obtain and are becoming the property of many men. The forces of the religious group must not be spent in defending historic dogma against the attacks of sound working hypotheses and science. A redefinition of religious objectives—I would almost say a restoration of the sense of mystery and worship as the basis for a point of view leading to a saner social philosophy —is, it seems to me, essential.

It is from that standpoint, and in an effort to place the significance of those social problems which are phenomena of the industrial revolution, that I wish to speak. I desire to stress the necessity of working out the problems forced upon us by this stream of scientific thought, and to point out that the burden of solving these problems lies upon groups in the community other than the scientists and particularly upon the business group.

The same things that have brought stress into

the structure of our religion have brought stresses and strains into our social organism, and the control of those stresses and strains, and the possibility of correcting their consequences, lie almost entirely outside the group of men who have created the problem. In a community full of idealists we have to an amazing degree a materialistic civilization. The idealism is so out of focus, so ill defined, and social values are so little understood that our current sum total is materialism.

The problems brought about by the success of these working hypotheses of science are all human problems; they are not mechanical problems; they are not materialistic problems. They come back to the old problem faced by every group in human society. You may call it the need for a better social organization. You may call it the necessity of finding out how to live together on a better basis. For all these mechanical and materialistic developments have tended to make it less easy internationally, nationally, and individually for men to live together.

Now, for a moment, I wish to take a fresh point of view. Every human being must, if he is to have his own or his community's respect, do two things. He must work out his economic status, unless he be an invalid, a moron, or a tramp, and he must maintain his economic status as a member of the community. Then he must work out some correlation between this economic side and his position as a part of the social structure. If one throws the balance either way to the exclusion of the other, the basis for self-respect and community respect does not exist. There is an inevitable conflict in every man's position between his individualistic economic point of view and his social obligations and responsibilities.

If one considers some of the great groups of men who are the leaders in the community, it is relatively easy for some of those groups—the teacher, the doctor, the research man, the church man—to harmonize those two inconsistent elements, because each one of these groups makes its living by working upon social problems. The economic side works out through the exercise of the social function, and in these cases there are relatively few moral issues that arise out of the conflict. Such issues exist of course in greater or less numbers for every man, but they are relatively less important for those groups than for other groups in the community.

For example, the legal group is constantly struggling with moral issues. There is hardly a part of the day's work that does not involve moral issues of extreme complexity. And that is likewise true of business. The differences between law and business, or some of the differences, are, however, worth mentioning.

So long as the lawyer was the sound counsellor of

his local community, the sage of his town, the adviser of those in trouble about their problems of living, the representative of his community in the larger social outlooks, so long as such was his position, there was little difference between his situation and that of the doctor and teacher, because the making of his living was to such a man as much an incident as it is to the men in the other groups of which I have spoken. That I conceive to have been the typical situation in the law from the Revolutionary period, when the legal profession of this country really started, to some such period as 1890. You cannot fix a date. But that situation has completely changed, and it has changed for a very interesting reason. The legal profession has gone to work for the business man. It has lost its independent professional status to a large extent by organizing great city law offices which are really auxiliary functions of business. The leadership of the community does not come from the servant class and there is here a certain abdication of leadership from which the community is suffering severely. Social leadership passed from the legal profession when the ablest men in the profession, men of outstanding ability, no longer practised their law primarily with social objectives as the things that they wished to accomplish, but primarily to make it possible for some part of the business group to accomplish business ends.

If we are to get control of the social consequences of this stream of materialistic developments from scientific thought, there is grave need that the legal profession be brought back to a more definitely social point of view about its job. I am rather hopeless of accomplishing this unless at the same time there can be created something of the same point of view, the social point of view, in the business group. If that becomes possible, the two can certainly be worked out together, because as they now stand they are so intimately related.

In any event it is essential to the working out of the problems brought about during the period of the industrial revolution, largely by the work of the scientist, that the business group should, to a large extent, acquire this social point of view and subject itself to the same kind of influences which exist in any truly professional group.

If you stop to think of it, neither the church, nor medicine, nor the teacher, nor the lawyer is typically at the storm centre of these problems. The control of the consequences of scientific development—which never existed in the scientific group even when they were creating the problems—in the largest sense centres in the business group. The business group, by the accident of fate, is in control of the mechanisms of production and distribution and finance, which are the fields where the problems resulting from these scientific developments exist.

The whole structure of business in its present scope is entirely new to the world. It is just as much a creation of scientific development as is the dynamo. Outside of trade and banking there is little left of the old business structure. It is almost entirely a creation of scientific development in the last seventy-five years. This is not true of any other set of phenomena in our social structure except that to a considerable extent our international problems are the result of similar conditions. Since the business group, by the accident of fate, is in control of the things which the scientist has created and let loose on the world, and since out of these forces the critical human problems facing our civilization largely arise, if these problems are to be worked out I definitely believe it must be largely from inside that group.

Our experience with legislative panaceas as cure-alls for social problems in this American community is varied and extensive, and it is conclusive that the legislative panacea will not work. We must get deeper into the ethical and social foundations of men than can be accomplished by legislation to compel particular groups to do certain things. The maximum that the policeman can do to protect organized society has apparently been growing constantly less and less in the last few years, and if we are to solve the problems that arise out of scientific developments, a large part of the solution must come from the business group. But unfortunately the business group to-day is not prepared for that task. It lacks a sufficient number of broadly equipped men. It lacks the requisite intellectual background. Thus, heavy social responsibilities have been rested by this course of developments upon a group which by nothing in its past has been prepared to cope with these responsibilities.

The intellectual background necessary for a profession, the ordered body of knowledge brought about by the joint action of large groups of men in the effort to learn how to work together and live together better, does not exist as the foundation for the profession of business to-day. And yet the need exists there and to an extent that it does not exist in any other segment of our whole social structure.

I realize that there can be a very good superficial case made out at the moment to support the thesis that there are no great dangers facing our organized society. We are in a wave of conservatism, a reactionary wave which is at the moment very impressive, as apparent evidence that our troubles in this country are behind us. This results largely from the shocking consequences of revolution in Russia, the generally disturbed state of Europe, and from a certain war-weariness which has grown upon our people. We have apparently taken hold of all sorts of problems and decided that the only thing that interests us is the most conservative and reactionary point of view.

But take any date which gives you even a little depth of perspective—obviously you need not go back beyond 1900—and make a comparison, really try to analyze the latent forces in the community, and then realize how rapidly the strength of such things as I have mentioned, the Russian Revolution, the post-war weariness and that sort of thing, will disappear as effective ways of minimizing the feeling of discontent. Your conclusion about the situation will be that such things as these, aided by a last effort of the fundamentalists to retain the old foundations of religion among the masses of people, simply give us time to reconstruct our foundations of religion and time to build up the intellectual background in the business group, upon which there have been placed heavy responsibilities with little in the way of preparation for the sound assumption of those responsibilities.

All these forces of conservatism are useful only as they give time for those who are interested in the orderly and progressive but not revolutionary progress of the community, who are interested in the effort to improve conditions without the risks of changes so radical that they become destructive in their consequences, to work out constructive programmes. All of us who are in that frame of mind may well be very grateful that these slowing down forces are so strongly in operation at the moment, and we may well use every particle of energy that we have in the effort to build up intellectual and social points of view and ethical standards.

We should not seek panaceas, for there must be a patient effort to solve particular problems by a consideration of the particular reasons that created those problems. We must do these things from the standpoint of a more idealistic working philosophy, a desire to learn better how to live together. We must not of course forget the great help that can be gained in the effort to construct such social points of view within business by using to the extreme limit of its usefulness the motive of intelligent and far-sighted selfishness. That motive alone is insufficient, in my judgment, to handle the problems that force themselves upon the community—problems which must be solved if we are to avoid the dangers of a debacle. But while insufficient, it is the most effective immediate tool we have for solving many of the problems. From the standpoint of influencing men this motive assists greatly where it is possible to lengthen the time elements and get men to consider things institutionally and not from a momentary standpoint. This alone leads to socially sound handling of many problems.

Over and over again, as the years go by, young men come to me querying in their minds whether there exists in the field of business an adequate opportunity for the man who desires to contribute what he can to the working out of the fundamental

problems of organized human society. If I am right
that the great bulk of the critical problems which
arise out of the industrial revolution must be solved
largely through the activity of the business group,
then the challenge to young men which is involved
in business can be exceeded by the challenge in no
field. As a test of intellectual quality I believe to-day
there is no single field where so much must be expected as in business, and there is certainly no single
field where the risks of failure in the broadest sense
from a low quality of moral fibre are greater than
they are in business. The temptation to prefer the
economic side to the social side of the correlation
worked out by each individual is certainly no
greater anywhere than it will be in the business
field. The difficulty of building up the intellectual
background which will enable a man to function as
he would like to is certainly no greater anywhere
than it is in the business field.

If I am right, the continued progressive stability
of civilization depends to a large extent on the
question whether we can create in the business group
a really substantial body of men who are working
with a sense of social responsibility within business.
As a community we are thoroughly familiar with
the fact that education and charities are supported
lavishly by business men. Many men in business are
already working out a fine correlation between their
individual and their community obligations. But a

large percentage of them are not doing it in the way that seems to me to be essential for the solution of this particular group of problems. We need a new focusing on ethical and social objectives. Often we find a man who is harmonizing his life between those two elements consecutively. Mr. Munsey's is the last case prominently in mind, a man who waited until the end to give recognition to the social side in the sum total of his career and then did something of great significance. There are many other prominent names that will occur to you of men who first made a great success of business, applying the standards of their time, and after that turned themselves into great and constructive philanthropists.

Then there is the group of men who support our local politics and most of our local community interests, who practise their business with their right hands, and with their left hands, after hours, work out their social obligations.

But neither of those groups, essential as they are, is sufficient to work out the type of problems that seem to me to exist within this business field. We must find an increasing number of men who will do everything that they do in their business from a social standpoint, who will think within business in terms of social values. We have the greatest need at the present time that there should be a revival of interest in social values in the religious group. There must be a realization on the part of the re-

ligious group that in this field of business they, and
the great army of unchurched but interested idealists
who desire to contribute to the orderly evolution
of society, have not only a great opportunity but the
heaviest kind of responsibility to think in terms of
sound social values and to get away from that naïve
materialistic point of view which Stevenson men-
tions.

DISCUSSION OF QUESTIONS

Question : Would you suggest any means by which
such a stimulating address as this could be brought
to the attention of five thousand members of the
university instead of the fifty in this room, and
secondly, whether you could suggest any way of
university extension in this field by which the ideas
you have been discussing could be brought before
the members of the business community now engaged in the active practice of their profession, and
if so, whether it would be feasible to include the
editors of the community, who are becoming more
and more the mouthpiece of the business interests ?

A striking example of what you referred to as the
materialistic point of view in social questions came
to my attention in the attitude of the editor of *The
Herald* toward Governor Smith's housing proposition
in New York. The entire interest in the discussion
of this matter seemed to be dictated by the fear that
the speculative real estate interests might in some

way suffer from the competition of any state co-
operation in the housing problem, rather than by a
recognition of the shocking social conditions which
have existed since the Tenement House Commission
made its report in 1901, and are likely to exist for
one hundred and twenty-five years more under the
present system and at the present rate of demolition of these unsanitary tenements.

Professor Donham: A man who goes into university teaching as a career deliberately makes a
partial type of religious vow, which is that he will
devote his attention to working with young men in
the hope of influencing them in their period of activity fifteen or twenty-five years later, rather than
turn himself into an immediate propagandist. I do
not believe the two things can be combined. Something can be done constantly, and certainly we always owe it to our profession to criticise constructively and to suggest constructively when and as we
can, but the great bulk of our accomplishment, I
think, will be through making possible the better
training of young men as the years go by. In other
words, I am avoiding the publicity problem and
passing it back.

Question: Do you think a redefinition of business
success embodying the element of social usefulness
is highly desirable to promote the social viewpoint?

Professor Donham: I am asked whether I think
a redefinition of business success embodying the

element of social usefulness is desirable to promote the social viewpoint. I very definitely do. One of the things that business education suffers from is the curious historic fact, not entirely unshared in our university communities, that the so-called learned professions are considered to be proper hoppers into which to throw young men of quality, but that the business hopper is thought of as reserved for sons who are not really quite up to the other jobs. I find frequently the feeling expressed that of course John did not go into law because he is not intellectual and so, "Shall we send him to the business school?"

But just think of what that means. A large part of the low ethical standards of certain of our racial groups has come unquestionably from centuries of oppression, from centuries passed under a hostile atmosphere. The merchant class in Japan during the centuries that it was oppressed by the Samurai class, attained a world-wide reputation for having the lowest ethical standards, a situation which Bishop Roots recently told me has been very largely changed within a brief period of twenty-five years through the constructive work of the higher commercial schools of Japan.

We certainly need a wide-spread community belief in the social importance of the responsibilities and problems faced by the business group and at the same time we need an entirely different and discriminating sense of the values which go into success.

The job of the man in the street in relation to the problems of which I have been talking is largely that of creating the atmosphere out of which the leadership necessary to solve the problems may come, because the type of leadership which is exerted by the leader is determined by the attitude of the tribe. To-day, to a shockingly large extent, our test is the dollar sign—that man makes a business success who makes X dollars or appears to have made X dollars. We should rather hold that the man makes a business success who does a real and constructive social and community job and at the same time preserves his economic status. Of course, the man who does not pay his bills—unless he has the alibi of invalidism—who does not clothe his wife and children, has little possibility of accomplishing really effective social service in any important sense.

Question: How would you reconcile the profit incentive in business with the social point of view that you mentioned?

Professor Donham: You cannot entirely. That is what I meant by pointing out that the motive of intelligent selfishness will carry you a long way but will not carry you the full distance. The motive of intelligent selfishness covers many definite anti-social results, and we have to find ways of controlling the opinions of the mass of men and bringing them to recognize that certain things are not being done.

Getting control of all these forces is not a simple

problem. It took two centuries for the English-speaking part of the race to get control of credits, of bills, mortgages, notes, and so forth, to the point that they ceased to be weapons of oppression of the most serious sort. The problems growing out of the industrial revolution are far more complicated. We face the necessity of socializing the results of science. We cannot depend entirely on the motive of intelligent selfishness, because intelligent selfishness as the sole motive would lead me to burn down my house; it would lead a bank officer to get his customer into a position where he could take toll from his transactions; it leads to many definitely anti-social results.

Intelligent selfishness will go a long way and is one of the major incentives, but I am one of those who believe that there is a real incentive in the desire to do something of social value in the community. If you can couple with that incentive, which I believe to be a definite and powerful incentive, the additional reward which comes from discriminating approval from those fellow men whose approval one likes to have, the two combine to make a really powerful incentive. I am not attempting to put this talk this afternoon on a plane so far out of touch with the facts of life that, to accomplish any of the things I am seeking to accomplish, it is necessary to assume the ability to make the whole race altruistic. That never has been and never will be done by the

theories of men. I believe that we can, by using the
forces of intelligent selfishness, by building up an
intelligent background for social points of view, by
demonstrating the inherent objectionable and unsatisfactory results that come from many things because
they are anti-social, do a great deal, and we can add
to these forces other motives and incentives which
are on a higher moral plane.

Question: What do you think of Rotary Clubs
and similar organizations in their attempt to make
the business man sensitive to his social responsibilities?

Professor Donham: One of the difficult things in
the whole problem is that in building this intellectual background for sound social decision of problems it is essential that we break down the tradition
which is so wide-spread in business groups, that each
man's business is a thing to itself and that he has
nothing to learn from any other group in the community.

One of the forces definitely at work in breaking
down that insular theory and creating a common
basis for theory is the growth of organizations like
the Rotary Club, and in that important sense I
think they have much social significance.

RELIGION IN LAW AND POLITICS

WILLIAM B. MUNRO

RELIGION has been one of the most powerful forces in moulding the course of social evolution. It has had a profound influence upon the development of law, political theory, and international relations. Without this influence, continuously exerted, it seems certain that some of the political and social institutions which we value highly at the present day could never have been evolved at all, or, at any rate, would never have taken their present form.

Law, in the first place, owes much to religion. Law had its origin in religion. Among primitive peoples there grew up the idea of taboo, that is, of frowning upon certain actions which were deemed to be offensive to the tribal gods. Thus first developed the rule of tribal custom, of custom enforced by the public opinion of the community, which later crystallized into the rule of a common law. Among primitive races there was no conception of law in the modern sense, that is, of rules made by man on his own initiative, by his own authority, and with man-made sanctions behind them. All law, in the earliest stages, was of supernatural origin. It was revealed, not enacted. Hence it was not within the power of man to change.

This conception of law persisted for a long time in human history; it continued even among nations which had attained a considerable measure of civilization. There was no distinction between laws human and laws divine, or between spiritual precept and the law of the land, for both had the same origin, the same sanctity, and the same punitive authority for their enforcement. In the Book of Leviticus, for example, we find the people enjoined to certain purely religious observances and admonished against sharp business practices, with no intimation that the one was in any way a matter of more strictly secular concern than the other.

Ye shall make an offering by fire unto the Lord every seven days.

Just balances and just weights shalt thou have, for I am the Lord, your God.

The Jews made no clear distinction between morals and law, nor did the Greeks, despite their marked advance over all preceding peoples in the practice of government. They did not attain to the conception of law as a body of rules controlled by the wishes of the people. We hear much about Athenian "democracy" and the mass-meetings of the citizens; but the Athenian citizen had no part in the making of the laws which regulated his daily life. The laws of Athens were a legacy from on high. They were committed to writing, once for all, by Solon, and

hence were not subject to change at the mere ca-
price of a mass-meeting. Changes in the laws of
Athens, by way of interpretation, could only be
made by the sacred Court of the Areopagus, which
spoke the mind of the gods.

It was the Romans who first effected the divorce
of law from religion. It was they who first seized
upon and put into practice the idea that while religious precepts might be fixed and immutable, the
ordinary day-to-day relations between man and
man should be governed by rules which could be
changed without any flavor of sacrilege whenever
the need might arise. The Romans brought about
this separation and by so doing made the greatest
single contribution to legal progress that has ever
been made by any people: *Tu regere imperio populos,
Romane, memento!* When law cut itself loose from
revealed religion, and became the enacted handiwork of man, it was then, and not until then, that
any real progress in the orderly evolution of law as a
science became possible. Christian Rome developed,
side by side, a great religious system and a great
system of secular jurisprudence. She did this because
her people separated the two. The state became a
community of law and politics, the church a community of religion and worship.

But although religion and law thus parted company, this does not mean that religion ceased to have
an influence upon law. On the contrary, the influence

of religious doctrines on both the substance and form of the law was very great during the Roman imperial period and even after the fall of Rome. Through the earlier Middle Ages the Christian religion was the one common bond among the peoples of Western Europe. It provided the one philosophy of law and order that lifted its head above the chaos. It is to the Christian church and its hierarchy that we mainly owe the preservation of those enlightened principles of jurisprudence which Rome developed and which form the groundwork of the civil law in half the countries of the globe to-day. Had it not been for the Christian church and its bishops, its abbots, and its monastic scholars there is little doubt that all this would have perished from the earth.

The mediæval churchman was a jurist as well as a theologian. He was learned in the canon law of his church, which in turn was canon law. It was Roman law adapted to the needs of an ecclesiastical establishment. The churchman often served as a judge in the feudal courts, for he was the only man in the community who had enough education to perform that function. When the kings and dukes and barons of Western Europe departed on the great crusades against the infidel it was the bishops and priors of the church who took over the administration of justice in their absence. Naturally they inoculated the laws of the land with their own high standards of right and justice. They tried to bring the legal customs and procedure of the community into line with the teachings of Christianity.

Let me illustrate the scope and importance of the churchman's influence upon the laws and legal system of mediæval England by reference to something that is already well appreciated by every lawyer, the origin and growth of the rules of chancery, or equity as we now call it. Back in the days of the Plantagenets the English king had a legal adviser known as the chancellor. He was the keeper of the royal conscience, and it was to him that the king referred the various petitions which came from individuals asking for redress which the ordinary courts of the realm could not or would not give. This chancellor was always a bishop or other high official of the church, with some knowledge of canon law, and presumably with sound ideas as to what constituted true justice between man and man. At any rate he began to lay down rules as to the scope and methods of the royal intervention in judicial matters and eventually these were elaborated by the chancellor into a body of jurisprudence known as the rules of chancery or equity.

So equity, in its origin and early growth, owed everything to religion and religionists. It owed both its content and its form. It represented an attempt to supplement the faulty handiwork of man, in the making and enforcement of the ordinary laws, by rules and remedies which conformed more closely to those precepts that good churchmen preached and which some of them practised. Had it not been that the Christian religion already provided, in those early days, a code of ethics which the chancellors could use as their guide, it is difficult to see how the development of equity in its present form could have been accomplished. Religion rendered its first service to law by cutting adrift, its second by aiding the development of what has become a mellowing influence on the rigidity of law.

There is a third and continuing influence which religion has exerted on the law. The student of institutional evolution has been too prone to look upon religion as a thing apart, a thing which is entitled to its day in court, that is, one day in seven. He has not always appreciated the steady, silent, unobtrusive pressure which religion exerts upon men and women during every hour of the other six days. "How can you have order in the state without religion?" Napoleon Bonaparte once asked that question and it was worth asking. We speak of the courts as the sanction of the law. We sometimes speak of them as the only sanction. We occasionally seem to go on the assumption that the fear of fine or imprisonment is the only thing that keeps people from violating the law. Were that the case our laws of whatever sort would be chiefly honored in the breach. Behind the courts are the power of public opinion, the influence of tradition, the innate sense of what is right. These things, which the religion of the people have a large part in moulding, are the fundamental sanction of the law. The conviction that wrong-doing will be punished and righteousness rewarded both in this world and in the world to come —that conviction among millions of men is the most powerful of all the incentives to walking in the straight and narrow way. Let that conviction be destroyed and how far would judges and jails avail to stem iniquity? We say that "laws cannot be well enforced if they do not have public sentiment behind them." What we really mean is that laws have a very inadequate sanction unless buttressed by a popular sense of what is right, just, and moral.

The influence of religion upon government, that is, upon the structure and functions of the state, has been equally assertive, although political scientists have not always appreciated the fact. In the countries of the Orient it furnishes the chief clue to an interpretation of political history. This is because the Orient has not yet reconciled itself to a complete separation of church and state, of religion and politics. It was the acceptance of Christianity by the Occident that made such a separation possible there, for among all the great religions of the world Christianity is the only one that actually encourages the church and the state to pursue their respective activities independently. It is the only religion that has shown itself able to thrive and spread without assistance from any secular power, yes, even in the face of secular opposition.

Yet curiously enough, Christianity was by no means so regarded in its earliest days. The first Christians were looked upon as the harbingers of a political revolution; indeed they so regarded themselves. They expected the Messiah to create a new secular government, to overthrow the Roman oppressors of Israel, and to lead the chosen race to its manifest destiny. That is why James and John, the sons of Zebedee, were so much concerned as to who would be prime minister in the new government. They were out for the spoils of office, as not a few of their successors have been. It is not surprising that the Master should have had political ambitions attributed to him by unlettered followers, for the doctrine of the Kingdom of Heaven on Earth, which was the main teaching of Jesus, was not one that could easily be interpreted as he intended it to be. It is small wonder that the disciples understood it in the light of the old familiar ideas of earthly kingdoms and kings and crowns. Time and again, it is true, their Master told them that his kingdom was not of this world, that his throne was in the hearts of men, that he had not come to destroy but to fulfil. But their minds could not grasp the profound largeness of these ideals.

It remained for the Apostle to the Gentiles to give the new religion its proper orientation toward the state. It was he, more than all others, who clarified the attitude of the Christian church toward the powers that be. In his epistles to the Romans he went more than half way in his proffer of the olive branch to the civil authorities, thus opening the way for a complete reconciliation between Christianity and imperialism, religion and patriotism, the higher law and the laws of man. If the Christian church had not utilized this Pauline philosophy to mollify the revolutionary teachings of the gospels, it is difficult to see how Christianity could have effected its conquest of Rome, the Roman Empire, and consequently of the entire Occident. The great Latin imperialism would not have surrendered to any sect of civil seditioners.

As it was, however, religion and government were able to form an entente by the terms of which they could be mutually helpful although dissociated and independent. When the Christian church grew strong enough, with a Pope as her visible head and with Rome for her capital, the idea of temporal rulership was again brought to the front. There was a shift from Paul to Peter for a justification of the revived ambition. But fortunately the church never succeeded in reducing the state to subordination and the dualism outlived the Middle Ages. During the past four hundred years it has strengthened and to-day the doctrine of a free church in a free state is accepted by nearly all the enlightened nations of the earth. It is not without significance, moreover, that the nations which earliest and most fully accepted this principle are the ones which have made the most striking progress in the practice of free government.

This separation of civil from ecclesiastical rulership has had one very far-reaching result. It made religious toleration possible. A certain measure of somewhat reluctant toleration is practicable, and is sometimes accorded, even where the church and state are unified; but a full and free measure of it is hardly conceivable. Religious persecution, as a matter of history, has been most rigorous where the civil power is dominated by ecclesiastical functionaries. It was so in Spain during the period of the Inquisition; it was so in France under "the Most Christian kings," and it was equally so in Puritan Massachusetts. But full religious toleration came with the separation of the church from politics; it came earliest in America because there the separation first took place. Religious toleration is probably the greatest of all America's contributions to democracy.

Now you may be surprised to hear me call religious toleration a "contribution to democracy," for you have probably not thought of it as having even a remote relation to the workings of secular government. But it has had a very direct and influential relation. In this way: the successful functioning of democracy postulates above all other things a willingness to respect the other man's point of view. It assumed that there will be differences of political opinion and belief, that those who hold diverging political opinions will be organized into political parties, each with its own programme or creed, and that each of these organizations shall readily tolerate the existence of the others. A democracy which is not based on these postulates falls far short of being a democracy at all. Toleration is an absolute essential in any democracy worthy of the name.

But how can a spirit of political tolerance be developed in any country? There is only one way— by long training in forbearance. It is not in the nature of men to be tolerant. Toleration is an acquired trait. It can be more easily developed, as history seems to show, in the field of religious opinion than in that of opinion relating to the social order. There are thousands of people in this country to-day who will readily concede a man's right to be a Catholic or a Protestant as he may choose, but not his right to be a Communist or even a Socialist. At any rate, toleration in religion usually comes first and paves the way. When people have learned to be tolerant in one field of thought it becomes easier to broaden their attitude in others. I do not contend that religious toleration has been solely responsible for that political tolerance which marks the progressive democracies of to-day, but I believe that it has had a large influence in promoting the latter.

Christianity is of all religions the most readily reconcilable with both the theory and the practice of democratic government not only for this reason, but for another, namely, for the emphasis which it places upon human equality and on the obligations of the individual. The teachings of Christ with respect to human equality and brotherhood must have given a rude shock to those who heard them. Here were disciples and followers of the Jewish race, the chosen race, with an intense racial patriotism. For generations they had regarded themselves as the holders of a first mortgage on the true religion. They were accustomed to render thanks that they were not as other men. And now to be told by a Nazarene teacher that as a race they were no better than any other, and that the true religion was not their exclusive patrimony—it must have come with a very discordant sound.

But if there is any one thread that runs like a golden strand through the teachings of this Nazarene, and indeed through the whole body of Christian doctrine, it is the principle that there should be no purely artificial gradations among men, that the true worth of every man is determinable by his own efforts and actions, not by his inheritance, nativity, or allegiance. And what a great, though ofttimes invisible influence, this doctrine of equality and individual obligation has had in moulding the social order! Its importance would be hard to overestimate. The principle of individual responsibility lies at the very basis of our whole economic structure.

People sometimes wonder why the Christian church does not take kindly to socialism. Socialist writers, like Mr. H. G. Wells, are at pains to point out that the founder of Christianity taught straight socialism to his disciples—good Marxian doctrine nineteen hundred years before Karl Marx was born. Where, indeed, can you find a better socialist sermon than is contained in the parable of the laborers in the vineyard? "To each according to his needs and not according to his labors." (I have noticed, however, that the socialists do not seem to be so keenly interested in the parable of the talents, for its implications as to the profiteering capitalist are not exactly to their liking.) In any event the socialists are fond of saying that Christianity has drifted far away from the teachings of its Founder, has developed a ritualism and an ecclesiastical organization wholly foreign to its spirit, and has become associated through this organization with large accumulations of worldly wealth. That, they say, is the reason why the Christian church (especially the Roman Catholic branch of it) has become the foe of socialism. In the United States the strongest, best-organized, and most unrelenting enemy of socialism, communism, and syndicalism is the Catholic Church.

It is the capitalistic system's front line entrenchment. It is the Verdun which socialism has not been able to pass.

But the hostility of the Catholic Church to socialism (in Europe as well as in the United States) does not arise from the fact that it is rich, or has a hierarchy, or follows a ritual. It is not because this ancient church has drifted away from the teachings of the gospels. On the contrary, it is because the church holds firm to a fundamental principle of the apostolic religion in all its implications. That principle, as I have said, is the principle of individual (as opposed to collective) responsibility. If there is any outstanding tenet of Christianity it is that righteousness is entitled to be rewarded and that unrighteousness entails punishment. It is by the individual's own faith and works that he must win the crown. All collectivist teachings are at the opposite pole from this. They do not enjoin the individual to determine, by his own exertions, the nature and extent of his reward. They assure him a reward according to his needs, not according to his deserts. Christianity places the responsibility on the individual; all forms of collectivism place it on the group. These two points of view are impossible to reconcile. Those who hold them must be foes.

There are many other ways in which religion has exerted an influence on the growth of law, government, and the modern social order. If time permitted,

it could be shown, for example, that the whole system of representative legislation grew out of the
monastic convocations and church synods of the
Middle Ages. Every jurist knows, moreover, how
greatly the evolution of international law has been
influenced by religious history. Many years ago I
was offered a position as a teacher of history in a
small sectarian college; but the offer was coupled
with a stipulation that "we do not want history
taught without a Providence in it." There was no
need to impose any such condition, because nobody
can teach history, or understand history, without a
Providence in it. The human race in all the ages has
been actuated, inspired, restrained, or otherwise
influenced, by a belief in some kind of a Providence,
and the motives which influence men are an integral
part of history.

LAW, POLITICS, AND RELIGION

ROSCOE POUND

As it stands upon your programme, the subject is indeed ambitious—"Law, Politics, and Religion; the Church and State, religion in practice of law, legislative and judicial pressure from the Church." Here is a wide range, reminding one of the Roman jurist's definition of jurisprudence as the "knowledge of things divine and human, the science of the just and the unjust." It suggests the mode of treatment adopted by the editor who, when called on to write upon Chinese metaphysics, read in the Encyclopædia Britannica under China and under metaphysics and combined his information. There is much temptation to say something about law, something less about politics, and still less about religion; this order, I fear, representing my competency to speak with some assurance in those respective fields.

I cannot undertake anything so ambitious as your programme demands. What I shall try to say has to do with law and politics in their relation to religion, and religion in its relation to law and politics. Moreover, by politics, let me say, I mean politics in the sense of the science of government, not politics in the sense of a profession or an amusement connected with the affairs of government.

If we begin down at the bottom—and those of you who have been listening to me in Criminal Law know that I like to have you begin at that point, if you can—I suppose if we begin at the bottom, we begin with the idea of human civilization. Not that we begin at the bottom from the standpoint of religion when we choose that starting-point. But in dealing immediately with law and government, as phenomena which we may study, no matter what our individual religious or metaphysical or economic standpoint may be, since we must live together harmoniously while holding diverse and conflicting opinions, we may find a common ground for all of us, at the bottom of what we may surely hold in common, by beginning with the idea of civilization. Human civilization endures. A continually increasing mastery of external nature and of human nature, an increasing control over external nature and over human nature, a raising of human powers toward their highest possible unfolding—this goes on while institutions decay and governments decay and every monument of human activity decays. And when we examine this phenomenon of human civilization we see that it rests upon social control. It rests on a control of the activities of each of us through the pressure of his fellows; through the pressure of the conditions of living with his fellows.

In the beginning, social control is an undifferentiated something out of which religion, morals (in the sense of the moral opinion of one's fellow men), and law emerge and become differentiated as the three conspicuous forms of control or agencies of control in the society of to-day. In a primitive society, social control is undifferentiated. There is an undifferentiated mass of religious rites, precepts of ethical custom, traditional customs of popular action, traditional wisdom of the kin group, traditional moral ideals of the kin group, and something that is beginning to be what to-day we should call law.

It is interesting to notice that as far as Greek thinking had advanced in other respects, much as the Greeks had done for the science of politics, the Greeks really had not differentiated law in the sense in which we understand it in the maturity of law to-day. The Greeks used the one word *nomos*, which we translate law, for this undifferentiated social control; so much so that in a dialogue called The Minos, attributed to Plato, which, however, I suppose we must concede to be somewhat subsequent to Plato—and that in itself is significant—the whole point of the discussion is this undifferentiated mass of agencies of social control called by that one word *nomos*. Socrates in that dialogue is reported as putting to his interlocutor whether a cook book is not the law of cooking. There are the customs of cooks, the wisdom of ages of cooks, set forth in that cook book; why isn't it law? He puts to his interlocutor the question, "Why isn't the gardener's manual a law book?" The customs of gardeners, the rules that have been proved by experience to be expedient in the work of gardeners, are set forth in that book. How does that differ from the book in which are set forth the customs of those who have ruled the city, the wisdom of those who have ruled the city in the past, the precepts that experience has shown as a result of ruling the city in the past, which are set forth in the form of sections of a code?

He puts along with those things religious rites, and speaks of the difference between the Greeks and the Carthaginians, in that the latter had the practice of human sacrifice; and perhaps the significant thing to remember is that this very human sacrifice was the origin of what we have come to think of to-day as capital punishment. The impious offender who offended the gods by his misdeeds, whose presence in the community threatened that community with the wrath of the gods, was sacrificed by the high priest of the city or of the people, to the offended gods, so that Socrates was not so far afield when, if it were he, he included this rite of human sacrifice among the Carthaginians in his term law. At any rate, it was a mode of social control; it was an item in that undifferentiated social control of primitive society.

Law, then, is a highly specialized form of social control, a social control through the force of politically organized society applied in the public administration of justice. Politics is the science of one specialized form of social control.

It is worth while to notice that law, in the sense of law as lawyers understand it, begins just at the point when it begins to be secularized, when it begins to be set off from religion. In the beginnings of Roman law the law was a tradition known to the pontifical college. If one wanted to know the law he had to learn it at the feet, so to speak, of the priest, who knew it and passed it down as an oral tradition in the pontifical college. The beginnings of law in the lawyer's sense, at Rome, were when the first plebeian pontifex maximus began to give audiences in public. When one wanted to know what the law was he could consult the pontifex maximus at a public consultation where students could be present and take notes, and thus there came to be in time a professional tradition. A class of professional lawyers grew up. The administration of justice and the advising of litigants ceased to be a priestly function and became a professional function of a profession of lawyers.

You could show the same thing—if there were time and it were worth while to do so—in the history of our own law. The decisive point in the history of our Anglo-American legal system was really when in the twelfth century the administration of justice passed definitely from the courts of the Church to the courts of the king, and a legal profession practising in the king's courts grew up to advise litigants, to argue before judges, and ultimately to sit upon the bench.

But there was something lost in that professionalization of the law, even if at the same time there was something gained. What was gained was what is always gained in any division of labor. By and large, men do things better when they are doing one thing at a time. The man who is devoting his whole heart and his whole energies to one thing is likely to do it better than if his energies are scattered among a number of things. On the other hand, for a time there was a loss in this definite setting off of law from the rest of social control. As a first stage in legal development, after law is set apart from morals, religion, ethical customs, religious rites, the primitive tribal taboos—after law is set apart from them we get a stage which I have been in the habit of calling the strict law. And in that stage of the strict law the law is so conscious of itself as being something set apart, it is so conscious of itself as being something specialized, that it can for a time ignore the moral aspects of human conduct, the moral aspects of human relations. The strict law asks simply one question—does the case presented to the judge come within the four walls, so to speak, of the legal compartment, the remedial compartment that has been made for it? In that aspect it would not matter that it was the greatest wrong in the world, if it did not come squarely within the letter of the appointed remedy. Also if a case does come within the letter of the appointed remedy, the result of applying the remedy may be a gross wrong; but as to those things the strict law is utterly indifferent.

One of the classical cases is the doctrine that obtained in our law until equity interfered with it, that if a man had given his bond under seal, acknowledging that he owed another a sum of money, and he paid that sum of money but he did not take back a formal release under the creditor's seal, the court would compel him to pay that money once more, because the only way known to the strict law by which the obligation of that bond could be dissolved was by the formal release under seal.

After a time men began to demand something more of the strict law than what it was set up for, namely, to give a certain order and certainty and system to the application of remedies through the force of politically organized society. With the development of moral ideals, with the growth of society under a political régime, men expect these precepts—and they have a right to expect them—to accord in their results with the results of the moral thinking, the moral sentiment of the time and place. For example, in the beginnings of the Roman law the strict law was that when a man died his property devolved upon those persons who were members of his household at the time of his death. But when his daughter married she went out of his household into the household of her husband or her husband's father. If a grandson was born he was not of any kin to his mother's father; he was of kin to his father's father, so that it might happen that if a Roman died and left no members of his household at his death, his property would devolve not upon his grandson through his daughter but upon all those persons at Rome who happened to bear the same clan name and, therefore, theoretically, were assumed to be related through a common ancestor. At a time when those Roman clans were made up of slaves made free by the members of the clans, you can see how repugnant that was to the moral sentiment of the people.

And so there comes a new stage, by way of reaction, in which there is an infusion of moral ideas into the law, a great liberalizing stage, which we see both in the Roman law and in the history of our own law; marked in the Roman law by the period of what is called natural law, and marked in our law by the rise of the court of equity or court of chancery. The point I want to bring home to you about that stage of legal development is that the controlling factor in that stage really is religion.

Now that might seem a bit difficult to prove in the Roman law; and yet I feel perfectly justified in asserting that the Stoic philosophy, which was the controlling factor in that great liberalizing era of

Roman legal history, was essentially a religion. It was the religious phase of it, the religious aspect of it, that was controlling in this liberalization of the Roman law through natural law. It was the idea of duty, the idea that there were certain duties devolving upon us outside of the law, beyond the law, and that it was the business of the law to give effect to those duties through its remedies, through its machinery of justice, that was the great liberalizing agency in that stage of the Roman law. The controlling idea was one of good faith, of the duty to do, not what the strict law demanded, but what good faith demanded of a reasonable man in such a connection.

Under the circumstances of the case, in view of what the parties had done and in view of what they had undertaken, what did good faith demand? The formula which the Roman prætor turned over to the judge truly displayed a magnificent confidence in the rectitude of that judge—"whatever in good faith the defendant ought to pay, to do, or perform for the plaintiff, in that condemn him." It trusted to his knowledge of what good faith demanded. And how was he to know what that was through anything that the law told him? The law told him to enforce a moral ideal, an ideal of the dictates of good faith in the given situation.

This stage of infusion of morals into law is superseded by a stage represented in the law of to-day by the nineteenth century and represented in the Roman law by the era from Diocletian to Justinian, in which we go back for a season somewhat to the ideas of the strict law; a stage in which perhaps we do not ignore morals but we contrast law and morals; a stage in which we cease to borrow from religion, in which we cease consciously to be affected by religion and yet, I hope to be able to show you in a moment, are profoundly affected by religion in what we actually do.

How does religion affect the law? How does it affect the administration of justice in this stage of the maturity of law? Well, there are two respects in which it does that. On the one hand, in such a stage of the maturity of law, just as in the strict law, we are not unlikely to get situations in which particular legal precepts, particular policies of administration, particular policies of legislation come into conflict with profound moral ideas, come into conflict perhaps with a deep-seated religious sentiment of some portion of the community. Let us remember a classical example in our own legal history—the case of the Fugitive Slave Law. There were before the Civil War many God-fearing men whose consciences told them not to be concerned in the enforcement of that law, told them even to resist the enforcement of that law.

How is law going to deal with a situation of that kind? Perhaps the law can only deal with it in one way. The law can only deal with it by doing its best through legal machinery, to give effect to the precept in spite of the opposition of those whose consciences lead them even to resist.

But certainly the political point of view must be different. From the standpoint of politics we are compelled to consider what we are to do when we are brought face to face with a conflict of that sort, and legal and political philosophers, from the time of Socrates, have found difficulty with what is indeed a very difficult question. On the one hand it is obvious that social control is at the very bottom of our civilization. It is obvious that by and large the legal order deserves and must have our respect, and after all, legal precepts are a good part of that legal order. When men have their eyes turned upon the security of social institutions, the result usually is a doctrine of passive obedience. Let us remember it is not entirely an accident that the doctrine of the divine right of kings or the doctrine of passive obedience was at its height in a society which had broken over the authoritarian régime of the Middle Ages, a society in which men had insisted upon the principle of private judgment, a society in which men insisted that the individual conscience was to be the measure of things.

Now, suppose you had to temper that doctrine by another. When you look at it from another standpoint you get such discussions as those which you forget to-day, but which are to be found in every elementary book on American law of a hundred years ago, namely, discussions of the so-called right of revolution. If you have on the one hand, in such a society, a doctrine of passive obedience, you are sure to have on the other hand a doctrine of the right of revolution. And the problem of reconciling them is not easy. It is one of the difficult problems of both politics and jurisprudence to determine how we are to fix some practicable line between, on the one hand the individual moral and social life and, on the other hand, the security of social institutions.

How are we going to do that? Well, I suppose most problems of politics and certainly most problems of jurisprudence get down at bottom to this question of values. In administration we have got to put values on competing policies. When you are called on to vote at an election your problem is to put values upon the policies urged on the one hand or on the other. In legislation the problem is one of values. There are conflicting class interests and conflicting group interests. Measures are urged which trench upon one person's activities in the interests of the activities of some one else, and you are called on to put values upon the claims of each. The judge in the every-day administration of justice has that same problem. He is called upon to put values upon the conflicting claims of the parties to the controversy, so as to be able to say what claims he will recognize, within what limits, and whether his machinery of giving effect to them will destroy more values than it will save.

How is he to judge of those values? That has been one of the debated problems of philosophical jurisprudence. In the nineteenth century, on the whole, we thought that we should value them in terms of the maximum of individual free self-assertion, that we should give effect to that claim or secure that interest which would promote the greatest amount of free individual self-assertion. To-day we are trying to substitute for that all sorts of theories.

One theory is that of the social utilitarian—Which one involves the greatest social advantage? Another school says we should think in terms of the ideals of the epoch—Which of these claims conforms to the ideals of the epoch? Another group says we should think in terms of civilization—Which one of them conduces the more to the maintenance or the furtherance of civilization? So, I could go on with many theories.

After all, doesn't it get down to this: Isn't what all of them are trying to do simply to weigh this policy, to weigh these interests, and to value them in terms of the highest good?

And where are we going to get our conception of the highest good? I will leave it to the teacher of ethics where we ought to get that conception, but I am perfectly sure, as I study legal history, where we do get such conceptions. We get them in large part and we always have gotten them in large part from religion. If any one doubts that, he has only to compare the solution of these questions, among different peoples in different times in different places, with the religious thought of the time and place.

There is another aspect of this matter that requires to be spoken of quite as much as the one upon which I have just been speaking, and that is the relation of religion to the ideal element in law. Now, in what I have been saying about values, I could speak both about politics and about law. I am not competent to speak about the ideal element in politics, but I do know that the ideal element in law is by and large the most important element. We think of law commonly as a body of precepts, something like a municipal code of ordinances. I am afraid some of you might think of it as you would of the football rules or the army regulations. But indeed that is the least part of law. The least enduring part of law, at any rate, is this body of precepts. These precepts change rapidly. They are like the hero of the freshman's theme who made himself "immortal for a great many years." Their average life, I suppose, is not much more than fifty years. Beyond that time, if they stay in the books, they are pretty sure to become obsolete by social and economic change.

Another element in the law is the art of the

lawyer's craft, the traditional art of developing and applying the precepts and of using them as materials for the decision of cases; the art of finding the grounds of decision in the traditional precepts.

The third and most enduring and, in the end, most important, is a body of traditional ideals taken as authoritative by the profession, by which the interpretation and the development of legal rules is governed and legal materials are given shape. Take, for instance, a precept that is of every-day application at Washington, that no state shall deprive any person of life, liberty, or property without due process of law. There is your precept. But if we had that precept and nothing more it would be pretty hard to know what to do with it. It does not tell us much. It is fairly easy to say what life, liberty, and property are, although there have been differences over both the words liberty and property. But, what is due process of law? The words do not tell us anything. Our historical legal technic tells us something. It tells us that it is a phrase going back through legislation of Edward III to Magna Charta. Well, that is something. And through that bit of history and our mode of handling historical materials through our traditional technic, we know that it means that no state is to deprive a person of life, liberty, or property arbitrarily and unreasonably. That is something more. But where do we get our idea of what is unreasonable? The law does not tell us what is reasonable or unreasonable. The legislature of a state says a thing is reasonable, and the court is called on to hold that it is unreasonable. How is it going to determine that? Why, the only way it can determine it and the way it does determine it is to have recourse to certain ideals of what organized society is about, of what the state is for, of what social control is trying to achieve, and of what legal precepts ought to be in the light of those ideals and what, therefore, it is reasonable for a state to do and what is unreasonable.

If any one doubts, he needs but to go back a bit, so as to get beyond the economic and social and political prejudices of to-day, and see how such provisions have been applied. I know of nothing more interesting as an example than a decision of one of the great states of the Southern Confederacy during the Civil War, at a time when the very political life of the Confederacy was at stake. When a confederate conscription act was before the Supreme Court of Georgia that court decided that the doctrine of state's rights was a part of an ideal of reasonable government and that any legislation that ran counter to the doctrine of state's rights was unconstitutional, without the help of any constitutional provision anywhere. That is because that political ideal was a part of the court's apparatus for the decision of that question.

Where do we get these ideals? In part, of course,

they are traditional. They are received. They enter into our professional education through our reading of the great books of law, the text-books, and the judicial decisions. But they change from time to time. Although they change slowly, they do change. If any one doubts that, he has but to read the writings of Lord Coke, the oracle of our law, who wrote in the whole spirit of the Middle Ages, with the ideal before him of the relationally-organized society of the Middle Ages, and then look at the books of to-day, where the ideal is the competitive industrial society, the society of competitive economic activity, in which we have been brought up.

What is the controlling agency in the construction, the shaping, and changing of these ideals? There, again, it is palpable that it is religion. I will give you two examples and that must be enough. I have already spoken of the influence of Stoicism on the Roman law. Stoicism was able to have that influence precisely because it gave shape and content to the ideal element. But we have even a better example in our own law. In the formative period of American law I think the controlling force was Puritanism. I believe that to be true both for American politics and for American law. The Puritan ideal was consociation, not subordination. As John Robinson says, "We are with one another, not over one another." The Puritan ideal of a willing covenant of conscious faith led him to think of the state as a political congregation. The ideal of private interpretation of the Scriptures, private, independent interpretation, led to the same idea with respect to law and government. To the Puritan the ultimate authority must be that things conform to the individual conscience. And if we Americans to-day are charged with being a bit lawless, we have come by it honestly. For generations it has been our habit to apply our individual judgment and conscience to political measures. If in the crowded world of to-day we need a little more passive obedience and a little less of the "right of revolution," we have to remember that passive obedience was not adapted to the pioneer conditions of our fathers and that the conditions that seem to call for a little more passive obedience have come on us rather suddenly.

The Puritan idea of consociation rather than subordination led American jurisprudence to be very slow to introduce any element of prevention or individualization; and the things that we conspicuously need in the administration of justice to-day are individualized application of legal precepts and the development of preventive justice.

The Puritan believed there ought to be a formula dictated in advance and that the magistrate ought to be able to do nothing but apply the exact measure of that precept. He objected to the doctrine of common-law misdemeanors worked out in the Star Chamber, and he objected to administrative individualization; and those are the very things which in the crowded urban industrial communities of to-day we are compelled to develop.

Well, what is the bearing of all this on anything that we have to do to-day and to-morrow? I think it is just this: I imagine that the stage that I have called the maturity of law has pretty well run its course. In one way or another, all recent writers on the science of law are going back to a certain subordination of jurisprudence to ethics, of law to morals, and are saying that after all this specialized social control through the law is an agency for giving effect in a certain limited field, to what as a whole is in the great field of morals. It is evident that we are entering or are about to enter upon a new era of legal growth, and in that era I undertake to say, exactly as in eras of growth in the past, religion is certain to be a great factor and, very likely, a controlling factor. For through religion we shall get a definite content for our ideas of value. Through religion we shall get some tangible conception of a highest good; and that ultimately is what we are using for our scale of values. Through religion we shall give a definite content to our ideals of the social, the political, and the legal order, and thus our picture of what it is we are trying to do through the law will acquire some definiteness of outline.

And so an awakened, a deepened religious feeling could not but be a powerful agency in the era of legal growth which undoubtedly is at hand. I think an era of political growth is also at hand and, if so, in that era of political growth one can say no less confidently that religion will be as powerful an agency as was Stoicism in the liberalization of the Roman law, as was the Reformation in the liberalization of the strict law which had grown up during the Middle Ages, and as was Puritanism in the formative era of our American law.

RELIGION OF THE FUTURE

WILLIAM ERNEST HOCKING

I

THERE are only two ways of discerning the future of a great human interest. One is to observe from outside the curve of change from past to present and follow the law of its unwritten arc. The other is to consider, from within, what is essential, and to assert as an optimist that this is what will prevail. Most prophecies about future religion are of the second variety; they are hardly prophecies at all, but rather literary devices for describing what we think valid, in terms of what we expect to survive.

In the case of religion, to attempt to discern the future is simply for each one of us to examine and clarify the religion of his own mind at the present moment. For one who professes that the religion of the future will differ from his present religion admits that he holds that present religion with a reservation: if he takes it as destined to be outpassed, he no longer quite believes it.

This follows from the nature of religion, which represents man's hold on what is eternal. The power of grasp varies, but the eternal itself presumably does not change. In whatever is genuine about the religion of any moment, it will join hands with the religion of all future and of all past moments. And while it is somewhat in the temper of the present day to suppose that we are chiefly interested in change, and that the permanent, if there is any such thing, has no great importance for us, there is a demonstrable fallacy in this view of our own interests. For that is as much as to say that we are interested in wind but not in air, in waves but not in water, in hills and valleys but not in the stable earth. The changing always gets its significance from a fundamental constancy. And especially in the case of religion, the perennial human sense of a trait in reality which calls for devotion and worship holds the centre of importance.

We shall assume, then, that the religion of the future—if the future has a religion—will be the true religion; and that the true religion is true now. But we can hardly assume without a pause that the future will have any religion at all.

I once thought that religion, founded as it is on enduring human wants, could never disappear. It now seems to me wholly conceivable that religion should vanish. For I am impressed by the ease with which men forget their wants, and the ease with which they mistake one want for another. There is in human nature a permanent need for beauty; but under misery and gross feeding men may forget that

need. There is a permanent need for honor and esteem, but there are conditions of panic or the
break-up of the social order in which this need may
be buried. There is surely a persistent craving for
mental exchange, and for the give and take of social
judgments; yet under conditions of physical pri-
vation and long continued solitude that need of
companionship and of conversation may decay with
the decline of the power and habit of intercourse.
The Roman Catholic Church sometimes speaks of
a supernatural sense, and reminds the human race
that there is a sense for spiritual things which may
be dulled and lost. Is the church saying through
this idea that there are conditions under which men
may forget that they need religion? It seems quite
possible that a generation should some day emerge
that has grown up somewhat as orphan children grow
up without the care of parents—children in institutions, who realize that there is something missing,
but not having known what is meant by home, never
find out what it is that they need. The wants of the
spirit must be kept alive partly *by being satisfied;*
and this implies that there is a tradition which points
out the way to their satisfaction. Religion is kept
alive by the presence in the world of those who
have known what religion is, and who interpret it
to us; and of these interpreters we have to say, as
the old Greek saying had it—many are the thyrsus-
bearers but few are the mystics.

Professor Whitehead has pointed out how much the interest in religion has fallen off on the continent of Europe, mentioning as one of the causes of that falling off a mistaken attitude toward truth on the part of the teachers of religion, on the part of the church. Conspiring with this cause there are others we may take note of. In our own country, material prosperity has had some effect in creating a sense of human self-sufficiency. The successes of applied science, to the present moment, have invited the human spirit to make the world of experience its home. But while prosperity may sometimes induce decay of religious sensitivity, misery also may have a similar effect. No one, I think, can observe the changes in the literary interest in Germany in the last few years, since the war, without feeling that Germany has suffered not only in material respects; with that material suffering has gone a serious decline among the masses in the interests of the spirit.

But while it is entirely conceivable that religion should disappear, I do not believe that it will disappear. Any falling off in religious interest may be interpreted in one of two ways. It may be the beginning of a great decline, but on the other hand it may be something like *taking a vacation* from religious attitudes and expressions, an experimental and tentative exercise of freedom. I believe that this vacation-taking is on the whole salutary—a fast, as it were, taken not for the sake of rejecting cosmic responsibility, but for the sake of recovering a fresh hold upon its meaning. I believe that we ought to take a vacation in our minds occasionally from all particular aspects of religion, from church, from the outlook of Christianity, in order to see whether those things which we put out of our lives will reassert themselves, and whether we can find for ourselves as an original need that which we have been told we need and which we have accepted too much on the strength of being told.

The difference between a permanent decline and an experimental vacation may be indicated by the *persistence of religious sensitivity* and of moral concern. I have spoken of Germany, and yet I cannot forget that Germany at the present time is turning with a new eagerness toward the Orient as a source of religious instruction—not only toward the occult and the exotic side of the Orient, but toward that side in which the Orient has a great deal to teach the West. With a true instinct, it seems to me, Germany is finding in the great religions of the East something which Germany had lacked, and something which we also had lacked. Let me see if I can call to your minds a picture of what I mean by this turning to a new interpretation of religious need.

We have all been impressed by the career of Mahatma Ghandi, and we have been interested, no doubt, in the peculiar method which he takes to recall his followers to their better reasons when, in spite of his injunctions of non-resistance, they fall forcibly afoul of each other or of the British Government. Ghandi imposes a fast, not upon his followers, but upon himself, as it were a personal penance. Surely, this is but a freak of Oriental fanaticism that a man should feel himself guilty on account of the sins of his followers! Yet we recall a similar attitude in Tolstoi, when shortly before his death he issued a manifesto of repudiation. The Russian Government had shot to death twelve peasants without trial, and Tolstoi in this statement declared in effect, "I repudiate my share in the benefits which the Russian Government offers me. These deeds are done in my name, and I am not satisfied until I dissolve my moral connection with those actions." Tolstoi was carrying out in principle what Ghandi was carrying out in deed. Has it not always been true that the finest natures of the world have been the most sensitive to the common guilt, and have been most ready to take that common guilt upon themselves even when they themselves have been guiltless?

Professor Anesaki, in his absorbing story of the Buddhist prophet, Nichiren, tells how he felt that the task of awakening his countrymen rested solely on his shoulders, and that he would have failed in his personal duty if the nation were unfaithful to his religion. He regarded his hardships, while the community was suffering under the menace of Mongol invasion, as the "remorseful expiation of his sin" of not having thus far accomplished all that he was sent to accomplish for his unique truth. Is that not another expression of the same principle? And I do not need to instance a prophet of still more ancient times who took upon himself in a more radical way the sins of a wider world, as if to say, "While you sin, I cannot hold myself immune."

These expressions of a spirit which I should call religious are all remote and oriental or semi-oriental. But we need not go to ancient times nor to the Orient for manifestations of this spirit. Only a few years ago a graduate of Harvard College made a strange journey to the village of Coatesville, Pa. Coatesville a year before had been the scene of a lynching, and this man, Jack Chapman, went to hold a penitential service. The members of that community were invited to attend. Chapman himself had had no hand in that lynching, but he felt that the disgrace of it went beyond that village to the state and to the nation, and became thereby a disgrace to himself. He held a penitential service, I believe with one hearer. He held it at some personal risk; but he held it as an expression of his distress of spirit that such deeds should be done in the group of which he felt himself a member. Now, apart from the exaggerations which mark these men, or these deeds, as fanatical and symbolic, we may find, if we look through the literature of this present moment, that the spirit of

Jack Chapman, of Nichiren, of Tolstoi, of Mahatma Ghandi, is not wanting among us, nor even, in essence, rare. For there is, after all, a vigorous and much-appreciated literature of self-judgment, one might say of penitence and confession, voicing an appeal to the sensitivity of this country, which in its prosperity is indeed becoming aware of its need for things which it momentarily has forgotten. The sense of a common guilt or sin is not absent; and this means to me that the religious spirit is not vanishing, though it may be dormant.

This sense of sin, and of communal sin, is not, I think, the *essence* of religion; but it is a *symptom* of religion. When a person perceives that we are miserable until we love holiness the substance of religion is in him. And when a people knows that prosperity alone leaves us empty, and that we remain empty until we as a community hunger and thirst after righteousness, the essence of religion is there.

If I am right in this judgment of the closeness of the essence of religion to the sense of sin, we may be led by this fact to conclude not only that religion will not die out, but that the religion of the future whatever it is will not be a religion of mere healthy-mindedness. It will not be a religion from which everything corresponding to hell and the wrath of God is absent. Abolish these things, and religion dies with them. For religion, I should say, is a *pas-*

*sion for righteousness and the spread of righteous-
ness felt as a cosmic demand.* Its severity is but the
shadow cast by the flame of that passion, and the
importance with which it dignifies human life.

The moral nobility of Judaism and Islam consists,
more deeply than in any other respect, in this, that
in these religions there is no attempt to smooth over
the fact of human fallibility and of communal
unrighteousness as the central problem of religion.
A recent interpreter of Islam has said: "Between
God and man there is no likeness whatever, nor is
it desirable that there should be." This is an emphatic, an overemphatic, statement of the gulf that
lies between us and our own ideal. It leaves man too
helpless. It leaves the cure of that situation too
much at the discretion of an arbitrary deity. But
reinterpret it, reinterpret it in the spirit of Nichiren
as a duty laid upon us to succeed, so that we are
guilty unless we do succeed in this task of bringing
about the spirit of righteousness, and we shall see
that here is the place for a sense of sin which is not
abject, which has nothing of the character of the
sick soul about it, and yet which introduces into
religion the note of authority, the needful grit of
sternness and of moral order. If this is a true account
of the essence of religion it will make clear, I think,
a number of ways in which we might say what the
future of religion will or will not be.

II

It is easy to prophesy by prolonging straight lines, and on the basis of this kind of prophecy many men feel, and particularly thinking men, that the religion of the future will be without a creed. Natural religion is exuberant. It mixes art and feeling with its surmises to create a world of myth and fancy. It fills the vast emptiness of super-nature with figures, places, personages, events; and a large part of the progress of religion consists in clearing out this supernatural garret, with its accumulations of rubbish. We can see the creed-content of religion gradually simplifying itself; and on the basis of that tendency it requires no seer to predict the result. A process of subtraction, sufficiently prolonged, must end in the reduction of creed-content to *nothing*. On this basis, the religion of the future might be a form of morality touched by emotion, a temper of good-will lighted by an unspecified poetic fancy.

But if religion depends, as we thought, upon regarding rightness as a cosmic demand, it cannot be creedless; for it must contain a conception of the cosmos which can place such a demand upon us. Such a conception may be in terms of symbol, myth, figure. Yet it means to be a way of laying hold of verity, not of dream. It enters the region of man's deepest earnest; and if it is the irony of his mental fate that he can see what is nearest to him only through the small angles of vision, and if he can make clear what he sees chiefly through poetry, he still lives by the element of literal reality in his imagery. No religion of the æsthetic sense, no religion of psychological conditions, can endure. Religion must have its belief; and its belief must be about ultimate objective reality.

Those who read religious history as a history of diminishing dogma forget, perhaps, that it is of the nature of insight to accumulate. The whole truth seems to be that the process of eliminating old dogmas goes hand in hand with a process of *finding the method* of religious knowledge. I am inclined to think that the creeds of Christendom and other-dom have indeed to face still further reduction—that the simplifying trend has not reached its culmination: but I believe, further, that the present moment is one in which religion is finding its method; and that when we do find how religion is related to science, and how we can use the insight of the religious leaders of the past, we shall recover the normal status in which the content of religion grows rather than declines. I admire the attitude of Buddhism, which does not state the conditions for the admission to its orders in terms of a theory. Its confession is a confession of the bent of one's will. "I take refuge in the Buddha; I take refuge in the law; I take refuge in the community." That seems rather truer to the religious sense than to hold up one hand

and say "I believe" in this or that. But, after all, one does not take refuge in unrealities; and within the statement "I take refuge in the Buddha" there is a belief in the Buddha; and behind the statement "I take refuge in the law" there is a belief in the validity of that law. The will cannot operate in the unreal. The religion of the future will not be creedless.

In the second place, the religion of the future *will not be a religion of humanity*. One of the directions of religious advance is that of a diminishing interest in super-nature, in the other-worldly. We dwell less on heaven and hell. We are much more concerned with social justice. We are much more concerned with behavior, morality, peace on earth—and so we should be. And the end of this process, too, is easy to see if we prophesy on prolonged straight lines. The end would be a religion not without a creed, but a religion whose creed was humanity, and whose God was the spirit of the race, or possibly the spirit of the nation. The tendency to reinterpret theology in terms of sociology is particularly strong among educated men; for thought does tend to humanize religion. But this tendency, given full swing, becomes one of the superstitions of the academic mind. For humanity alone cannot maintain the conditions for its own satisfaction; taken as a God, humanity is altogether too fallible, its unwisdom is too palpable, too cruel in its effects. Its blunders are irremediable, and it has no outlook beyond death either for the future of the individual or for the future of the race.

The essential difficulty with the religion of humanity is that *man, the individual, does not stop at humanity*. Each man includes within himself something of the whole universe; as he touches the limits of the world in his thought, so the whole of things enters into his being and alters his destiny. His religion can be nothing less than a religion about the cosmos, about the whole of things. Cut off the infinite fringe of human existence, and you cut the nerves of even its present worth, for the meaning of the part is derived from its commerce with the whole. No *value*, whether of life or of art, can live without this reference to the whole; try to discard this reference, and you succeed only in reintroducing it. Let Omar Khayyam serve as evidence; for Omar, in his quatrains, is the type of all those who would invite the human spirit to take refuge in the moment, and yet the whole romance and beauty of his poetry depends upon his unique power to invoke the image of infinity.

> "When you and I behind the veil have passed,
> Oh, but the long, long time the world shall last,
> Which of our coming and departure heeds
> As the seven seas should heed a pebble cast."

There is the appeal of the moment, but there is the moment in the frame of eternity; and that is what the human spirit will always claim for itself. Man cannot be less ambitious in his religion than to deal with the whole of the universe.

I have said that the religion of the future will not be without a creed, and that it will not be merely a religion of humanity; but I must add at once as a third point that it will *not be identical with metaphysics*. There is a tendency among thinkers, and perhaps among philosophers particularly, to identify religion with truth, and to decide among religions on the basis of theoretical truth. They are inclined to read the direction of religious progress as one of dropping away the historical, personal, accidental elements of faith until—prolonging the straight line —nothing but the pure essence of truth universal is left. Now, religion must be true; but to say that religion consists in truth, or that truth is the essence of religion, is to make of religion a timeless and unhistorical affair, which it is not, never has been, and never can be. Some years ago, in a course on ethics, I asked the students in an examination to give a comment on the course, and some of those comments were memorable. One of them was by a Jewish student, Cohen by name, who said this: "I do not believe that the teaching of ethics is of any real value. It is impossible to prove that a man should love his neighbor, and if you could prove it, that proof would not in the least help him to do so. I can understand how a Jesus Christ or a Nietzsche might turn the world upside down, but I cannot understand how a college professor could turn the world upside down." My friend Cohen had touched the difference between religion and theory. I do not think he was entirely just, perhaps, to the teaching of ethics, but in this point he was right: religion must be something more than the truth of its propositions.

Religion cannot be communicated simply as truth. Although I do believe it is a matter of life and death that we have the truth, and that it is far from being a matter of indifference which of various philosophies we finally adopt, it is clear that a certain tolerant objectivity is necessary in the inquiry after truth, a certain detachedness which leaves the crucial question unmet, "What is your passion about the world, and what in the end are you to do about it?" Religion has to be communicated as a union of truth with passion: its concern for truth is a part of its passion for righteousness. It has to be a handing on of a revolution in the will, as determined by a radical insight.

But even in the winning of its truth-content, religion does not grow purely as metaphysics, without reference to the lines of history. Note the way in which men make use of one another's perceptions in the building up of religious traditions. It is not always the clear and finished thought of a thinker that is used by his successor; it is frequently the thing that is vague and inchoate in a man's mind that is most useful to those who come after him. We value one another for our *directions*, quite as much as for our achievements; and in the decanting of truth from one mind into another; that which was vague in the previous thinker becomes a little clearer in the succeeding thinkers, until after a hundred of these decantings of the spirit you come from murkiness into light. The historical order of the movement of man's minds is just the reverse of the physical principle of opacity. If you set up side by side, or on top of one another, a number of translucent plates, you can in time cut out all the light and arrive at darkness; but if you set up in succession a number of translucent thinkers the time may come when you reach a transparency. The order of growth in religious knowledge needs to be an historical order, largely because in the progress toward truth the human race needs to use the principle of cumulative vision. The direction of the minds of the seers becomes the direction of the mind of their race.

III

Now to these negations, can we add a few positive statements about the religion of the future?

Certainly this may be said: that the centre of religious thought must always be *the conception of God*. In a dead world, man is already dead. Unless he has a living universe, he knows himself to be ultimately lost. Some conception of this life, that is, of God, must exist if there is any religion; and in this conception there is always an attempt to meet two requirements. God must embody in himself the *divinity* of the world—he must be that holiness for which religion is the passion; but he must also be the *supreme power* of the world. God is the divine, God is the glory, and the glamour, and the aura of the world; but God is also necessarily the ultimate source and the ultimate reality. And now the difficulty in religion consists very largely, and always, in bringing these two demands together; because power as we find it in experience seems essentially brutal or indifferent—not at all divine; whereas divinity seems essentially ideal—not at all powerful. On the one hand there is the evident evil of experience, whereby the power of the world becomes a symbol for all that is repellent, prodigious, indifferent; on the other hand, if we look toward our ideals and ask what reality they have, there is the appalling silence of God. Although the history of religion has been full of so-called revelations, their very multitude shows chiefly man's need for revelation, as if he were knocking on an unanswering door. The divine thing in the world seems essentially the non-evident and the impotent thing.

The discovery of God depends in part upon the discovery that silence—this silence—has its paradox; for a silence may be itself an eloquent silence, like the silence that followed Pilate's question, "What is truth?" Two thousand years have heard the echo of that question, as if every man could hear the response, "He who desires the truth shall know what it is." It is conceivable that the all-silent God may be the all-speaking God if we know how to listen, for if we imagine that God should speak in some din, or even in some tinkling bell in the back of our mind, we realize that such a voice as a partial voice could not possibly be divine. The voice of God can only be the voice *of the world* speaking with a constant and universal impression that forms the background of consciousness, not its saliencies. We might indeed regard such speech as indistinguishable from nothing, were there not those who feel that the silence of God is full of meaning, were there not some who find that silence so oppressive with presence, that they must needs, like Nietzsche, declare God dead in order to find room for themselves and their own expansion. The insistence of Nietzsche that God is dead appears to me a confession of a haunting sense of a presence unwelcome to the man who felt the need to become the superman.

We must learn the meaning of silence; for that there is such a meaning I verily believe. The silence of God may mean that God will not speak where men can speak for him, and that God will not occupy any room in which man can grow and should grow. The silence of God may have some meaning in regard to evil; for when we regard evil as the negation of God, as it certainly is in some respects, the sort of hostility we set up between God and the evil of the world depends on the kind of God we have imagined. We do well to reconsider our view of what God is, remembering that mere insulation from evil, or mere hatred and dread of an evil which exists in spite of him, can never be the whole truth of God's relation thereto. William James was following the track of a true instinct when he made the statement that God is no gentleman. He cannot in any case be one who must remain out of touch with the mud and scum of things, or even with the hellish possibilities of existence. It can hardly be the lot of the human race to be delivered from all evil in the sense of hardship and suffering, but it belongs to the profound doctrines of religion that if men have to descend into hell, God descends with them. And while he remains silent regarding the origin or necessity of that evil, we who are not delivered from suffering may by that fact be delivered from despair. The evil that admits companionship is neither devoid of hope nor devoid of meaning.

And further, the silence of God may have a meaning with regard to this apparent powerlessness of the divine. For the powers which work evil in the world are the blatant powers, and God is certainly not in the field with them—he is not their competitor. Whatever the power of God may be, it is not a power in which God needs to exert himself, as though he were strained by the opposition. He need not labor nor contend. His power, whatever it is, is more like the repose of the sea which Thor tried to drink in a goblet, or like the repose of that serpent which Thor tried to lift. God's power is like the unassertive but all-quickening power of light—and like the light which shone in Plato's cave, it fills the world from behind us, so that we do not see its source.

These are only suggestions of the possibility of God—the possibility of a solution; they are not solutions, they are not proofs of God. It remains true that some such insight as this must bring us to our conception of God, and must in some way explain these two profound mysteries of evil and of silence.

But, suppose we have gained a conception of God which successfully solves these mysteries, will this suffice for the religion of the future? I think not. For beside the conception of God, religion must always depend upon a *perception* of God. And this also will be true of the religion of the future.

Here I find it a matter of great difficulty to put into words what I mean. I may attempt it by considering the silence of God in a new light. God does not speak in concepts; he does not define in terms what he is; he does not argue with the arguer; he does not deny him who denies his existence. He contends with theories no more than he contends with forces; it is as if here, too, he knew that "When me they fly, I am the wings"; he has a mode of presence deeper than that of conscious thought. What is that mode of presence?

We know in our own finite way what it is to be undisturbed by varieties of opinion. We frequently recognize the religious quality in men whose theories are critical of religious conceptions. While religious feeling, as a passion for the spread of righteousness, is therewith concerned for the spread of religious truth, it is still keener to recognize its affinities of motive under whatever variety of intellectual garb. The good bishop in *Les Misérables* kneels before the dying Conventionist and asks for his blessing. The great religious spirit becomes great in his hospitality; he transcends all sects, including his own; he finds his brethren among Buddhists, Jews, Mohammedans, Christians, also among the philosophers and the atheists. It is as if he saw that the pantheist, the God-denier, the God-hater, might each in his way be recognizing and serving God. How can this universal sympathy go with a burning concern for the spread of truth?

Perhaps the secret of this absolute hospitality, an echo of the divine tolerance itself, is, like that, an expression of an ultimate security: every sincere seeker of truth is on the way to a perception of deity, and each one is dimly aware that it is this which he

seeks. For to all of them there is a need for understanding, sought first in the human context, a need
which cannot be fully satisfied by that human context in its own right. Nietzsche needs and desires you
and me as his understanders and interpreters; he
had addressed himself to us: Spinoza, in his solitude,
writes for us, and confesses the same need. It is the
unexpressed need of every prophet that he shall be
understood; and it is a part of the instinct of the
prophet that while he addresses himself to us men,
he knows that he cannot be satisfied with our judgment—he looks for something beyond it. One who
should meet in experience a judgment so true and so
searching that he felt it to be final would be led to
say "God is here."

Now we mortals, again by instinct, make a brave
attempt to hold one another up by mutual understanding; but we know in our more self-conscious
moments that we are attempting to stand to each
other in the place of God, and that we do so only
symbolically. But human love, and the religious
spirit in its more hospitable understandings, seem
at times to reach an authority beyond themselves.
An element of absolute right enters into and co-
operates with the human judgment; and we find God
as we find the glint of absolute validity in these
human understandings and interpretations. *God is
the touch of validity in human evaluation.* God is
the promise of immortality in what deserves to be

immortal. And when across these human judgments there runs the awareness that one is being perceived not by the neighbor alone, but by truth itself, the impulse arises to say "Thou" to the universe as though the universe in finding one out had already said "Thou" to that person. Religion, as the perception of God, is the ability to say "Thou" to the universe, as God is the "Thou" of the world.

After all, it is of little value that a man shall believe in the omnipresence of God, as an abstraction, unless he can verify that consequence of omnipresence which alone counts, namely that God is here and present. The religion of the future will recognize that its vitality depends on leading every individual to make this demand of his world; he must have his own conversation with its reality, in immediate experience, and not alone through his speculations or through his institutions or through the saints and seers who form the tradition which he accepts. His personal intuition must be his guide to his authorities and his reasons. The religion of the future will have its element of mysticism.

But, finally, the religion of the future will be a positive religion. It will be for each person one of the positive religions now existent. It will not be a new religion; for a new religion is a religion no man wants. Because the full vision of religious reality is a composite vision, in which transmitted elements join with one's own, worship, for each man, must be a joining with his ancestors in worship; he joins with them first, and with his race afterward.

Does this mean that there will be a contest among the present religions for the supremacy of the world, or for the position of "the world religion?"

This is hardly the way to put the matter; for it seems to forget the fact that there *already is a world religion*. Despite the differences in the thoughts of God in different traditions, the meaning of God in terms of experience is the same for all men. The worship of God is the deepest of all common bonds in the human family.

And further, there can be no contest among religions for *displacement*. This has been a misconception of the burden of missionary effort which is gradually being overcome. No man, if we are right, should abandon the religion of his ancestors; for the Hindus, Hinduism; for the Chinese and Japanese and Siamese and many other Asiatic peoples, Buddhism as modified by Confucian or Taoistic or Shintoistic currents; for others, Islam; and for others, Judaism.

But while there can be no contest for displacement, there may be, and must be, a contest for *inclusion;* for some religion, better than others, will represent the whole of what man's cosmic ambition craves, and will place the partial truths of the rest in their right setting. It will be a contest, in part, of *truth;* but this is a contest which usually settles itself in a simple way, for the truth of religion belongs to all religions, and religions quite readily appropriate one another's ideas and tend toward identity on the main points. But it will be chiefly a contest of *motive powers*. For a religion is a way of life in relation to the divine; and contact with the divine power of the world is what lends motive power to men and societies. Now the great positive religions differ in their motive power; and we cannot say that so long as he has a religion of his own it is a matter of indifference which religion any man has. Let me illustrate this fact by a parable.

We have been trying to get rid of the trade in opium. We have been trying to attack that problem through the League of Nations; and that is a very good way to approach it. But it is not enough to approach that problem through the agents of the various governments concerned in the traffic. Let us consider the position of a Chinese farmer who has a field of poppies, and a market for those poppies. Now the problem of getting rid of opium is, at bottom, a problem of dealing with that farmer and others like him, farmers who have poppies and a good market for them. That farmer is now called upon by you and me to give up his income, and the only practical question is, "What motive can you give him for doing that?" He may not be among the consumers of his poppies. What you have to do is to implant in this man's mind a concern for his neighbor which he has not. You have got to bring him to a state of mind in which he will say: "This is lucrative, nothing else can bring me so much, but there is something for which I care more." You have got to do for him what Cohen wanted the course in ethics to do, you have got to create in him a new love for his neighbor, and a new perception of who his neighbor is. Religion must give men their adequate and decisive loyalties, and I ask you whether every religion will do this as well as every other. The Chinese farmer does not find in his own spiritual atmosphere a sufficient motive for abandoning his profit. And the same may be said of many a man in our own neighborhood. The problem is the same everywhere.

Now the religion of the future must satisfy the whole man in all of his instincts. It will not be a religion of repression, nor one which asks him to leave this world to find the scene of his success. It will not be a religion which requires of him the abandonment of a belief in life and its possibilities. It will be one that insists that men shall succeed, shall satisfy their wills to power, shall work miracles, shall achieve what Nichiren wanted to achieve—a success which includes the spread of righteousness— even though that success be through radical sacrifice. For it must at the same time be a religion that is at home in the suffering and the despair of men and which promises them—as Chesterton represents

the image of May as promising King Alfred—
only this, "that the night grows darker yet, and the
sea rises higher." It must be a religion that lures
men, not by visions of rest and ease, but by demands
of infinite effort, infinite achievement, giving them
at the same time the power of accomplishing that
success.

I know of only one religious tradition which demands these things of men, and hence only one
which is in a logical position to supply the motive
power to fulfil such demands. But I believe that
the contest of religions in respect to motive power
is a contest whose future is to be decided by the
Socratic method. Socrates did not pledge people
into accepting his truth. He said, "Let me ask you
questions, and let us find out what in our combined
resources we have." And the result was a common
movement to a common goal in which Socrates'
ideas were also developed and clarified. Missions
as one-sided proclamations of final truth have had
their function to fulfil, they still have a function.
But I believe that there is a greater future in a new
form of the intercourse of religions which has for
its presupposition the common quest for an adequate
motive power for the tasks of life, and the common
concern that the completest truth and the most
adequate motive power shall be the possession of all.
Religion has no call to obliterate the variety of the
ways of insight; it has a call to extend the unity

of truth, and the deeper unity of human aspiration.

Religion of the future can live only as a universal religion, and it is not a slight issue whether it shall or shall not continue to live. Whether men shall come to look upon their lives in terms of a cosmic demand, and also in terms of a cosmic concern for their good, is no less a matter than the ultimate life or death of human society.